RONALD A. KEITH

With a new introduction by Sean Rossiter

BUSH PILOT WITH A BRIEFCASE

THE INCREDIBLE STORY OF AVIATION PIONEER GRANT McCONACHIE

DOUGLAS & McINTYRE
VANCOUVER/TORONTO

97 98 99 00 01 5 4 3 2 1

Douglas & McIntyre Ltd.
1615 Venables Street
Vancouver, British Columbia
V5L 2H1

Canadian Cataloguing in Publication Data

Keith, Ronald A.
    Bush pilot with a briefcase

    ISBN 1-55054-586-8

    1. McConachie, Grant, 1909–1965. 2. CP Air—History. 3. Bush pilots—Canada—Biography. I. Title.
TL540.M22K4 1997   387.7'092   C97-910393-2

Cover design by Peter Cocking
Cover photograph of Grant McConachie courtesy of Canadian Airlines Archives
Some of the photographs that appear in this book are courtesy of "Red" Rose, CP Air and the McConachie family.
Printed and bound in Canada by Best Book Manufacturers
Printed on acid-free paper ∞

The publisher gratefully acknowledges the support of the Canada Council for the Arts and of the British Columbia Ministry of Tourism, Small Business and Culture.

PREFACE

He was once described as "an airline president who goes about with a worried look—on his assistant's face." For more than twelve years, that face was mine. During the previous fifteen years I was privileged to occupy a front seat at the McConachie flying circus, first as aviation reporter for the Edmonton *Journal* in the late thirties, then as editor of *Canadian Aviation Magazine*.

For enthusiastic support in the research and writing of this biography I am indebted to many, including Barry Broadfoot, Tony Craig, Don Cameron, N. R. Crump, Glen Fenby, John Gilmer, Ian Gray, Arthur Hailey, Bill Herbert and the CBC, Frank Lloyd, Hugh Main, Mrs. G. McConachie, Barney Phillips, "Red" Rose, Bill Roxborough, Ian Sinclair, and especially to my wife, Dorothy, for her encouragement and forbearance.

This book is a personal tribute to Grant McConachie—a fascinating personality, an inspiring colleague, a congenial companion and a true friend.

Ronald A. Keith

Vancouver
1972

INTRODUCTION

The great visionaries of this century were the airline-builders. They somehow foresaw in the stick-and-wire, fabric-skinned biplanes of the late 1920s the intercontinental airliners of the past twenty-five years. Aviation history sings the praises of such pioneers as Eddie Hubbard, who formed United Airlines; Juan Trippe of Pan American, who pushed for bigger, faster aircraft; and, of course, Howard Hughes, whose airline, Trans World, conceived the first money-making transport, the DC-3.

All three were Americans, which explains why their achievements have been widely celebrated. But there was a Canadian airline-builder who started out with not much more than personal charm enough to keep his Ford Trimotor aloft. He operated with one hand tied behind his back by the Canadian government, which ran its subsidized airline, Trans-Canada, in competition with his own. Yet he equalled Hubbard in buying up his competitors and Trippe in visualizing a way to span the oceans. He was every bit as colourful as Hughes. He was Grant McConachie.

McConachie was a big man with a smile that could light up a hangar. Like Russ Baker, founder of Pacific Western Airlines, McConachie was a natural but not especially accomplished pilot, and he was raw enough as an engineer to have had the exhaust manifold of his Fokker removed to augment its engine's power—

and increase its payload by half—thus gassing himself with carbon monoxide whenever he flew it. Sometimes his bonhomie was all he had to cement the loyalty of his employees. Great aviators, such as Sheldon Luck, Canadian Pacific Air Lines' first chief pilot, flew for McConachie despite the frequent absence of pay cheques, on borrowed aviation fuel. Luck and McConachie appeared in a wartime issue of *The Saturday Evening Post,* credited in the photo caption with building CPAL "out of baling wire." Hugh Main, McConachie's first secretary at CPAL and later Vancouver's chief tourism promoter, called him "everybody's pal."

By 1941, his own Yukon Southern Air Transport absorbed by the Canadian Pacific Railway, the thirty-one-year-old McConachie was the unlikely regional manager of airline routes combined from ten bush operations—most of them run by men far senior to him— including outfits founded by such bush-flying legends as Leigh Brintnell of Mackenzie Air Service and Canadian Airways' Wop May and Punch Dickins. McConachie probably got the job because, while he certainly had rivals, he did not have enemies.

The western operations of the new airline were at first run from the CPR's offices at Royal Alexandra Station in Winnipeg, where McConachie was a breath of fresh air in what had become over most of a century a quasi-government bureaucracy. He bicycled to work and nipped out over the lunch hour to the Y with his secretary, Main, for a swim and a workout.

Harry Porteous, later treasurer of CPAL, first encountered McConachie in his new boss' small office. McConachie was sitting on the floor, "which was covered with maps. Right away he started to show me how he was going to fly to the Orient and to Australia. It was a tremendous revelation to me. I had never even thought of anything beyond the two ends of the railroad."

Eddie Hubbard was an early test pilot who flew the first international airmail from Seattle to Vancouver's Coal Harbour, with Bill

Boeing as his co-pilot, on March 2 and 3, 1919. (They were forced down overnight by bad weather.) One of Hubbard's brainstorms was to urge Boeing to introduce the Model 40 mail plane in 1927. This was a major change for a company that had not built a civil aircraft in seven years. Within a year the two passengers each Model 40 could carry—later enlarged to four—were generating pure profit while mail paid the freight. Boeing soon dominated the U.S. airmail system, and the profits made possible the amalgamation of Boeing Air Transport, Pacific Air and the other Boeing-owned airlines that became United Airlines on December 18, 1928. The next day, Hubbard died.

Howard Hughes became a household name by flying a Lockheed Model 14 Super Electra around the world in record time. (Trans-Canada Airlines was organized in 1937 with similar but smaller Lockheed Model 10 Electras, the type of aircraft Amelia Earhart was flying when she disappeared.) Denied the "three-mile-a-minute" Boeing 247 airliner by United's corporate connection with that manufacturer, TWA issued the breakthrough specifications that led to the legendary DC-3.

Juan Trippe's Pan American Airways led the way to routine transoceanic schedules by prodding three aircraft manufacturers (Boeing, Martin and Sikorsky) to outdo each other's prewar flying boats in size and range, making transoceanic flights not just possible but as luxurious as Pullman car journeys. Trippe's last coups were to lead the world into the jet age with the Boeing 707 and into the wide-body era with the four-hundred-passenger 747—for both of which Pan Am was Boeing's launch customer. *The Airline Builders,* a book in the popular TIME-Life Epic of Flight series, calls Trippe "the man who shrank the earth."

There are elements of each of these stories in McConachie's. When McConachie's company and nine other bush operations were bought by the CPR, the resulting airline merely shrank Canada. The Canada-wide route system ranged "from the Yukon in the far northwest to Labrador on the Atlantic," in the words of one history of bush flying.

But nowhere in the accounts of these American pioneers do today's polar routes to Europe and Asia appear. The idea, not of shrinking the globe but rather flying over its smallest parts, was McConachie's contribution to commercial aviation. As with most visionary ideas, this one preceded the means to realize it. But when the time came to fly over the coldest regions of the globe after the Second World War, McConachie somehow managed to find aircraft that could do the job. Locating the right aircraft and acquiring them dirt cheap was one of McConachie's specialties.

One key to Yukon Southern's value when it was taken over was the fleet of Model 18 Lodestars that McConachie charmed Lockheed salesman Carl Squier into spiriting from the U.S. Army Air Force's order, right off the assembly line, camouflage paint and all. Although the paint later had to be sandblasted off the planes for airline use at the cost of hundreds of man-hours, the camouflage did pay off during their delivery flights in free refuelling at the Great Falls, Montana, army airfield stop. McConachie, a master promoter, advertised the new airplanes as "the fastest commercial aircraft in the world." And they were.

For building a national airline out of bush outfits, McConachie was awarded Canada's highest aviation award, the McKee Trans-Canada Trophy, in 1947. He was thirty-eight, and then only on the verge of his lasting contribution to air travel: CPAL's transpolar routes.

Perhaps it took an actual bush pilot, one with thousands of hours over the far North on his log, to know by the seat of his pants how much smaller the world is at its poles than around the equator. McConachie's northern route is one of those insights that revise the way we see the globe. He didn't shrink the world; he flew the shortest straight lines over it. By the time McConachie's idea had been fulfilled by the everyday routine of a flight schedule, he was long since legendary for inflating the plastic beachball globe he carried in his briefcase to important meetings and taping pieces of yarn to its surface to show how much shorter his route would be once pressurized airliners became available to overfly the North.

McConachie became president of CPAL in 1947 and began the airline's international services by flying back-door routes that the government-owned TCA did not want. One condition of the deal with Industry Minister C. D. Howe that gave CPAL access to international routes was that the airline had to buy Montreal-built Canadair Fours, the high-flying but loud and vibratory North Stars. McConachie kept the routes but soon ditched the North Stars, which were eventually replaced in CPAL's fleet with smoother, longer-legged Bristol Britannia turboprops built in Britain.

Another condition was that CPAL also service Australia. No problem: that had been part of McConachie's plan all along. If CPAL wanted access to Europe, it would have to use Amsterdam as its terminus: TCA would retain its exclusive rights to London and Paris. McConachie didn't mind flying into Amsterdam, either. He had figured out that the destinations CPAL flew to were less important than his ability to negotiate connections with other airlines to bring further cities within reach. He was thirty years ahead of his time in understanding how critical networking would be for airlines. CPAL flew not only to Tokyo and Hong Kong, which became rich markets, but to most major cities in South America.

The account of all this and more, the book you are now holding, is among the best-written aviation biographies ever published, an award-winning ten-year labour of love by McConachie's personal assistant and publicist. *Bush Pilot with a Briefcase* was published seven years after McConachie's death in 1965, and it sold 20,000 hardback copies in Canada alone between October 1972 and March 1973 before appearing that year in the PaperJacks edition.

Ronald Keith broke into print on January 26, 1936, with a two-page profile of Mohandas Gandhi that appeared in the *Toronto Star*. He instructed pilots in the British Commonwealth

Air Training Plan during the war at Trenton, Ontario, joining Maclean-Hunter in 1949 as editor of *Canadian Aviation*. He was able to get his immigrant friend Arthur Hailey a job at *Canadian Bus and Truck* magazine, where Hailey married a member of the steno pool and became a literary celebrity with his thriller *Flight into Danger* and subsequent best-sellers. Grant McConachie lured Keith away from magazine journalism in 1952 to become his much-needed personal organizer, and, eventually, publicist for an airline that, during the 1950s, seemed to launch new routes monthly.

Keith wrote this book in the little spare time he had left over from building a network of PR people in every CPAL destination city. It was time he could not have spent typing, then a noisy pursuit, without that supportive mate so many authors gratefully acknowledge. When Dorothy Boyd Booth married Ron Keith in 1962, it was the second marriage for both. Still, she had no idea what she was getting into.

"He always packed his portable typewriter with him on our holidays. He had dry spells, which were bad enough, or he'd be up at 2:00 a.m. pounding that typewriter," she chuckles. "At times it got to be a pain in the neck to me. Every waking thought, in the middle of the night—his mind would be elsewhere. I don't know how he did it and carried on his job."

During an era when there were few book awards of any kind, *Bush Pilot with a Briefcase* won the 1973 James Strebig Award "For Outstanding Excellence in Aviation Writing or Reporting." Ron Keith died in 1985. If he had time to write only one book in his lifetime, and manage that only by dint of long nights on vacation, this is the one to have written.

One of the virtues of *Bush Pilot with a Briefcase* is that its seamless parade of anecdotes is left uninterrupted by claims for McConachie's place in the annals of aviation and commerce. But all the necessary evidence is here. At the time this book was published, CP Air had established itself as a better-equipped and more reliable airline than Air Canada was.

Since then the saga of CP Air, more recently Canadian Airlines, has entered a survival phase all too common among the visionary carriers. Pan Am is gone; United is owned by its employees; TWA is a shell of its former self. Canadian Airlines' next set of interest payments could be its last. If Canadian can hang on long enough, though, McConachie's legacy, those routes to Asia that few other than he wanted, might yet be the airline's salvation.

SEAN ROSSITER

1. RESCUE FLIGHT

October 1932

The message clicking in to the Army Signal Corps post on the outskirts of Edmonton was halting and so garbled that it was almost unintelligible, but it told a story of anguish and despair.

The two Sens brothers were in desperate need of rescue. Returning to their wilderness hut from a routine patrol, they had tried to light their stove, fed from a near-by natural-gas pocket. The leaking stove blew up in their faces.

Both of the brothers were seared blind. Their faces, hands, arms and chests were severely burned in the flaming explosion. But, using his elbow on the telegraph key, Joe Sens was able to hammer out an agonized plea for help.

In the meantime, a neighbouring trapper, alerted by the roar of the explosion, had arrived at the cabin. He could do little to relieve the suffering of the blast victims, but under their gasped directions, he was able to rig a telephone on to the telegraph line and converse with the Signals authorities in Edmonton to explain their predicament.

Unless they got medical treatment soon they could not hope to survive. They would face a slow and painful death in their remote cabin, 150 miles north of Edmonton in the bleak Canadian wilderness.

Rescue appeared hopeless. There were no roads in that

wilderness, and no flat areas where a plane could land. Normally, the local rivers and lakes provided natural runways for the planes that were their only link with civilization. In summer the planes landed on the water on pontoons, in winter on the ice on skis. Between seasons, when the forming or melting ice was not strong enough to support a landing, nothing flew in that area.

It was between seasons now.

In Edmonton Major Jim Burwash, C.O. of Army Signals, himself a weathered veteran of the northern telegraph patrol on which the Sens brothers served, paced the brown linoleum of his small office.

"Those two boys are going to die and there's damn-all we can do about it! Any pilot trying to land on the river or lake ice would crack up and go straight to the bottom. But get one of those bush pilots out here right away. At least we can talk about it."

Half an hour later the warped storm door of the shack was yanked open, and along with a gust of cold air and a flurry of snow, a tall broad-shouldered young man clumped into the room. Major Burwash had asked for a bush pilot; he had got Grant McConachie, the youngest and wildest of them all.

While McConachie shook the snow from his rumpled brown hair and his windbreaker, Burwash quickly told him the story. McConachie immediately picked up the phone to Pelican Rapids and confirmed with the trapper that despite the cold snap there would be no hope for an ice landing on the Pelican River or on any of the lakes in the region. And the solid timber all around made a landing on the ground apparently out of the question.

But McConachie tried another tack. The nearest lake? Ten miles from the Sens cabin along his trap-line trail. He had a small shelter on the shore. Yes, the water would be low at this time of year. There was a fairly level strip of beach.

Couldn't say for sure, but there might be just enough spread between the tree line and the water for a small plane to get down.

"I'm going to try a landing on that beach," McConachie shouted to the trapper over the makeshift phone line. "You take the boys over to Oboe Lake at first light tomorrow morning. When you get there, be sure to light a fire so the smoke will give me the wind direction for landing."

He outlined his plan of action to Major Burwash. The blue Fokker he had been flying on the barnstorming circuit all summer was still on wheels in the Edmonton hangar. He could take off before dawn with a doctor, a mechanic and medical supplies. They might have to pancake on to the beach and probably would damage the plane, but he was sure that nobody would be injured.

The doctor could look after the blast victims. Then they would just have to wait till the lake froze over solidly enough for a plane on skis to come in and pick them up.

The grizzled Signals veteran squinted dubiously at young McConachie. "It's a wild scheme. Mebbe just crazy enough to work," he said. "But I can't be responsible for taking a chance with a doctor. If you and your mechanic are prepared to make the try on your own, you've got my blessing. You can fly in with the medical supplies, and the doctor can give you full instructions. You'll just have to do your best."

As he negotiated the snow-covered dirt road from his home in Calder to the Edmonton airport in the five A.M. darkness of the following morning, the young pilot's mind was on the Fokker's most serious shortcoming as a wheel-plane . . . no brakes. Instead of brakes the Fokker was supplied with a hook attached to the tail which was supposed to plough into the ground and halt the plane. In theory, and on soft landing strips, it was fine; on the frozen lake beach it would ski along uselessly.

Landing on a narrow strip of shoreline less than a thousand

feet long without brakes—well, even he had to admit that there was an element of sheer madness in this mercy flight.

Another fact nagged at the big twenty-three-year-old's confidence as he thought about the rescue venture. He knew that as a plane loses flying speed on landing the force of the slip stream diminishes, making the rudder ineffective. For steering, the pilot has to use a touch of brake on either wheel. No brakes, no steering. Not a cheering prospect with the spread between the lake and the trees only slightly more than the Fokker's wingspan. The slightest misjudgement would send him careening against the trees or into the lake.

As he pulled up on the grass ramp at the airport McConachie was happy to note a light in his corner of the hangar, which meant that Chris "Limey" Green was already at work on his checkout of the engine and airframe.

Limey was a bush pilot's best form of insurance, a skilled and dedicated mechanic. McConachie had filled him in about the flight the night before. Green was aware he would be riding blind in the enclosed cabin during a perilous landing, but his only remark had been a question, "What time do you want the ruddy beast ready to go?"

In the murk of the empty airfield McConachie lowered himself into the open cockpit of the Fokker, switched on the twin magnetos and prodded the starter. The Jacobs belched loudly, then roared to life. He went through the familiar drill. Flex rudder, elevator and aileron controls, flick a finger against each instrument on the panel . . . altimeter, fuel level, engine revolutions, oil temperature, cylinder head temperature . . . As the engine warmed in the crisp air he pulled a helmet over unruly brown hair, buckled the chin strap and watched the oil temperature needle move slowly from red to green.

Then he lowered the heavily-padded goggles. He advanced the throttle, tested both mags. at full power, eased back on the revs., waved the chocks away and jockeyed the aircraft over the uneven surface of the cow pasture that served as Edmonton's airport.

As the Fokker slanted upwards into the early morning sky the young pilot exulted once again in the thrill of release from the bonds of earth. But now the familiar exhilaration of flight was spiced with the anticipation of a challenging adventure. Climbing steadily on a northerly compass heading, he watched the ground recede gradually into a featureless haze far below. Soon the first slanting rays of the sun were glinting on the lacquered fabric of the Fokker's wing. At least the weather would not be a problem this day.

At altitude, the continuous thunder of the engine exhaust stacks directly ahead of his windscreen diminished perceptibly as McConachie throttled the Jacobs back to cruising power. He adjusted the elevator trim for level flight, fanned a practised glance across the altimeter, airspeed and tachometer readings on his instrument panel, then relaxed at the controls.

As the blue Fokker droned northwards McConachie found himself reflecting on the intimate relationship that soon evolved between a pilot and his aircraft. The Fokker responded to his slightest pressure on the controls more like a living thing than a mere assembly of fabric and metal.

During the long year past, most of his waking hours had been spent in the cramped and solitary world of this cockpit. Now he felt as if he were almost an integral component of the blue Fokker. He could anticipate every quirk and whim of its airborne behaviour, could sense its predictable response to each swell and current of the restless air ocean in which it swam.

McConachie was aware that he possessed a native aptitude for flying, so he had no doubt of his ability to pull off at least a survival landing in the wilderness. He recognized that his arrival might well prove to be what the wits would call an "organized crash." The Fokker might take a knocking about. But he and Limey would come out of it intact. And so, he prayed, would the wooden carton lashed to the centre of the cabin floor. He was acutely conscious of its contents: carefully padded bottles of tannic acid, assorted quantities of special ointments, bundles of antiseptic gauze, rolls of bandages, and the doctor's typed instructions for the treatment of burns. He winced as his thoughts turned to the victims waiting at Oboe Lake.

High over the white spume of the still-unfrozen cataract he identified on his map as Pelican Rapids, McConachie eased the control column to the left and applied a touch of rudder, banking into a steep turn on to a westerly heading. Minutes later he sighted his destination and throttled back, sloping the Fokker into a steep gliding descent, to circle at low altitude and size up the situation.

He remembered the subsequent events well:

"It was by now a bright sunny morning and there was no problem of visibility. It was a big lake covered with thin ice. I could see the trapper's cabin and three men on the shore.

"The shore line, which appeared to be clear of obstructions, was frozen marsh overgrown with bullrushes, and there was a narrow margin of sand, just enough for one wheel, between the overgrowth and the lake ice. I figured if I could set one wheel down along that sand margin, the other on the flat shore ice, there was just enough room for the wing tip to clear the trees. Nothing to spare, though.

"The trapper had followed my instructions and had a fire going so the smoke would give me the wind direction, but he got a little overenthusiastic and there was so much smoke that it blinded me completely as I flew in low over the beach on the landing approach.

"After two attempts I had to give up that idea and decided that instead of landing into the wind, which is normal so the head-wind will give you the slowest possible ground speed, I would have to try a landing down-wind. This, of course, stacked the odds higher against me because the wind would be pushing me along faster instead of acting as an air brake.

"However, there was no choice, so I had to rely on my experience with this particular aircraft to bring it in at the lowest possible airspeed. It was like treading an invisible tightrope. Just a shade slower and I knew the plane would stall and drop from the sky out of control. I kept the nose high, with a lot of power on, so we were actually wallowing down through the air in a power stall, practically hanging on the propeller. Then, just as the wheels were rattling over the first of the bullrushes on the shore, I chopped back the throttle completely. I cut the ignition switches to minimize the danger of fire if we cracked up, and pulled the control column full back to complete the stall and uttered a small prayer.

"It was pretty rough as we plopped down into those bullrushes. I thought the first impact would drive the undercart right up through the floor. Then we bounced and jolted along the beach. There was a frightful moment when I thought we would keep on going right through the trapper's cabin. Without brakes, and with the tail-skid hook dragging uselessly on the rock-hard surface, there was nothing I could do to slow the landing run. Luckily, we rolled right up to the door of the cabin and came to a stop almost beside the bug-eyed trapper and his two patients.

"It was quite a shock to see those poor fellows at the cabin. You couldn't even recognize them as human beings. They had been burned so badly they had great white water-blisters hanging down from their faces right down to their chests. There were angry red welts covering their hands and spreading right up their arms. Their faces were so badly seared and swollen they couldn't see. They weren't actually blind but their eyes were swollen tight shut. Their noses were almost burned right off. It was a terrible thing to see."

It was clear that if McConachie waited for the ice to freeze, the Sens brothers would be dead. They would have to make the return flight at once.

While McConachie applied first aid, Limey inspected the

aircraft. The Fokker had not escaped undamaged—in fact, its fabric underbelly was split from end to end. Apparently, it had caught the stake of a muskrat trap as they landed. Limey sewed it up in hopes that it would hold together for the return flight. McConachie then gave his attention to the problem of taking off from the short strip of beach. As he put it, "With no brakes on the Fokker there was nothing to hold the aircraft while I could rev up the engine to full power before starting the run down the short strip of beach. The strip was so short that it seemed certain I would run out of runway before I could get off the ground.

"We hauled the aircraft back as far as we could up a slight slope and tied the tail to a tree, running the rope over a stump we could use as a chopping block. I told the trapper to stand by with his axe while I ran up the engine to full power, then to chop the rope when I waved my hand.

"Meantime, Chris had loaded the heavily bandaged patients into the cabin and made them as secure and as comfortable as he could.

"We were taking off into the wind, and I figured that with the down-slope and starting with full power we had a good chance of making it. I pushed the throttle wide open, waited for the engine to pick up full revs, then gave the signal. The trapper swung his axe, the rope parted and away we went rumbling through the bullrushes.

"With the full power from the start, the blast of the slip stream over the rudder gave me full control, so it was not too difficult to thread the needle of the narrow beach between the trees and the lake. We didn't seem to hit any obstructions, but suddenly, just before the wheels left the ground, there was the most terrible vibration. I thought it would shake the plane to pieces.

"I throttled back as much as I dared but by this time there was no other choice. We had to either take off or crash, so I manoeuvred the Fokker out over the lake, just skimming over the tree-tops, figuring it was better to crash through the ice than into the trees if we had to go in.

"The shuddering continued. It increased when I put on more power, diminishing as I pulled the throttle back, but I couldn't figure out what it was. The engine seemed to be working all right. Chris couldn't find any damage to the fuselage. However, we were able to gain some altitude and continue the flight."

It was a long trip home with the plane trying to shake itself apart all the way. But, finally, McConachie shut off the engine for a dead-stick landing on the Edmonton airport where police cars, ambulances and doctors were waiting.

As the injured men were whisked off in ambulances, McConachie clambered wearily down from the cockpit and was surrounded by reporters and photographers. Meanwhile, Limey studied the propeller. Shocked, he called Grant over to see it. It had split right down the middle as it chopped through the heavy bushes on the take-off. The only thing that had saved it from flinging apart was the metal binding. They had flown all the way home on a thin strip of metal!

The story has a happy ending. After four or five months the Sens brothers recovered and returned to their solitary cabin at Pelican Rapids. They owed their lives to the "wild scheme" thought up and pulled off by the brashest young bush pilot of them all, a man destined to become one of the most colourful and controversial figures in the world of aviation—Grant McConachie.

2. CALDER WORE OVERALLS

Grant McConachie was born in April 1909 in Hamilton, Ontario. At the age of nine months he was bundled up by his parents and taken on a 2,500 mile expedition in a wooden train coach through the deep freeze of a Canadian winter. Sleeping on a straw mattress on the slats of a wooden bunk that swung down from the ceiling, and warming their provisions on a cast-iron stove that puffed dry heat into an atmosphere pungent with the odors of peeled oranges, stale bread crusts and hot human bodies, his mother received a harsh initiation into pioneer life. This was very different from the luxury Elizabeth McConachie had known at home in Buffalo, where her father, the son of an Astor mother, was a wealthy brewer.

It was a little easier for William McConachie. After all, he was a third-generation Canadian, descended from hardy Scottish pioneers who had hacked a clearing in the forests of Upper Canada long before Canada existed as a nation. And he was used to long trips as a Santa Fe railroader. On one of them he had come east, met Elizabeth, persuaded her to break off an engagement and, despite her parent's objections, married her. Since the marriage in 1908, he had visited the booming railroading city of Edmonton and decided to make his home there. So as they travelled west, he knew what lay at the end of the line.

His wife didn't. She had caught some of the excitement of the new land, but to her the five-year-old Province of Alberta was just a name. As the white sahara of the wintering prairies drifted past the frosted window of the coach for long days she began to realize what lay in store. But when they finally did arrive in Edmonton it was still a shock to her.

"Mercy," she recalled, "I thought I had come to the very edge of the world. The bitter cold of Edmonton in January. My, it must have been thirty or forty below. It just made you gasp, took your breath away . . ."

The taxi from the station was a home-made cutter pulled by a scrawny Indian pony. She and her child were bundled under furs in the open sleigh to travel for miles between huge parapets of snow, out beyond the fringes of settlement until finally they pulled up in front of what appeared to be an unpainted woodshed submerged in the snow. This was the second dwelling in the "suburb" of Calder, across the tracks from Edmonton's east end. McConachie, on his previous inspection trip, had put together this three-room shanty to house his family until a proper home could be built in the spring.

The rest of that winter was an ordeal for the young lady from Buffalo. There was no plumbing. Water came from snow melted in a tin tub on the kitchen stove. Kerosene lamps provided illumination. The nearest stores were miles away in the city. Several days a week Mrs. McConachie pushed the baby sleigh for three miles through the snow to the trolley line that rambled downtown to Edmonton.

When the snow melted, causing a quagmire of prairie gumbo, the foundations were laid for the two-storey McConachie dwelling. The slab-sided house, yellow with green trim, and with a boarded verandah and black-shingled hip roof, was to be Grant's home for the next twenty-four years until his marriage.

As young McConachie grew up, Calder also grew, becoming a lively and colourful community, a mixture of many races and cultures—Scots, Russian, English, Yugoslavian, Ukranian,

French, Irish, Chinese—homogenized into a soot-grimed fraternity of workers-on-the-railroad. During his school years
there was always the hiss of steam from the huge black
locomotives that clanked past.

In the days of Grant McConachie's youth, Calder wore
overalls. Wherever men gathered and youngsters listened, the
talk and the banter concerned the skills of the railroad; of
mastering the great engines, of running on time, of stocking
the firebox to keep up steam, of "stretching out" trains properly
to prevent slack building up between each car which could
lead to a snap so violent that it would "pull a draw bar" and
break up a train, of slow freights "going in the hole," pulling
into a siding, to be "scooped" or overtaken by a faster train.

Since Calder was a railroad town, it was only natural that
William McConachie, as district chief master mechanic, should
be its uncrowned mayor. Short and rotund with direct, penetrating brown eyes and wispy blond hair neatly brushed along
the sides of his bald dome, he had the large, sinewed, competent
hands of an expert mechanic. He invariably wore a carefully-
brushed blue serge suit, white shirt and black tie, a large
gold watch chain across his vest and polished black shoes.
When he arrived at work he changed to overalls in the little
red yard shack that was his headquarters.

He always carried a black Gladstone bag to work as his
duties frequently took him out on the road. He was, in effect,
a "check pilot" on the railroad, responsible for the mechanical
and operational efficiency of the equipment and manpower in
his district. This meant that young Grant often didn't see his
father, particularly in winter when trains suffered from freeze-
ups.

There were many freeze-ups. With all those hose joints and
connections dripping water or spouting steam, in sub-zero the
lines froze, the pans froze, connections burst. The master
mechanic was a nomadic foreman monitoring the performance
of men and engines under these arduous conditions.

With this background it is hardly surprising that William McConachie had very firm ideas about the value of work. Work, he believed (as his Presbyterian ancestors believed) was good: It was the perfect antidote for laziness and mischief. He told his wife: "Keep Grant busy and he'll find no time to get into trouble. The devil can soon find employment for an idle youngster."

So Grant was kept busy. From the age of six until after he left high school his time was fully occupied. At home there was always a stock of boxcar lumber in the back yard to be sawn and split for firewood, kerosene lamps to be trimmed, polished and refilled, snow to be shovelled, the basement to be cleaned, and other regular domestic chores to be performed.

He discovered early, however, that persuasion could ease his burdens. As an eight-year-old he was told to pile a huge stack of firewood against the back of the house. The pay was twenty-five cents, a good wage. Grant sub-contracted three pals, in the best Tom Sawyer style, to help him stack the wood; he paid them two cents each, which was not a good wage.

Outside the home, he did every job that it was possible for a young, healthy, small-town boy to do: after school there was a paper route, and a job as a salesman and delivery boy for Turner's General Grocery at $2.50 a week. A private side-line selling Christmas cards earned him a .22 rifle. On his afternoons off he used the rifle to shoot rabbits, which he sold to the Chinese restaurant. They later appeared on the menu as chicken chow mein.

All through high school he supplemented these earnings with a succession of summer jobs. He bundled lathes in a lumber-yard, ran a planer in a sawmill, laboured on a farm, wheeled ashes for a steam plant, acted as night watchman and hostler for the railroad and as fireman on a threshing machine. These were rugged jobs for a boy.

It is no wonder that McConachie's childhood friend Glen
Fenby summed up his memories of the lean and gangly lad:
"The thing I remember about him, he was always working."

He added a significant note: "Grant had quite a charm for
the women on his grocery route. Even as a lad he seemed to
have all the social graces. He was very deferential to women
—and they all remembered his smile."

Others were to remember McConachie's smile, in a bemused
and often rueful way. Already, despite his father's beliefs,
Grant was finding time for youthful devilment; the prankish
sense of humour was already making its appearance. On one
notorious occasion he conspired with a school chum to spike
the teapots of the Ladies Aid Society with liberal lacings of gin.
Then they hid in the stairwell to watch developments as the
pillars of the feminine community gathered in the McConachie
living room for their Wednesday afternoon social.

The meeting never did come to order, nor were the pro-
ceedings ever recorded in the official minutes of the Society.
But it was the liveliest meeting in the Society's annals. The
two lads began to have misgivings as the discussion mounted
to an uproar, with tipsy matrons swaying on their feet and
clamouring for attention. Finally, the meeting dissolved in
confusion. The members of the Ladies Aid, Calder Branch,
stumbled off to their respective homes in various stages of
befuddlement. There were quite a few late suppers in Calder
that night. Questions were asked, but never answered. It was
only after a safe passage of years that McConachie ventured to
disclose his involvement in the great teapot scandal.

Because of his heavy work load during school months,
Grant was given special dispensation to play hockey after
dinner with the older boys. As a teenager, he developed
rapidly, his sinews toughened by work and sports activity.
By the time he graduated to Victoria High School, he was a
young giant, excelling in football, hockey and basketball; he

was unbeatable in marathon bicycle racing over the 200-mile grind between Edmonton and Calgary.

It would be difficult to suggest that he had a normal childhood. He worked like a galley slave, although the family did not need the money he earned. The Protestant ethic was deeply ingrained in him, and he worked harder and longer than most full-grown men.

And there was tough, proud William McConachie to contend with, more boss than father to the resourceful boy.

As always, the family car was a source of friction. In the Calder of 1925, a car was a luxury, a status symbol appropriate to the CNR's chief master mechanic of the division and a leader of the community. Apart from his house, which he maintained so proudly that it always seemed to be newly painted, the dark-blue MacLaughlin-Buick was the only real luxury the thrifty railroader had ever permitted himself. To young Grant's and his mother's considerable chagrin, his dad demonstrated more interest in polishing and grooming the car than in driving it. Whenever the roads were muddy or if there was even a hint of rain, the automobile stayed in the garage to be shined, tinkered with and admired. The car was so like a convalescent that its occasional ventures on to the roads—in perfect weather—were family events.

Mrs. McConachie shared her son's impatience with the Buick's back-yard immobility and supported his ambition to get behind the wheel of the precious automobile. Their chance came when McConachie took off on a ten-day business trip to Winnipeg. But, cannily, he removed the carburettor and locked the garage. Grant soon borrowed a carburettor from the neighbourhood garage, picked the garage lock and liberated the MacLaughlin-Buick. Mother and family had a glorious series of outings before restoring the car to its original situation in time for father's return.

Later, his dad and mother left in April for a month's vacation in Chicago and sixteen-year-old Grant knew that this was his great chance. William McConachie, a suspicious man, had changed the garage lock. He also had hidden the car keys. No problem. Young McConachie soon found the car keys. Then he unscrewed the hinges, laid the heavy garage doors flat and backed the car out over them. So simple.

He recalled:

"My pal Cam and I had a wonderful time. We toured around town, took our girl friends for drives out to Saint Albert, went on picnics up the Sturgeon River. We had very little time for school, of course. This meant we had to compose quite a few notes to explain our absences from the classroom. I had my aunt die, my grandfather die, my uncle die, and so on until suddenly I realized my grandfather had died twice, so I suppose the hookey was bound to catch up with us.

"When Dad returned, I had the car in the garage and the doors screwed on again. But when he opened the garage I nearly died. There were big muddy tire marks running up the insides of the doors. To my great relief he didn't notice them and we scrubbed the marks off, but the hookey playing caught up with us."

In one disastrous day Grant got the word that someone had tattled to his dad about the car and also that Mr. Hicks, the school principal, wanted to interview him about his absences from school. He held a conference with his fellow-conspirator, Cam Richardson. The jig was up. The combined retribution of parents and principal was just too much. They'd run away. Go to Vancouver, by train, and join the Navy.

Grant's mother said later: "I was out in the front yard cutting some pansies when Grant came out and smiled at me and told me I was the best mother in the world. I should have known right there something was not quite right. Then he asked if he could stay the night with Cameron so they could study. I agreed, but what I didn't know was that the rascal had already slipped a kit bag out the back window."

The next morning Cameron's mother came looking for her boy, thinking he had spent the night at McConachie's. The lads had disappeared. Grant had drawn his two-hundred-dollar savings from the bank, and they'd gone downtown and bought a gun, ammunition, stout breeches with leather facings, windbreakers, and other provisions appropriate for life on the open road. Later they had boarded a CNR passenger train and headed west to join the Navy.

The mystery of their disappearance didn't last long. The conductor, a good friend of the McConachie family, recognized the boys in the first-class passenger coach as the train rolled through Stoney Plain just beyond the western limits of the city. The word was flashed back from the next station.

The runaway touched off a domestic crisis in the McConachie living room. William McConachie, apoplectic with rage, was inclined to let the "rascals" run as far as they wanted. His wife pleaded Grant's case, even threatening to leave home unless her husband fetched him back.

So action was taken.

As the CNR Super Continental steamed into the log station at Jasper, deep in the Rockies west of Edmonton, the section superintendent, acting on orders from the chief master mechanic in Edmonton, swung aboard the first of the passenger coaches. Minutes later he was escorting two rather sheepish youngsters to the station platform. The Royal Canadian Navy had just lost two potential recruits. The boys were locked in a storage room in the basement of the station until, three days later, Grant's father and Cam's big brother arrived. As soon as he saw his dad, Grant bolted down the tracks. His father commandeered a local yard engine to give chase, but his quarry cut off into the woods. The youngster soon realized the futility of flight, however, and returned to face his father's fury. It was a grim and silent journey home to Edmonton.

The family council that followed was a painful one. The tearful reproaches of his mother and his younger sister Phyllis were every bit as bad as the ragings of his father. And the questions. Why had he run away? Why this, why that?

Finally goaded to rebellion, he exploded. He accused his father of failing to understand that a boy needed some freedom, some free time away from work. It wasn't fair to expect him to work every second of his waking hours. And another thing. What kind of life was it for a sixteen-year-old if he had to be home at nine o'clock regardless, no excuses. The guys all thought he was a sissy, having to leave hockey games before the end, to get home by nine because his dad insisted. Or taking out a girl! And having to be in at nine!

Miraculously, the outburst worked. Father and son both calmed down and reached an agreement that if Grant passed his Grade Ten examinations he could do what he wanted, go wherever he liked. It was a great victory—for both McConachies.

The next two months were tough ones. "As runaways my friend Cam and I were treated like social lepers. It was a strict society in Calder, and a person who ran away from home was really bad. Like someone who had robbed a bank or been in jail, almost." School was rough, too. ("I was so far behind, I didn't know what the teachers were talking about . . .") But Grant buckled down and with some special tuition, he somehow passed his Grade Ten exams.

Now he was on his own.

3. SWEATED LABOUR

His father was as good as his word. Through his railway connections he got the boy a job wheeling ashes in the stationary steam plant that provided electricity for the mountain resort town of Jasper, Alberta.

So in the summer of 1925, Grant McConachie was a freewheeler, on his own, living away from home for the first time. This posed some unfamiliar problems.

With some difficulty he found lodging in a rooming house, but he had to eat his meals in restaurants. Accommodation in Jasper was so scarce that his bed was shared by two other men in round-the-clock shifts. It was like a comedy skit. Grant would roll out his bedding on the cot from midnight till eight and then the next man would shake him by the shoulder to claim the bunk.

Grant's work shift was four P.M. till midnight. The lazy, incompetent day fireman stoking the big furnace left all of the ashes from his shift. When McConachie came on he had to shovel and wheel the huge pile of ashes of the past eight hours from the pits to the dump outside, and somehow keep up with his own shift to leave the ash pits clean for the midnight crew. It was hard labour for any man, and he was a lad of sixteen. For the first few days he stumbled from job to cafe to cot to job in utter exhaustion. He thought his muscles would never stop aching. But gradually he got into the swing of it and was able to take pride in his ability to handle a real job. He was soon as tough as any man.

By the standards of McConachie's railroad upbringing, a top stoker was always greatly admired, and the sixteen-year-old soon developed a hero-worshipping regard for Tiny Johnson, the fireman on his shift. Tiny was a bull moose of a man rearing six-foot-seven in his bare feet. He was so powerful he used a snow shovel to heave coal and would joyfully impress Grant by doing it with one hand. This incredible prowess and Tiny's gentle kindliness quickly won the devotion of the youth from Calder.

"This was a very important and formative period of my life, the first time away from home on my own. I grew very fond of Tiny Johnson and he taught me some lessons I never forgot. I was surprised at the kindness shown to me by a complete stranger, and I found everyone responds to kindness. It became apparent to me that no matter how big you are you can't shove your way through life, but if you try to help people, you make friends, and they come to your aid when you're in trouble," McConachie recalled. "Years later, when Tiny went half blind, I was very glad to be able to employ him, and he had a job with me for about twenty years. As long as he wanted."

The weeks at the ash pit dragged on, and while the work was less agonizing now, it was dirty, and it would always be a dirty job.

There had been really no fun that summer for young McConachie. Just work, sleep, eat, work, sleep, eat. No girls. Or sports. Was this all there was to freedom?

He thus began to entertain his first misgivings about the so-called joys of independence. He was at first reluctant to admit even to himself that he missed the security and comforts of home. But Jasper seemed to be only hard work, sleeping, eating, and paying out his hard-earned money. Everyone wanted his money. He even tried to save by doing his own laundry. But his costs always seemed to overtake his wages. At home he had been able to save most of his earnings.

One afternoon late in August he was hunched over a tub hand-washing socks when his glance caught a pair of gleaming black shoes, an unusual sight in the plant's furnace room.

Surprised, he looked up to see his father watching him. "Have you thought about coming back to school, son?" His father's tone was casual, almost indifferent.

"No, Dad. I'm on my own now. No more school for me." There was no argument.

"It's up to you, my boy. It's your life." Then his father added, "Oh, by the way, Rex is in good shape. Thought you'd like to know. I think that dog misses you. Seems sort of lost around the place. Oh, yes, your girl sends her regards. She was over at the house the other day talking to your mother, and she was asking about you."

After more casual conversation his dad left.

Ten days later, on September 4, Grant quit his job, bought a one-way ticket, went home, settled gratefully into his own familiar room, and enrolled for Grade Eleven at Victoria High School.

His savings from the two months hauling ashes and firing were a lousy twenty-two dollars. He bought a snappy new double-breasted topcoat at a "Walk Up and Save Ten" cut-rate clothing store, and had enough left to take his girl out for an evening of dancing. At the dance, the coat was stolen.

But the summer of hard labour had its rewards. Independence at sixteen had lost much of its glitter and McConachie was able to appreciate his home life. Even high school became attractive, though not the classroom. That autumn and winter Grant, his muscles developed by the hard physical work, emerged as the number one sports hero of Victoria High, excelling in football and basketball.

"I hadn't realized that all my bicycle riding, and particularly

the work at Jasper, had put me in such good shape. I wondered why everybody fell down when I hit the line on the football field," he said.

At basketball he excelled even in the men's league, as a first-
string member of a team that made a strong bid for the provincial championship.

At home, he had outgrown the crisis of being sixteen and
was getting along well with his father, and the stigma of his
runaway had been erased in the community.

Although he was a reluctant student, his personal warmth
and enthusiasm ensured his popularity with teachers and
students. His grades were about average, but he failed utterly
in Latin and this proved disastrous to an early ambition to become a doctor.

His principal, C. O. Hicks, years later, appraised his former
student: "He was a young man of unusual determination and
personality. When he played football and found he could not
penetrate the opposing line he vaulted over it. That seemed to
sum up his attitude to other problems as well. I can't think of
him without remembering his wonderful smile, radiating friendship and sincerity. It seemed to envelop you and hold you en-
thralled, for it was the magic of a great personality."

That smile again!

The last summer of his high school career, he worked at the
CNR's Kinsella Pits which in 1926 were the source for fine
gravel to ballast the main line out of Edmonton. He worked as
a night watchman on the six-to-six twelve-hour night shift and
became familiar with the maintenance of the big "iron cows,"
the freight locomotives. He qualified to check them out and
move them into coaling or loading stations.

The working hours were long, but the seventeen-year-old
relished the thrill of mastering the great locomotives, wearing
the striped overalls of a railroader and sharing the bunkhouse
with the work gang.

Then suddenly his world was shattered by a minor disaster.

He had the misfortune to bring a locomotive to a halt with its wooden cowcatcher directly above a glowing dump of ashes.

The cowcatcher was burned to cinders, Grant was fired, and the man who tried to cover up for him by reporting that the cowcatcher was demolished by a rock on the track was punished for turning in a false report. Young Grant was fired by the big boss himself, the chief master mechanic—William McConachie.

At home the lad was in disgrace. He was despondent. His bright hopes of learning the railway trade seemed dashed. But to his astonishment the union local decided to intervene. The union argued that Grant was being paid only as a watchman, not as a hostler or engine jockey, and ought not to be punished for inefficiency in carrying out extra unpaid duties.

In the end, the top boss, William McConachie, was forced to put him back on the job with a substantial bonus of back pay for the hostling duties he had performed. His father was furious for weeks afterwards. There was silent hostility in the McConachie household.

The next summer he was fired once again, this time from his job as timekeeper. A hostler named Stepkov demanded that he falsify the time sheets in his favour. Grant's indignant refusal led to hot words and Stepkov swung a fire shovel, gashing McConachie's face and knocking him to the ground. Livid with rage, McConachie picked up a long-handled sledge hammer and chased the big hostler out of the locomotive cab and right across the rail yards.

"I had it timed beautifully, swinging that great hammer. Every four paces I took another swing at the bastard. By this time he was scared witless, running for his life and just half a pace ahead of that swinging hammer head all the way. He could hear it swishing past his ass. Finally, just outside the bunkhouse, I clipped him with a glancing blow. It knocked him right off his feet and I jumped on top of him."

Workmen running behind the pair broke up the fight and

the foreman fired McConachie and Stepkov on the spot. Later, however, when the facts were reviewed by the union grievance committee, the youth got his job back.

But by now a railroading career had lost its allure for McConachie. He was to don the striped overalls again, but only to earn enough money to qualify for what he considered a much more exciting destiny. By the time he had finished high school McConachie was lost to his father's sooty but honourable trade.

He was now eighteen, bull strong, incredibly naïve, but experienced enough to realize that a life of grime, hard labour and long hours was not his chosen destiny. By the code of Calder, where he had grown up, the definition of success was— work hard and stay out of trouble. It was no longer McConachie's personal code. Education, he decided, was part of the formula. He registered in Engineering at the University of Alberta in September of 1927.

4. EDMONTON FACES NORTH

In the 1920s Edmonton posed as a civilized and sophisticated metropolis. The fine and prestigious University of Alberta lay just across the river from a downtown that embraced the marble halls and the stately dome of the parliament buildings as well as the medieval castle-like Macdonald Hotel with its grey-stoned aura of solid distinction. The Women's Musical Society, the Celebrity Concert series and other cultural overlays all helped the city to sustain its veneer of urbanity.

But deep down, Edmonton was still frontier. Stilted boardwalks traversed rainy-season quagmires in many of the residential areas. Children got lost in bushlands within the city limits. Weeds flourished between streetcar tracks. The chamber of mines was as important as the chamber of commerce. Stores that dazzled their customers with copies of the latest Parisian creations were outnumbered by outfitters featuring snowshoes, trapline gear, bush boots, moccasins, mukluks, fur parkas, big-game artillery, ammunition and prospectors' supplies.

Ladies of the Women's Musical Society were sometimes jostled on downtown streets by rough-clad trappers, free traders and prospectors who had come "outside" to Edmonton to squander their boodle. These men roved the sidewalks, swapped coarse banter in the saloons and celebrated riotiously in the hotel rooms. And soon the numbed survivors of these

revelries would stumble on to the bush planes at Blatchford
Field to vanish into the northern skies, into the wilderness of
the Mackenzie delta and the Barrens, to refill their pokes and
to thrive on the harsh frontier existence of the trap lines, the
trading posts and the gold claims.

As they winged into the north, rumpled, unshaven and hung-
over, they were the new breed of airborne pioneers who were
opening vast virgin territories suddenly accessible by bush-
plane. Just as the railroad had cracked open the west in a
previous generation to create and sustain cities like Edmonton,
so in the '20s the airplane was penetrating the north. The new
frontier started two miles from the heart of Edmonton, at the
hay-meadow airfield, jump-off point for the small single-
engined bush planes heading down north.

Down north! In the Edmonton of the '20s the phrase spelled
rugged adventure and the hope of quick riches. Down north!
To the oil-oozing tar sands of Athabaska, to the fertile reaches
of the Peace River country, to the gold-bearing quartzite of
Yellowknife, far north beyond the icy waters of the Great
Slave Lake, more than a thousand miles north to the broad
delta where the Mackenzie River emptied the silt of a quarter
of a continent into the Arctic Sea.

With mounting excitement Edmonton looked north to this
vast and promising hinterland . . . northern Alberta, upper
British Columbia, the Yukon Territory and the Northwest Territories, two million square miles of still-to-be-discovered treasure—gold, silver, copper, uranium, furs. The new-era folk
heroes of Edmonton were the young men who flew the bush
planes down north.

During McConachie's school years the front pages of the
Edmonton newspapers extolled the heroics of these northern
air pioneers. The episode of the moose-glue propeller was
typical. As first reported in the press, it was indeed a fantastic
story. Stranded 850 miles north of Edmonton with a broken
propeller, a bush pilot and his mechanic had shot a moose,

chopped down some birch trees, and then fashioned a new prop of birch laminations bonded with glue stewed from the hide and hooves of the moose.

The true story was almost as remarkable. Two planes were marooned at Fort Simpson with propellers shattered by ice hummocks. Replacements were laminated out of oak sleigh boards using glue (from moose hides) acquired from the local Hudson's Bay trading post. Both planes made it back to Edmonton with their moose-glue props.

Fostered by such publicity, the bush pilots became Edmonton's celebrities. Wop May, a First World War hero and the best-known bush pilot of them all, drew a throng of thousands to the Edmonton field merely by arriving there on the routine delivery flight of a new bush plane. The frenetic "air age" excitement of that era in Edmonton can be sensed in the prose of a page-one editorial in the Edmonton *Journal* lauding a mercy flight made by Wop May and Vic Horner to deliver serum to a snowbound outpost threatened with a diphtheria epidemic.

> Canadians were thrilled to read of this heroic exploit. The feat, which was nothing more or less than a sublime gamble with death, on an errand of unalloyed mercy, must forever be associated with the great deeds of men since time began. It rivals the heroism of Balaclava and Lucknow. If anything it outshines them. . . .

It was not surprising, then, that young McConachie's boyhood romance with railroading should yield to a new fascination with the burgeoning north and the bush pilots who symbolized the new age of exploration and high adventure.

During his final year at high school, the youth dawdled many a school-day afternoon at the Royal Signals shack near Calder. He was first attracted there because a friendly mechanic would lend him tools to tinker with the decrepit automobile he had patched together for scooting around town. But soon he was spending hours inside the shack that provided radio communications for the entire Western Arctic. He was fascinated by the interchange of radio messages with the Arctic settlements . . . remote, romantic outposts of the fur traders, trappers, prospectors and missionaries. Names like Aklavik, Coppermine, Arctic Red River, Fort Norman and Fort Wrigley came alive through the big receiver in the corner. Here, too, he came to know the local folk heroes, the bush pilots; legendary men like Punch Dickins, Wop May, Walter Gilbert, Con Farrell, Stan MacMillan, Archie McMullen, Art Rankin and others who dropped by from the airport to hear from their friends on the far-northern sky routes. Grant listened to their stories with mounting excitement. Railroading, he had learned by harsh experience, meant soot, sweat, and the scant rewards of honest toil. It was then he began to consider a career in the sky.

Young McConachie's lifetime love affair with the flying machine actually began, however, in September of 1927 while he was on a brief holiday prior to going into first year engineering at the university. A low-wing Junkers damaged its propeller and undercarriage in a hapless landing at the Edmonton airfield not far from the McConachie home.

He became fascinated by the repair problem presented by the crippled Junkers. When the aircraft was finally pronounced airworthy the pilot invited the youth along on the test flight.

Hunched on the webbing of the jump seat, the eighteen-year-old experienced his first sensation of flight. His view through the unwashed cabin window past the wing was restricted to flashes of landscape, a patchwork of farmlands, a pattern of streets and houses, a glimpse of crazily-tilted horizon. Then he was back on earth again. A quick flight, but unforgettable.

A few days later a visiting commercial pilot from Winnipeg took him up in an Eagle Rock cockpit plane. The exhilaration and thrill of this flight made an even more vivid impression on the youth. This time he wore helmet and goggles and was able to sit beside the pilot in the cockpit.

As the small aircraft rose steeply above the tree line and banked in a climbing turn over the Calder rail yards, he was in a new and exciting world. The familiar terrain of his boyhood was now spread below him as the plane wheeled and soared in the freedom of the sky. The slip stream swirled over the visor to fan his cheeks, the roar of the engine drummed its rhythm against his leather helmet. He could watch the pilot's deft and easy use of the throttle lever, the control column and the rudder pedals. This was an astonishing machine, a wonderful machine. He was hooked. He determined to fly.

But first, Grant had to play the role of an engineering student. To attend lectures, since he couldn't afford gas for his jalopy, he had to travel twelve miles by streetcar from Calder through downtown Edmonton, across the High Level Bridge and then to walk the last mile to reach the university. He often avoided the tedious journey to and from home by the simple device of skipping lectures or by overnighting with friends on the campus.

A friend, Leo McKinnon, remembers him as a young man of many enthusiasms and formidable persuasive power. Frequently he used to bunk in with McKinnon and his dormitory room-mate, Neil Stewart. He somehow managed to persuade his two hosts to share one cot while he stretched his lanky frame on the other. In the morning he usually cajoled them into sleeping late and missing breakfast, which gave them two meal credits with which they could host McConachie for lunch and dinner.

Reflecting on the young man who so often came to dinner and stayed, McKinnon said, "That McConachie could charm you right out of your socks without taking your shoes off . . . and make you like it."

He joined in the social activities of the Students' Union, played handball, basketball and rugby, and on Saturdays sold ties and socks at the Hudson's Bay store to earn walking-around money. All the while his mind was on flying and the glamour of the northern skies, but he had neither cash nor credit to finance the restless urge to fly.

In May of 1928 as the university final exams approached, McConachie realized that he had no hope of passing. But he was not particularly concerned. He had learned that the Canadian Government was offering free flight training at Camp Borden in Ontario in a program to train a reserve force of "provisional pilot officers" for the Royal Canadian Air Force. He put in his application, was accepted, and started a search for transportation to eastern Canada. In the meantime he didn't bother to write the exams—or to tell his parents what he was doing.

The trip east was a disaster. It started well when Grant got the job of chauffeuring a friend's new car to Ottawa. Free transport. Unfortunately, the friend, who couldn't drive, decided to take the wheel for the last few miles to impress his hosts with his arrival. The car smashed into a tree.

Then, before he could report to Camp Borden, McConachie broke out with a scarlet fever rash, had to miss the training course, and returned to Calder as reserve fireman in the cab of a CNR locomotive.

During his absence, his parents had searched in vain for his name in the newspaper lists of University Examination Results—First Year. On his return his admission that he had not written the exams once again put him in disgrace at home. "What will become of the boy?" his mother wailed. The boy himself had no clear idea.

Except that he wanted to fly.

5. "EVEN THE AIR
SEEMED ON FIRE"

Because he was so unpopular at home Grant was glad to locate a job for the rest of the summer. He became the night watchman for the crew on a locomotive ditching machine, a complicated piece of equipment with sixteen levers that operated steel arms extending laterally from each side of the locomotive. At the end of each arm was a scoop shovel used to clear out the drainage ditches beside the track. By shrewd observation, Grant was able to figure out how to work the machine.

So when the regular operator booked off on sick leave, the foreman put young McConachie on the job. Everything went well until one night, drowsy from eighteen hours on shift, he ran the gouger through a highway intersection, scooping up the roadway, knocking out the power lines, blacking out the entire town of St. Albert and halting traffic for more than an hour. Miraculously, he escaped blame for the incident and finished the rest of the summer as the ditcher engineer.

In the fall of that year, 1928, he made the big decision. He decided to find a job rather than have another try at university. He would use his savings and earnings to take flying lessons at the Edmonton & Northern Alberta Aero Club. He told himself he would some day graduate as an engineer, but he'd get his pilot's license first and then see what happened.

He hired on as fireman on a pile-driving engine working
along a spur rail line north of Edmonton, and worked ten
hours a day firing. Soon he was working as a watchman, an
easier job, where all he had to do was keep steam up and check
the engine. In his spare time he played hockey, switching
from one team to another as the crew moved from town to town.
He would play for North Fork one week, then in the next game
would be teamed with Greencourt against North Fork, then
with Whitecourt, Mayerthorpe or Sangudo.

On week-ends he flew. When the winter job ended he
promptly blew all his savings from it on his lessons at the aero
club. Very slowly and very expensively he was building up
towards the number of hours in the air that would qualify him
for a commercial license.

He tried, without success, to find a job in or near Edmonton
that would pay enough to support him and pay for his flying
lessons. Finally, he had to sign on with the Northwest Lumber
Company as fireman on a logging train running out of Greencourt, shuttling timber from the outlying camps through dense
bush country to the Greencourt sawmill. Home now was to be
a peeled-log bunkhouse in a clearing beside the tracks twelve
and a half miles down the line from the Big Bear lumber
camp, about eighty miles northeast of Edmonton.

Grant's job was to keep the logging train engine, or shay,
fired up with coal. The shay was tiny, only half the size of an
ordinary locomotive, and its top speed was less than five miles
an hour at full throttle. But it was a powerful machine, and
it gobbled up coal as fast as it was shovelled in.

This was sheer bull labour. The hours were six to six, seven
days a week, one week off after each full month. As he flopped
on to his cot at the end of the twelve-hour day, drugged with
fatigue, Grant felt like a galley slave, shackled to a scoop
shovel, heaving coal into the insatiable furnace until every
muscle ached in protest.

But the pay was good and money meant flying time, the precious ten-dollars-an-hour air time needed for his commercial license. He had now made up his mind to become a commercial pilot. His commercial ticket was a passport to freedom from a life of brute labour, a passport to an exhilarating new life in the air.

So all through the long summer months the strenuous routine of the bush railroad continued. During his week off each month McConachie returned to his home in Calder and spent his pay cheques building flight time in the cockpit of a Gypsy Moth biplane.

But back in the woods the slow and tedious journeys through the long green tunnels continued day after back-breaking day. There was no break in the monotony.

Until August 22, 1929 . . .

That morning the sun was a pale disc as it rose over the tree line, its rays filtering bleakly through a smoke haze.

"Forest fire," muttered Brockey, the engineer, as he and McConachie clambered into the engine. "Hope to God we don't run into it!" The brakeman and conductor were already aboard the caboose at the end of the long train.

As the train moved slowly through the woods towards the lumber camp McConachie noticed that it was getting darker.

The air tasted bitter. As they chugged along, billows of wood smoke began to swirl through the cab of the donkey engine. When they reached Big Bear and were ready for loading, the bush fire was not far away. Showers of black ash and burning cinders were now falling from the sky. Hurriedly, they hitched up the log train and got underway. But it quickly became obvious they were not escaping from the fire. A wind shift had spread the flames in a wide encircling movement and soon McConachie could see trees on both sides of the right-of-way bursting into flame. One moment a tree would be standing there green and silent: then, suddenly, with a loud angry crackle it would explode into a flaming torch. The heat was becoming so intense that breathing was painful. Smoke reduced visibility to a few yards.

In desperation they uncoupled the train of flatcars so that the shay, with only the water tender in tow, could move ahead faster. The iron flanks of the engine were now as hot as stove lids and the interior of the cab was an oven, but McConachie continued to shovel coal, working like a robot. At least it was something to do. The situation was desperate.

The brakeman, who had been sent ahead with a lantern to check the tracks, staggered out of the smoke and swung aboard the shay, blackened, gasping, and apparently half-dead. He rasped, "We're trapped! The fire is all round us. The ties up ahead are burning. We're goners."

Flames were now stabbing at the black iron walls of the donkey engine and the heat in the cab was almost beyond endurance.

Then the shay heaved and listed to starboard. The supporting ties had burned out and the tracks were sinking.

The crewmen scrambled down the side-plates as the shay tilted crazily before toppling beside the tracks.

"I was sure we were done for," McConachie recalled. "The fire was all around us. The smoke was so dense I couldn't see and choked on every breath. My overalls were starting to smoke. I tried to protect my face and hands with my cap and handkerchief. My eyes were streaming so badly from the soot I was just staggering around blindly."

Somehow he found himself with his mates hugging the ground under the shelter of the tilted water carrier which was attached to the upset shay. The water in the big tank acted as a buffer protecting the men against the searing heat. As near as Grant could estimate, they remained there for five hours, greedily sucking oxygen from the thin layer of smoke-free air close to the ground. As the fire subsided, the trainmen crawled out on to the tracks again. The right-of-way afforded a narrow passage between the desolation and for some reason they all began to run along the tracks.

"I don't remember being scared," McConachie later recalled. "There was so much excitement and a sort of desperation. I was caught up in the urge to get out of there alive."

Even the air seemed to be on fire. It parched their throats and seared their lungs. They clutched handkerchiefs to their faces, trying to filter out the smoke and heat to protect their eyes and their lungs. They had violent fits of coughing, and vomited as they stumbled blindly along.

Suddenly, the ground fell away under their feet and the four men slid and tumbled down a steep embankment. Then, mercifully, they were splashing in the water of a stream. The log bridge had disappeared in the flames and they had fallen into the gulley.

The forest continued to send clouds of black smoke churning over their heads and spiralling upwards on drafts of super-heated air. But the men knew that they had stumbled on to their salvation. The gulley had trapped a pocket of relatively cool air in which they could breathe freely. McConachie soaked the blistered skin of his hands and face in the stream. He was alive!

At last the refugees clambered out of the stream and sprawled exhausted on the blackened slopes of the embankment. McConachie was astonished to discover his heavy coal shovel lying near by. For some unaccountable reason he had clutched it during the frantic dash along the tracks. Blackey, the brakeman, though he could not remember having done so, had rescued a crate of eggs from the cab of the donkey engine. Men do weird things under stress.

Now these unexpected possessions were put to good use. McConachie set his water-filled scoop shovel over a pile of embers. When the water began to boil, Blackey dropped in the eggs.

"I don't think I ever enjoyed eating as much before or

since," McConachie recalled. "Perhaps it was just that the miracle of our survival had sharpened our appreciation of everything. We ate every egg—about eight each."

Thus fortified, the crew set off on a ten-mile trek home. Long after midnight they trudged into the clearing to find their log bunkhouse still standing. The flame-break of the surrounding meadow had saved it from the holocaust that had devoured everything else for miles around.

There were no more complaints about monotony in camp that summer.

6. "NOT A LAD TO STICK BY THE RULES"

Captain Maurice "Moss" Burbidge, the Edmonton Aero Club instructor, called Grant McConachie a "natural flyer." This was rare praise from Burbidge, an ex-R.A.F. martinet of the old stamp . . . clipped moustache, clipped accent, ice-blue eyes, no ruddy nonsense . . . He seemed to regard his flying students as cadets in mufti, giving the impression he'd have appreciated a salute in acknowledgement of his instructions.

It was only Grant's easy skill at the controls of the Moth that spared him the lash of the Burbidge tongue. He was lucky. The fact that the Aero Club students were paying the princely sum of twelve dollars an hour for dual instructions did nothing to lessen the bite of their instructor's invective.

Fortunately, during his military and civilian flying career, Captain Burbidge had acquired a supreme mastery at the controls of a biplane. The skill and precision of his demonstrations must have been responsible for whatever competence his pupils achieved, for everything else seemed to conspire against the learning process.

Aloft, the mysteries of controlling the progress, direction and altitude of the Gypsy Moth with proper use of throttle, stick and rudder, were less baffling than the frustrations designed into the flying equipment, presumably by some envious groundling.

The strangest of these flying "aids" was the Gosport Tube, designed as a means of communication between instructor and pupil. It was nothing more than a length of garden hose connecting the speaking funnel of one cockpit with metal-disc earphones fitted into the flying helmet in the other.

Even in the relative hush of the locker room, Burbidge's normal flow of exasperated cockney was difficult enough for the most attentive student to comprehend. But when borne aloft in the Gypsy Moth, garbled through the length of the Gosport tube, then churned in the maelstrom of engine exhaust and slip stream in the forward cockpit, the instructor-to-pupil communication conveyed nothing more intelligible than an overtone of rising fury.

Sometimes the instructor gave vent to his exasperation by thrusting the speaking funnel into the slip stream, sending a seventy-mile-an-hour ram of air through the tube to batter the ears of the student. "Clears the wax out of the blighters' heads," Burbidge would explain.

The goggles provided by the Aero Club were fitted with great sponge-rubber blinkers, a safety feature that succeeded only in blocking what little side vision remained from the venetian-blind effect of the biplane wings and the spiderweb of flying wires strung between them. Contributing to the visibility problem was an early-plastic windscreen invariably so pitted and blemished as to sustain the impression of flying through a perpetual haze.

It was not, then, altogether surprising that those air pupils with the determination and the native talent to survive these frustrations went on to become skilled and resourceful pilots.

Grant McConachie was an able and enthusiastic student pilot. After his first two hours at the controls his chief concern seems to have been a mounting impatience to unload the instructor and soar into the unfettered and less-costly status of solo pilot. After a mere five and a half hours of dual instruction even martinet Burbidge had to allow that

Grant, the best student he had ever had, was ready to fly solo.

Technically, Grant's progress as a pilot was first-class. What caused him, and everyone else, a lot of trouble was his utter disregard for regulations. The director of the Edmonton Aero Club, Captain Jimmy Bell, put it succinctly: "He was troublesome, just not the type of lad to stick by the rules."

Bell found this out very early in Grant's flying career. As a director of the Aero Club, Bell received a phone call congratulating him on "that fine young pilot of yours who's been out in the Whitecourt area taking people up for five-dollar rides in one of your cockpit planes."

No such assignment showed on the club's flight log. A subsequent investigation exposed the "fine young man" as Grant McConachie, the twenty-hour-wonder, who still lacked thirty flying hours to qualify for a commercial license and the legal right to carry passengers for hire.

When Grant was grimly summoned by Bell and Burbidge to explain himself, he listened meekly to the airport manager's indictment.

Then he explained that he'd been operating on the premise that the rides would help aviation in general and the club in particular. Most of the passengers were rail construction men with money to spare, and if they could be interested in flying they would join the Aero Club. So, McConachie had rented a plane and charged them for rides. A meadow near the construction camp had served as a runway, and he had filled up with tractor gas whenever he ran low.

Burbidge and Bell listened, fascinated by the rascal's wide-eyed sincerity.

But, for once, the McConachie smooth-talk failed to produce the required results. After delivering a lecture on the significance of air regulations, Captain Bell grounded him indefinitely.

Three weeks later, however, Captain Burbidge found himself cajoling the airport manager into lifting the ban for the good of the club. They needed McConachie's stunt flying to headline their forthcoming annual air show. His "spine-chilling specialty," as proclaimed on the handbills advertising the show, was the "spin of death."

As a climax to the show, McConachie put his yellow-and-black biplane into a spin from five thousand feet, spiralling down seemingly out of control to disappear and, apparently, crash behind a high-treed hill. His trick was to make a low-altitude recovery, circle behind the screen of trees, then roar suddenly over the heads of the audience.

Bell gave in and McConachie got his wings back. The stunt was a smash-hit and the air show a success, but all this did not put an end to the airport manager's problems.

Several weeks later, Bell got reports that private pilot McConachie had again fractured air regulations. This time he had flown a commercial passenger to southern Alberta where he landed in the customer's barnyard.

Jimmy Bell chose to let that one pass, pretending he hadn't heard about it. But a short while later McConachie disappeared with one of the club Moths and was unreported for four days. As soon as he returned to the Edmonton airfield, he was summoned to the upper office. This time it was rumoured around the hangar that he had flown a mining man across the border into the United States, simultaneously fracturing three sets of regulations: customs, immigration and rules of the air—in two countries.

"I really can't explain how he talked his way out of that one," Bell later told friends. "Somehow he got the conversation turned around to the future of aviation, and we never did get back to the matter of his transgressions."

McConachie could not have chosen a diversion better calculated to distract Jimmy Bell from the matter at hand than the future of aviation, a subject on which the diminutive airport manager regarded himself as a leading authority. Reporters, visiting dignitaries, even casual visitors to the grass-patch airfield could rely on the self-appointed prophet of the air age for an oratorical vision of the flying future.

Bell's designation of his airport domain as "aerial crossroads of the world" was to be realized much sooner than even he could have anticipated.

In 1931 Edmonton was selected as a refuelling and overnight rest stop for Wiley Post, the one-eyed aviator from Oklahoma, and his Australian navigator, Harold Gatty, on their record flight around the world in the famous *Winnie Mae*. The course had been from England to Moscow, across Siberia then over the Bering Sea to a sandy beach at Solomon, Alaska, and now, on the home stretch, to Edmonton.

Captain Bell, and the Edmonton airport, basked briefly in the floodlights of world attention. The airport manager devoted a sleepless night to overseeing the numerous arrangements. Fuel and servicing for the *Winnie Mae*. Special police cordons to restrain the wildly cheering throngs. Installation of telephone, telegraph and radio facilities for the press corps. Rest and seclusion for the weary flyers.

Unfortunately, the *Winnie Mae*'s arrival on June 30, 1931, was preceded by torrential rain which turned the field into a lake. The plane got down safely, but taking off appeared to be hopeless.

Captain Bell came up with the solution. All night, as Post and Gatty slept, workmen were stripping the electrical cross-wires from the two-mile concrete stretch of Portage Avenue running in a straight line from city centre to airport.

In the first light of dawn, the white Lockheed monoplane roared down Portage Avenue, wing tips skimming past light standards and hydrants, then slanted upwards to continue its journey around the world. Late the same evening, word was flashed back to Edmonton that Post and Gatty had landed at Roosevelt Field, New York, having circled the globe in record elapsed time of 8 days, 15 hours and 51 minutes.

The visit of the *Winnie Mae* stirred the people of Edmonton with the glamour and aura of great adventure, and probably no one in the entire air-minded community was more deeply impressed than student-pilot Grant McConachie. The event did more than stoke the fires of his flying ambitions. He noted and was later to apply the practical lesson in aerial geography spelled out by the Post and Gatty epic, a lesson that went unnoticed by most observers at the time. The *Winnie Mae* had flown over the roof of the world. It had come in from the north. The shortest distance between Edmonton and the Orient was north rather than west. It was young McConachie's first inkling of round-world thinking, which later was to have a pronounced influence on his own destiny.

7. THE YELLOW-TAILED CROWS

Despite his frequent brushes with authority, by the fall of 1931 Grant McConachie was approaching the fifty-hour mark in his logbook that would signal his qualification as a commercial pilot. He had passed the written and flight tests and now needed only a few more hours of solo flying experience.

He could hardly have chosen a less opportune time to launch a flying career. The Great Depression, combined with drought, had hit western Canada very hard. Prairie farmers were hitching horses to their fuel-starved jalopies. People were selling up and moving on, some joining the mobs of drifters who rode the freights in a hopeless country-wide search for work.

For pilots things were rough. The government of R. B. Bennett had cancelled the prairie air-mail contracts. Aircraft were rotting in silent hangars across the country. Commercial and transport pilots with hundreds of hours' flying experience were out peddling brushes, vacuum cleaners and life insurance.

Then word reached the Edmonton Aero Club in November that the Chinese Government had set up an agency in Vancouver to hire Canadian commercial pilots for an air service to be based in Shanghai. The pay was to be three hundred dollars a month, a fortune in 1931. McConachie rode a cattle train through the Rockies to Vancouver, passed the Chinese flight

tests and interviews, and was ready to leave for Shanghai.
Then he talked to Uncle Harry.

As far back as Grant could remember, the escapades of
his father's youngest brother had been the subject of tight-
lipped conversation around the family dinner table. Uncle
Harry provided the family with a spectacularly black sheep.
He never worked, at least not at any trade recognizable as
work. Yet, to the rage of his industrious brothers, he was
always sharply dressed and able to throw money around. It
was this mysterious affluence, even more than his low regard
for work in any form, that had honed the cutting edge of
family censure.

There had been one brief spasm of family approval when
Uncle Harry, at last responding to the pressures of conformity,
had taken a job firing a steam engine for the Grand Trunk
Railway. Grant's father, as district chief master mechanic
for the railroad, was proud to have the convert in his territory.

He never forgave Uncle Harry the scandal of his departure
from the Grand Trunk. Young Grant later heard the details
from his unrepentant uncle.

It had happened one hot summer afternoon. The engine
Uncle Harry was firing was chuffing up a long grade. He had
paused to mop the unaccustomed sweat from his brow and to
ponder the shortcomings of honest toil. The engineer barked
at him, "More coal! More coal! Get that Goddamned steam up,
man! Jump to it!"

Uncle Harry opened the firebox door, heaved his coal
shovel into the flames, stepped down from the slow-moving
cab, and, without a backward glance, walked away from railroading forever.

Uncle Harry's activities had always fascinated Grant, and
he had looked forward to the happy renegade's visits to the
household. These visits had occurred whenever the summer
circuit of country fairs passed through Edmonton. For Uncle
Harry had a keen eye for a fast buck and a slow yokel, and he

ran a midway concession of dubious fairness at an enormous profit.

Now, on arriving in Vancouver, Grant went along to his uncle's hotel suite. As always, Uncle Harry was a memorable sight. His bald cherubic features dignified with silver-rimmed spectacles could have identified him as a kindly professor or a family doctor—except for his attire. He was resplendent in a sports coat of many colors, maroon bow tie, yellow vest, tan slacks, maroon socks and white shoes with brown trim. He toyed with a gold cigarette case as he listened with close attention to his young nephew's account of the great opportunity to fly for China at three hundred dollars a month.

To Uncle Harry, a natural cynic, it seemed too good to be true.

It was. On checking, they discovered that before signing up for the government airline Grant would have to give up his Canadian citizenship and become a national of China. In a war, he could be drafted into the Chinese Air Force.

As McConachie's enthusiasm for China skies evaporated, Uncle Harry came up with a new idea. Why not go into the flying business in Canada together? He would put up some money to buy a used bush plane. There were a lot sitting idle around the country, weren't there? Grant would rustle up the business and do the flying. They decided to set up a company, Independent Airways, with good old Uncle Harry as president.

That same evening, Grant rode an overnight freight through the Rockies to Edmonton where he bought a blue Fokker monoplane for $2,500 of Uncle Harry's money. Independent Airways was in business.

In fact, Independent Airways was in business from the minute that its pilot could legally fly for hire. Literally. For while Grant was circling the Edmonton airport putting in the last twenty-five minutes of his mandatory fifty hours, his first customer was waiting impatiently on the ground below. Professor Archibald Rowan was not alone in his impatience; the two hundred other passengers who were destined to go aloft on the first commercial flight of Independent Airways all jostled and squawked.

The other passengers were crows. Not ordinary crows, but elite crows that had been chosen by Professor Rowan for a special mission for which they had been adorned with sporty yellow-painted tails and leg bands. Rowan planned to use these crows to prove his theory that birds flew south in the fall and north in the spring because of the effect of the diminishing and increasing hours of daylight on light-sensitive cells in their optic systems. To test this theory he had collected two hundred crows in his laboratory. There, by artificial lighting, the daylight hours of midsummer for the crows had been extended right through until December.

Young Grant McConachie's role was simply to ferry the crows as far south as his fuel would allow. Rowan would then free the birds and give a five-dollar bounty for each leg band of a yellow-tailed crow, with precise data where the bird was shot or captured, mailed in to him at the University of Alberta.

If most of the birds were caught far to the south of the release point, it would prove the birds had not been fooled by Rowan's make-believe summer, and his light-cell theory would fail. But if they were scattered in all directions, some even north of the take-off point, it would prove that the birds were confused, which would support the Rowan claim.

The flight south was without incident. In their cages the birds were quiet, model passengers. Finally, McConachie selected a snow-covered field near Drumheller as his landing strip.

The Fokker's skis skittered over the snow as he executed a smooth landing, then advanced the throttle to taxi to the back stoop of a near-by farm-house. The farmer and his brood of sons, who had never seen a flying machine at close range, were puzzled but delighted to assist with the unloading of the crates and the release of the Rowan crows, which seemed uncertain about what they were supposed to do.

Leaving them hopping around, the men all trooped into the farm kitchen where, over tea and oven-warm bread, the professor could not resist telling his hosts the story of the great experiment. He also mentioned, quite casually, the offer of the five-dollar bounty.

As the daylight waned, the Fokker took off for home. McConachie decided to circle the field for a friendly wave to the hospitable farmer and his family. The farmer and his two boys were too busy for waving. The pen-conditioned crows were still hopping about in the stubble, apparently reluctant to test their wings. To Professor Rowan's considerable chagrin he saw the farmer and his sons blazing away with shotguns, obviously intent on bagging the yellow-tailed birds for their five-dollar bounty. It was too good a chance for a depression-hit family to miss.

As soon as he reached Edmonton, Rowan launched his press and radio appeals. He alerted hunters and bird watchers all over the country to be on the look-out for yellow-tailed crows, and stressed the five-dollar bounty.

Rowan got reports, and leg bands, from widely scattered points in the western provinces of Canada—and some from the United States. He got a letter from the remote Magdalen Islands in the St. Lawrence River reporting that his crows had *not* been spotted there. He also received fifty dead birds and a claim for two hundred and fifty dollars from the hospitable farmer near Drumheller.

The Rowan experiment did not prove to be a major scientific break-through. It tended to confirm, but did not prove conclusively, the light-cell theory of bird migration. Probably its greatest significance lay in its contribution to the flight of man-made birds. It launched the commercial flying career of Grant McConachie.

8. FLYING FISH

The flight of the yellow-tailed crows got Grant's Independent Airways off to an unusual and profitable start. But then there was no more work. As his blue Fokker sat eating up rent in the Edmonton hangar young McConachie had lots of free time to ponder the harsh realities of trying to start an airline in the middle of a depression. No private businessman could afford to hire a plane and pilot. As for the government, Grant had quickly discovered that the glamorous air mail and charter routes extending north from Edmonton through the western Arctic were the preserve of seasoned airmen. A sixty-hour novice with a brand new commercial ticket could not hope to crash the elite fraternity of the far-north bush pilots, when experienced flyers were working as store clerks or were on relief. Times were tough.

Then, in December 1931, by good fortune, Grant happened to meet the president of the Cold Lake Fish Company, Jim Burwash, in the lobby of the Corona Hotel in Edmonton. They talked fish. Burwash told the inquisitive youth about the big winter yield of whitefish being taken from the lakes north-east of Edmonton. He described how the fish were harvested and conveyed to the markets. Long ropes were used to string the commercial nets under the ice between specially-dug water-holes. With the lead lines frozen in at either end, the nets remained suspended under the ice overnight. During the day, the fishermen were occupied chopping out the lines, breaking open the water-holes and hauling up the nets, loaded with whitefish. The fish were dumped into the snow where they froze solid in minutes. Horse-drawn sleighs hauled the frozen fish for distances up to fifty miles over rough bush trails to the railhead at Bonnyville, where the cargo was shipped to city markets in refrigerated freight cars.

The big market for his Cold Lake operation, Burwash said, was in Chicago where the substantial Jewish community showed a religious preference for the fresh-water fish. Too bad, though, the fish had to freeze. The Chicago market would pay a premium of four cents a pound for *fresh* lake fish. But what could you do when you had to haul the cargo in sleighs for ten to fifteen hours in sub-zero weather?

McConachie saw his opportunity:

"From what you've told me, Mr. Burwash, I figure there must be some way we can put your fishing and my flying together so we both come out ahead. Suppose instead of a ten-hour sleigh haul you had a twenty-minute *flight* from the lake. I could use my Fokker to deliver those fish to the freight cars still flopping. Maybe you wouldn't have to freeze the fish. You could sell them fresh and get the premium price!"

Jim Burwash had eased forward in his big chair as McConachie expounded his idea.

"By God, you may have something there, son," he said. "Let's go back to my office and see if we can't work out some kind of a deal."

Soon the pilot and the fishmonger were deeply engrossed in the economics and the logistics of a great new era in fish peddling. Burwash at first doubted that one man and one plane could handle the job but eventually was persuaded to give McConachie a trial contract to fly a minimum of thirty thousand pounds of fish a week over the thirty-mile air distance from Cold Lake to the railhead at Bonnyville. The rate would

be one and a half cents a pound for the fish-lift. Grant
quickly calculated this would cover his gas, oil and living
expenses. What more did you need? Let Uncle Harry worry
about profit and loss. He and Burwash had a deal.

The flight of the blue Fokker to Bonnyville bore slight
resemblance to the perilous air journeys that were making
the northern pilots famous in the early thirties. McConachie
simply followed a branch of the Northern Alberta Railroad
that meandered northeast from Edmonton, flying over the
bleak desolation of wintering farmlands, frozen swamps and
scraggy timber country. When the steel ran out, there was
Bonnyville, a nothing place, consisting of a rail yard and a
street set by the edge of a lake known as Blackwater Slough.
But for the young pilot it held all the allure and hidden promise
of a new-born career.

Banking his plane over the town as he lined up for a
landing on the frozen slough, he was puzzled to see, etched
in the snow, the black blotch of a burned-out building. Then
he realized the charred debris must be the remains of Bonnyville's only hotel. Smoke still curled up from its ashes. The
hostelry, which was to have been home for him and Bud
Sutherland, his one-legged mechanic, must have burned to the
ground overnight.

The true scope of this disaster did not become evident to
McConachie until after he had landed and taxied to the town
water-front. With Bud, he ambled up the main street in search
of lodgings. A thermometer outside the hardware store informed
them that the temperature was 28° below zero.

The store proprietor's information was just as chilling. No,
there was no other hotel. No, there was no room anywhere
else for them . . . unless they wanted to try their luck at "the
harem."

Bonnyville's only boardinghouse catered, the storekeeper explained, exclusively to young ladies. Consequently, the ram-

bling two-storey building on the water-front was known to
local sports as "the harem." But any notions of a water-front
seraglio were effectively dispelled by the vigilance of its proprietor, Madame Lamontagne.

Madame had been jilted by her husband and still nurtured
a deep suspicion of mankind. She found expression for her
maternal instincts in dedication to the safety and welfare of
her young ladies. No gentlemen visitors permitted beyond the
front hall, was one rule. There were many others.

McConachie had to find lodging in Bonnyville at once or
give up the fish-haul contract. Obviously, his only hope was to
persuade the vigilant widow to adopt him and Bud into her
all-female boardinghouse. His most effective ploy, he decided,
would be to exploit the novelty of being the first birdman ever
seen in Bonnyville.

He taxied his Fokker to the widow's front gate, easing the
flying goggles up on his helmet as he emerged from the cockpit
and presented himself at the front door of the boardinghouse.
Madame Lamontagne confronted him with unpromising severity.
She was lean, hunched, her gaunt sallow features framed
with iron-grey hair and surmounted with a bun.

"Yes. What is it?" The tone was forbidding from long habit,
but McConachie took hope from a glint of interest in the dark
eyes. A bright-eyed young giant of an aviator with an infectious
grin was not to be shooed off her veranda like one of those
pesky rounders up the street.

"I am very sorry to disturb you, ma'm." McConachie smiled.
"I'm going to be flying from the water-front here, and I would
like to discuss the possibility of renting your boat shed to
store my gas and oil drums." Better ease into it.

"Well, I must say this is a bit unusual, young man. But
come into the parlor and we can discuss it over a cup of tea."
Cheers. The widow had already broken rule one. Perhaps
there was a chance after all.

Deferential, eager to please, McConachie left his snowy

boots on the porch, removed his helmet and windbreaker and settled comfortably into an overstuffed chair in the widow's parlor. Gradually, his sad story was revealed to her. Now there was no hotel, no place to stay, and he would lose his big chance for a career as a commercial pilot. There were no other flying jobs for a lad of his limited experience. His mother had been so proud of his contract with the Cold Lake Company. She would be terribly disappointed.

The widow gradually relented. There *was* that empty storage room over the kitchen. Perhaps it *could* be fixed up with a couple of cots and an old bureau from the basement. Perhaps some new curtains on the window. Maybe a wash basin and a mirror. Really, it might be quite comfortable. As she was to tell her young ladies at dinner that night, she was sure the nice young boy and his friend would be no trouble. It would be quite exciting to have a pilot living in the house, wouldn't it? All the young ladies nodded vigorously.

In later years, McConachie was to look back on the winning-over of the widow Lamontagne as one of his most challenging ventures in persuasion. Certainly the news that the pilot and his apprentice mechanic had moved into "the harem" caused a sensation in Bonnyville, confirming the prevalent view that a pilot was indeed no ordinary mortal. Now Bud and he were all set to start flying fish.

Bud Sutherland was not a licensed mechanic. Indeed, his only qualifications for the job were his ability to carry out the simple though arduous chores required to service the Fokker outdoors in winter, and the fact that he had a wooden leg. The latter circumstance, which had resulted from an accident while working on the railroad, entitled Bud to a modest pension. This made it possible for him to support his needs on the Independent Airways salary: fifty dollars a month and experience. After two years of such experience, Sutherland could qualify for his air engineer's ticket.

The mechanic's daily routine started before dawn when

he stumped out of the boardinghouse through the snow to fire up the pot-bellied iron stove in the boat shed. This was to heat the lubricating oil he had drained from the engine the night before to prevent it congealing. While the oil was heating, Bud was busy stripping off the heavy canvas wing covers. Then he ducked under the tent that shrouded the prow, and used a blowtorch to warm the cylinders of the radial engine. From there on, it was a race against cold—shut off the blow-torch, strip the engine tent, funnel the hot oil into the engine, rush to the cockpit, try to start the engine. If the engine did not catch in the first three or four tries, it would be too late. The oil would start to congeal as the cylinders cooled. Then he would have to drain the oil out of the engine and start all over again. Many bitterly cold mornings Bud Sutherland cursed himself into a frenzy.

It was a tough way to start the day, seven days a week, but there were compensations. While McConachie was in the sky, Bud hung around the boardinghouse strumming his banjo and singing popular tunes. He enjoyed this recreation, especially on Saturdays and Sundays, when the young ladies were home and he had an appreciative audience.

But he still got only fifty dollars a month for one of the world's grimmest jobs.

McConachie's day began when he was awakened by the rumble of the Jacobs engine down on the water-front. After breakfast, he put on two suits of long underwear, heavy socks, flying overalls, fleece-lined boots, leather helmet, goggles, fur-lined mitts, and a leather face mask he had designed to protect his face from the freezing blast of the slip stream in the open cockpit.

McConachie was later to refer to his first winter on the fish haul as a triumph of ignorance over reality. He did not know there were limits to the number of hours a pilot should fly in a given period. Subsequently, airlines were to establish this safe

limit at eighty-five hours a month. During his first month
hauling fish McConachie was to fly 240 hours.

Great for the logbook, but an almost intolerable strain on
the pilot. He recalled, "I wondered why I seemed to be
exhausted all the time, dog tired. I didn't realize it was because
I was doing too much flying. I thought it was just like any
other business—you got up in the morning and put in a full
day's work. I flew as long as there was light, sometimes even
after dark."

He stayed in the cockpit from first light until long after
sunset. Despite the face mask, he usually froze parts of his
face on the first flight each day. He found it less painful to
remain in a numb condition all day, thus enduring the discomfort of thawing out only once, after the last flight.

In his eagerness to fill out the contract, he was sometimes
caught in the air after dark but he developed a method of
"feeling" his way down. From the night sky, the lake was a
grey patch surrounded by the darker margin of the tree line.
McConachie would descend in a long flat glide with enough
power on for a low rate of sink. As soon as the skis touched
the snow, he chopped back the throttle and settled for the
landing, hoping he would not have the ill luck to hit an ice
hummock.

To McConachie, weather was not a flying problem. When
the blizzards struck or the cloud ceiling closed down, he simply
flew that much closer to the tree-tops.

The legal maximum pay load of the Fokker was eight
hundred pounds, but McConachie soon discovered that his
bush plane would stagger into the air with 1,200 pounds of
fish in the cabin. That promptly became his standard pay
load.

In the wisdom of later operational experience, McConachie
was to reflect on the business aspects of his first flying winter
with rueful amusement: "If there had been a bonus for
ignorance, I would have made a fortune on that fish haul. As

it was, I was going broke happily, losing money on every hour's flying, but I thought I was making money."

His was a simple, in-the-head accounting method. The gas and oil and his living expenses were his costs. He gave no thought to depreciation, funding for major overhaul, wages, other indirect costs or profit. Later, he once calculated that on the fish run he lost about fourteen dollars for every hour he flew.

This weird, dangerous underpriced venture was saved from utter ruin, however, by a freak of good fortune. Unusually heavy snow that winter closed most roads and all bush trails. So the lone fish pilot worked up a steady traffic in groceries and other supplies from Bonnyville to the snowbound settlements in the Cold Lake area, thus getting good loads on the empty back-haul leg of the shuttle. Not knowing any better, he charged only the fish contract rate of one and a half cents a pound for this unexpected cargo.

There was also a trickle of passenger traffic in both directions. His tariff was underpriced too, at three dollars per person for the one-way trip, but, of course, the accommodation on McConachie's first air service could only be considered low-grade steerage. Out-bound from Bonnyville, passengers sat on the floor of the unheated cabin saturated in smell.

The return journey was even less luxurious. The passengers, including an unfortunate bride and groom on one trip, huddled and shivered on sacks of cold wet fish.

Maintenance of the aircraft was rudimentary, for Sutherland's working knowledge of the airplane engine could scarcely have been less. After all, he was still learning—the hard, cold way. It did not occur to him that the spark plugs should be checked, cleaned or replaced. When an accumulation of engine maladies resulted in a drop from 1,800 to 1,600 revs. per minute on the tachometer, he cured the symptom while disregarding the ailment. Ignoring the loss of power, as reflected in the rev. drop, he simply took the metal propeller of the

Fokker into the shed and hammered the metal blades into a
finer angle of pitch. This permitted the prop to revolve faster
at the same power, thus boosting the r.p.m. Bud was ignorantly
happy with this solution. So was McConachie.

Government air regulations specified that a commercial aircraft must be signed out as airworthy every day after inspection by a licensed air engineer. McConachie could not afford
a qualified man, but this technicality did not interfere with his
flying operation. On the rare occasions when he flew to
Edmonton to visit the folks or to have a long overdue check-up
of the faltering engine, he managed to cajole an engineer
friend into signing the back entries in the Fokker's logbook.
A bottle of rye squared the account.

The widow's boardinghouse was considerably less exotic than
the Garden of Allah envisioned by some of the more fanciful
townsmen, though it did prove to be a delightful haven for
the flight-weary pilot and his banjo-strumming mechanic. Their
fellow-residents included several nurses, a schoolteacher, a
switchboard operator, a secretary and a hairdresser. McConachie was not oblivious to the discreet rivalry for his attention
amongst the young ladies, but at the end of his long stint in the
cockpit, his one, dominant interest was sleep. Alone.

Even so, after a long day in the sky, it was blissful to bask
in the heat of the big wood stove in the kitchen in an aura
of fluttery femininity with soft white hands massaging the
warmth back into his frost-numbed features and dainty volunteers struggling to remove ice-encrusted flight gear.

But there were bad days, many of them.

Taking off from Cold Lake one afternoon with a heavy load
in wet snow and poor visibility, McConachie overran the
trampled runway, struck an unseen ice hummock and jolted
into the air. As his overloaded Fokker wobbled over the
trees and struggled for altitude, he was stunned to see that
one ski had been knocked sideways, at right angles. This was
real trouble.

In fact, this could be disaster. Bush pilots never carried parachutes. There was no escape, no choice but to continue his flight to Bonnyville, ride the crippled plane down and hope. With a cabin full of fish, and wing tanks near the brim with high-octane gasoline, the minimum landing speed would be sixty miles an hour. The moment the heavily-loaded aircraft settled, the sideways ski would snag in the deep snow, spiralling the plane into a dreaded ground-loop. It required little imagination for McConachie to visualize the crumpling of the wings, the crushing of the fuel tanks, himself trapped in a jumble of twisted tubing, a geyser of raw gasoline spouting over the wreckage, sparks leaping from twisted metal . . .

McConachie said later he was not conscious of being frightened. He knew his luck would look after him.

When the now-familiar blue Fokker droned over Bonnyville, few townspeople bothered to look up; but Bud Sutherland had spotted the sideways ski from the veranda of the boardinghouse. Suspecting the pilot might be unaware of his danger, he started a frantic dash for the landing area. As McConachie flew low over the shore line he could see his mechanic floundering and signalling but making little progress as his wooden leg kept plunging through the crusted snow. Finally, in frustration Bud just lay panting in the snow, helpless and worried sick.

Circling over the landing area, McConachie saw the means of his salvation. The fresh overflow of a creek had created a narrow path of glare ice a few feet wide across the snow surface in a reasonably straight line for several hundred yards out from the shore line. He manoeuvred the heavily-burdened plane with familiar skill, drifting in at minimum flight speed, near the stall.

His undercarriage brushed the top branches of the shore-line trees. The Fokker levelled over the lake, touching down gently with the good ski in the soft snow, the crippled ski skidding sideways along the pathway of sheer ice. The bush plane lost momentum, wobbled precariously, then slid unsteadily to a stop on the frozen surface without further damage. To Bud Sutherland it was an incredible performance.

The local blacksmith heated the twisted metal axle in his forge and hammered it back into shape. The fish haul resumed.

The episode of the crippled ski had a sequel a few weeks later when McConachie flew to a more remote lake, about eighty miles over wilderness from town, to pick up a load of humpback whitefish at a premium rate. As he was taking off with the load a ski hit a rock-hard snow drift, snapping the repaired axle in two. He was able to close the throttle and stop without further mishap.

There was an Indian fishing camp on the lake, but the people there were making good money fishing so they refused to drive him by dog team the eighty miles through the bush to Bonnyville. McConachie had never handled a dog team but, in desperation, he decided to try.

"I guess my language wasn't strong enough in those days," he later recalled, "because the dogs didn't pay any attention to me. Whenever I did manage to get them untangled from the harness and started along the trail, they would just circle around and head back to the fish camp. After several of these vain attempts, I gave it up and decided to bunk with the Indians for the night.

"I was hungry as a lean wolf by this time and was delighted when the Indians invited me to dinner. We sat around a big pot of muskrat stew. The fish were too valuable to eat. Everybody was dipping in with long spoons, and an Indian handed me a spoon and pointed to the pot.

"Well, sir, the first thing I came up with was the skull of a muskrat with the eyes still in it and staring back at me, so I was less hungry immediately! I finally got something more appetizing out of the mixture, but I wasn't too anxious to become the Indians' star boarder."

Next morning, having abandoned hope of getting out by

dog team, McConachie hired an Indian to help him improvise an axle. They whittled a sapling trunk to fit a wooden shaft inside the broken tubing of the axle, then bound it with birch splints encased in wet caribou thongs. When the thongs dried, they were tight as bands of steel. The repair was strong enough to carry the weight of the empty airplane for the take-off. During a turbulent flight back to Bonnyville, however, the jagged ends of the broken tubing chewed the wooden core so that it broke on landing. But, somehow, the weight of the Fokker was supported by the splints. It was another survival landing.

With the spring melt of the lake ice, the fishing season ended and McConachie flew back to Edmonton. In three months of intensive flying, he had logged more than six hundred hours in the air. After paying room and board and wages for his mechanic, he had enough cash left over to repay Uncle Harry the $2,500 loan for the purchase of the Fokker. By depression standards, it had been a good contract. The fish buyer was pleased, Uncle Harry was pleased, Grant McConachie was happy. This was the life, good times were ahead.

Then he received his first sharp lesson in the economics of flying. The Fokker would not be government-approved for further flying until it received a major overhaul. The very lowest estimate he could get for the overhaul was $1,800. McConachie had to borrow this money back from Uncle Harry to get his aircraft ready for the next venture, barnstorming.

9. BARNSTORMING

"Gee whillickers, Poppa," shouted Pete, "he's flying right into our field!"

"Gol-durn-me if he ain't!" Moose Magrichuk, now fully awake, leapt up from his rocking chair. "Is that feller plumb crazy? He's knockin' down my grain!" Flushing with anger, he was off the stoop and running towards the plane as its wheels settled into the soft furrows. Its struts and undercarriage flattened a broad swathe in the stand of wheat in the field next to the fair grounds where the annual Red Deer Summer Fair was about to begin. By the time the irate farmer had covered the distance to the field, the blue plane had wobbled to a stop. A leather-helmeted pilot rose out of the cockpit, pushed his goggles up on his forehead and greeted the fist-waving farmer with a grin.

"Sorry I bent some of your wheat, sir, but I'll be glad to pay you for it." He reached into a pocket of his flight suit and pulled a sheaf of bills which he waved in the air.

The farmer was nonplussed. Still simmering over the invasion of his property, he was awed by the flying machine, the first he had ever seen up close, and he didn't know what to make of the genial aviator with the bundle of cash. The pilot went on:

"How would you and the family like to come up for a free

ride in my airplane, then we can talk business." As he spoke, he was sliding to the ground as casually as any invited guest.

By noon the Magrichuks had enjoyed the thrill of their first ride in the sky. Grant McConachie, the pilot, and the farmer were seated on the back porch discussing compensation for the damage to the crop.

The birdman was a good fellow, after all, the farmer had decided. He certainly understood farm machinery, which they had discussed at length. He even had had experience firing a steam-operated threshing machine. The pilot had also shown a sincere interest in Pete and Wilbur, the Magrichuk youngsters, taking evident pleasure in explaining to them the mysteries of flying an airplane. And as for Martha's hot muffins, weren't they just the best he had ever tasted in his life!

According to Magrichuk's figuring, a settlement of thirty dollars would seem to cover the damage to his wheat crop. McConachie smiled broadly and allowed that sounded fair enough to him, even though it would take all his profit for the week-end of flying, since he had to pay a parachute jumper, and other expenses. He also wondered if some of the wheat might not straighten up again in time for the harvest, but of course the farmer would know best about that.

He then switched the conversation back to flying, casually dropping the remark that he expected to charge the fairground folk $2.50 each for their plane rides. He went on to enthuse about the flying machine and its future.

He hoped to earn enough money barnstorming in the summer and flying fish in the winter to buy more planes and build up a regular air service of his own. The time would come when the farmers of Alberta would no longer be snowbound in winter or mired on the muddy roads in summer. They would have an air service and, later, winged flivvers of their own to skim over the prairies, to commute to the cities in minutes.

The farmer was caught up in the young man's enthusiasm and began to think he should do something to help him to realize his ambitions. Besides, it was true that some of the wheat would grow up again—maybe most of it. Then, too, there were the free rides. . . .

The deal was finally settled for ten dollars cash and the two shook hands cordially. McConachie stayed for lunch with the Magrichuks. Then he climbed into his cockpit, adjusted his goggles and was ready for work.

All afternoon the Fokker roared into the air from the Magrichuk wheatfield, each time executing a wide sweep around the countryside and landing again for another load of thrill seekers. Inside the cabin, which was as barren as a boxcar, the four $2.50 passengers on each circuit sat strapped to canvas-webbed steel-framed jump seats. The high-wing configuration of the Fokker afforded them an unobstructed view of the flat countryside as it tilted, revolved and rushed past below the grimy windows against which their excited faces were pressed. It was a bigger thrill than the giant ferris wheel, they all agreed after landing.

At the end of the day, McConachie and Bud Potter, the parachute jumper, staked the airplane down in a corner of the field, munched on the cold sandwiches they had brought from home, pitched a small tent beside the plane and rolled out their sleeping bags for the night.

On Sunday evening, after a full day of passenger-hopping, McConachie shook hands with the Magrichuks, packed his gear in the cabin, and flew back to Edmonton. He carried $220 proceeds in the cash box after having paid out ten dollars to Potter for two jumps and another ten dollars to the farmer for the damage to his crop. It had been a profitable week-end.

It was in this way during the summer of 1932 that Grant McConachie was able to earn money to pay for the overhaul and repair of his Fokker after the strenuous winter on the Cold Lake fish haul.

Sometimes, but not always, the barnstorming venture was

blessed with fair weather and good crowds. Then his week-end take was a rich one. But even at best it was a fitful business, for the farmers and townfolk had little time for frivolities during the week.

At this early stage in his career, Grant McConachie became alert to the importance of aircraft utilisation. He learned to hate the sight of an aircraft sitting idle on the ground, consuming the profits with depreciation and overhead costs. He realized he had to keep the Fokker flying. Bugged by the mid-week idleness of the country-fair circuit, he went on the look-out for an opportunity to start a regular passenger run. At last he found what he was searching for, an isolated community with the makings of a landing strip near by.

The unsuspecting beneficiary of his proposed new air service was the tiny mountain community of Robb, Alberta, which consisted of a hole in the ground, the Robb mine, and a soot-stained cluster of shacks. It was the very isolation of Robb, deep in the Rockies and accessible only by coal train, that had pricked McConachie's air-pioneering instinct.

Back at the airport, he mustered a small group of "hangar rats," the youngsters who haunted the airport ready to swing props, pump fuel, sweep floors, run errands or peddle plane rides to the public, anything to earn a little money for flying or to cadge a free flip in one of the trainers. To this motley group of hopefuls McConachie explained that he was looking for volunteers to clear his landing strip at Robb. It was the beginning of a promising new air service, he told them. Direct air service to the isolated area would stimulate the mining and the growth of population, and who knew what would come out of it—probably quite a few flying jobs, opportunities for ambitious youngsters!

He had just the spot picked for a landing strip, he went on, a flat ledge on the slope of a ravine close to the town. All it needed was the clearing of a few trees and the air service could start.

"Red" Rose was the first to volunteer. He wanted desperately to become McConachie's full-time mechanic, to gain experience for an air engineer's ticket. A new air service might be his chance. He was joined by his pal Bill "Tiger" Pollard, an amateur boxer with professional aspirations. There could be no better conditioning for a boxer than pure mountain air, the good food of a mining camp, and the vigorous exercise of tree chopping, McConachie argued.

"Look at it this way," he suggested to Pollard. "I'm providing you with a free training camp, all expenses paid."

The third volunteer was the least enthusiastic. Only eighteen, "Souki" Bell stood six two and weighed 220 pounds, mostly flab. He was fond of inertia and found it difficult to imagine the benefits of chopping trees in the mountains. He had no special interest in flying. But Grant McConachie was his current hero. So Souki joined the little company of volunteers because he didn't want to be left behind.

McConachie's small band of reluctant pioneers rolled into Robb a few nights later, their axes, saws, shovels, bedrolls and tent stacked about them on the floor of an empty coal car. At Grant's suggestion Red had taken them in his dad's Buick from Edmonton to Edson where they took a coal train to Robb. During the long ride from Edmonton, their leader had regaled them with anecdotes illustrating the health-giving benefits of outdoor exercise. They were indeed lucky, he kept assuring them, to be treated to an all-expense-paid holiday in the mountains.

When he discovered, however, that the tab for grub at the mine cook-house would be a dollar a day each, his enthusiasm chilled perceptibly. He called his little band together.

"Listen, boys," he said. "We've got to get this job done in a hurry. At these prices we can't afford to stay here very long!"

For a time the work proceeded steadily. The silent woods echoed with the sounds of their industry from early dawn until nightfall as the volunteers felled trees, buck-sawed and hauled the logs, uprooted stumps, cleared underbrush and filled stump holes to create the rough semblance of a runway along the narrow shelf that clung to the slope of the gorge.

After some two hundred yards of narrow strip had been cleared, McConachie called his group together to make an announcement.

"You've made great progress, and you're in better physical condition than you've ever been in your lives," he said. "The big part of the job is over, so I'm taking the train back to Edmonton to pick up the Fokker. I'll be flying back a week from today. By then you'll have another hundred yards cleared and that will be all I need to land and take off. I'll fly you out to Edson and you can drive back from there in the Buick."

It sounded like a good plan, but with McConachie gone enthusiasm diminished and progress was slow. A week later when the Fokker appeared in the sky only another fifty yards had been cleared and the runway was still pocked with stump craters. As Rose recalls, "McConachie took one low pass over the strip and we were all sure he would wheel around and head for Edson. To our surprise he did a tight circuit and came in for a landing. How he escaped packing her up in one of those stump holes, I'll never know, but he pulled it off.

"He was visibly displeased with our lack of progress and told us we hadn't been working hard enough. He said he couldn't take off from the short rough strip with a load, so we'd have to stay and finish the clearing then come out to Edson by train and pick up the Buick there.

"Tiger Pollard had to get out right away for a fight, so McConachie agreed to take him in the cabin, but the rest of us had to stay and finish the job.

"Well, you've never seen such a take-off in your life! The ground was soft and humpy. The Fokker was slow getting up speed. It was obvious McConachie was going to use up all the runway before he could get off the ground.

"I stood there scared rigid, waiting for the crash I knew

would come. But at the last minute he kicked on hard left rudder. The Fokker veered sharply and dropped right over the edge of the cliff. There was a sheer drop, right down into the ravine.

"I shudder to think what it must have been like for poor Pollard, sitting in the cabin and sure his last day had come. But anyway, as it plunged into the ravine the plane picked up flying speed and McConachie pulled up into a climb over the hill on the other side. He was off to Edmonton and the two of us were stuck there with our axes and shovels."

Red Rose and Souki Bell finally cleared the remaining fifty yards of the landing strip, packed their gear and rode a freight caboose back to Edson where they expected to pick up the Buick for the drive to Edmonton. It was gone! They learned that on his first trip out, to get the Fokker, McConachie had taken the Buick in preference to riding the train.

The runway builders were tired, hungry, broke, and stranded in the mountains nearly two hundred miles from home. It was now late fall and the nights were bitterly cold. They had no choice but to hop a freight. Finally back in Edmonton, shuddering with cold and cramped with the pangs of hunger, they had to find what consolation they could in the knowledge that they had contributed in some small measure to the progress of air transportation.

Events were soon to prove just how small their actual contribution had been. The Robb air service was never to enjoy more than a fleeting success. One episode, however, does deserve at least a footnote in aviation history. For one incredible flight to Robb, McConachie succeeded in cramming nine hockey players, and all their gear, into the cabin of the Fokker. History does not record whether the team won or lost.

10. CRASH!

That summer of 1932 produced something more lasting than McConachie's barnstorming flips and his air service to Robb. For in July, with his usual astonishing good luck, he met a White Russian refugee, Prince Galizine, and his wealthy Maltese wife. The princess mysteriously owned two aircraft, a Fokker and a Puss Moth. She had used them to prospect, without success, in the north and to tour the prairie ranchlands inspecting cattle she might buy for her country estate and ranch west of Edmonton.

The Galizines were intrigued with bush flying, and the princess readily agreed to a three-way partnership with Grant and Uncle Harry. Thus, Independent Airways was formed. Its entire fleet consisted of the two Galizine aircraft and the McConachie Fokker. Three aircraft. No big deal, but a start. Uncle Harry was president, with the princess as vice-president and Grant as general manager. Without a doubt the carnival con man, the Maltese princess, and the big twenty-three-year-old formed the most unusual management team in aviation history.

But by early November 1932, Independent Airways had a contract to fly more than a million pounds of whitefish for MacInnis Fish Company between Peter Pond Lake and the railhead at Cheecham in northern Alberta. The rate was ten

cents a pound, which would mean a good profit if the contract
could be completed, but it would mean a lot of flying. McConachie, with the bounce and enthusiasm of youth, was anxious to
get started.

The previous night three inches of snow had fallen; winter
had come. Now skis could be used and the planes could start
working. So despite the cold, damp, foggy weather, as Grant
clambered up to the high-mounted cockpit of his blue Fokker,
his mind was on this year's fish haul.

He started the engine, fastened the helmet chin strap,
checked his goggles, adjusted the leather mask he had devised
as protection against the frigid slip stream, and flicked through
the familiar ritual of the cockpit check. The freight and passenger cabin of the Fokker was enclosed in the fuselage,
separated from the cockpit by a solid bulkhead, but he could
hear the thumping and cursing as Limey Green, his mechanic,
stowed away the supplies.

Noting that the oil temp. was up to green, McConachie
revved the engine, flicked switches to check both mags., noted
tachometer and cylinder temp. readings, adjusted his goggles
and was reaching for the throttle when there was a shout.

A nattily-dressed businessman had burst through the fringe
of spectators and was ankling through the spat-deep snow
waving frantically. Ye gods, Uncle Harry! McConachie reduced throttle to idle and hoisted himself out of the cockpit.

It was a typical Uncle Harry caper. Rolling in from Toronto
on the Canadian National train he had hopped off where the
tracks ran past the airport in the hope of catching his nephew
for a business discussion before he took off for the fish base.
Like many of Harry's chances, this one had paid off.

Leaving his engine idling in the cold fog, McConachie shuf-
fled off to the hangar for the meeting with his uncle. This un-
foreseen delay was to have fateful consequences.

Every detail of the episode was to remain etched vividly in

McConachie's memory forever after, and he was to recall it in the following words:

"While we talked Uncle Harry wondered about the fog, but I told him I could skim over the tree-tops and would come out in the clear at St. Albert. It was just seven miles north, so there was no problem. Then he noticed that my staff pilot, Lionel Vines, had taken a run down the field in the other Fokker without getting into the air. What about that, he wanted to know. I said not to worry. The temperature was just on freezing and perhaps the snow was a bit sticky for skis. I told Uncle Harry my plane had just been overhauled and was in better shape than the other one, so I would have no trouble getting off.

"My engine had been idling all the time I was talking to Uncle Harry, so when I climbed into the cockpit I was all set to go. Not a worry in the world. I had noticed some ice in the slip stream, but I knew we'd be out in the sunshine after a few minutes of flying, and once we got out of the foggy patch it would be clear sailing.

"I put on full power but the aircraft didn't pick up speed properly. It was damned obvious I wasn't going to get off. Well, I guess pride enters into these things, so I swung around in a big circle with the power still full on—I figured with the extra run we would pull the skis up off the sticky snow and then we'd be away.

"Starting my second run into the wind I already had about twenty-five-miles-an-hour head start, so with only my mechanic, a drum of oil and light cargo back in the cabin I was sure the Fokker would get off—without the least difficulty.

"When I got three quarters of the way down the field I realised we didn't have the speed we should, although by then I was committed to take off. When I hauled back on the stick to pull her into the air she mushed back on to the ground again. By this time I was beginning to get a little desperate.

"I was only about a hundred and fifty feet from the end of the field, and there was the usual collection of telephone lines on the edge of the airport. I got the plane into the air, all right, just over the fence, and I was sure it would climb right away, as usual. But it didn't. The plane just staggered through the air. I grabbed a quick glance at the instrument panel and everything seemed to be working perfectly, with the engine roaring at full power. But the airspeed needle was just on sixty, flickering there, near the stall, and if I tried to climb for altitude, she would start to settle towards the ground. In other words, I would crash.

"By this time I was over Calder and I seemed to be hopping from roof-top to roof-top. Radios had just started to become popular, so there were lots of high aerials on the roofs. Well, it seemed to me that I had flown through about three city blocks of aerials when I came to the CNR Calder yards, and there were the towers of the coal ducts dead ahead.

"I had to make a turn. Naturally. Dangerous as hell, too, near the stalling speed so close to the ground, but I had no choice. I know now I was holding that plane in the air by sheer will-power, but anyway I managed the turn and there was a clear space ahead. So I had a chance to take a breath. But then I saw there was a power line. Christ!! I couldn't get under it because of the trees or over it because I didn't have the power. I had to risk another turn. Here we go again, I thought.

"Well, the odds and everything else finally caught up with me right then and there. I banked into the turn like a big crippled turkey, and before I knew it the port wing tip had snagged the ground. Yes, *the ground*—that's how rough things were.

"It's amazing the things you notice at such a time, but just before the world went crazy I saw old Jake Carter going along the road in his open delivery sleigh. The horses were bolting in panic and Jake was grabbing every which way to hold on to them without taking his eyes off me. By this time I was putting on quite a show.

"The newspapers were to give me a lot of undeserved credit for keeping the plane in the air to avoid the houses and managing to crash in the only open area around. Actually, it was a sheer case of survival; I was just trying to manoeuvre my way out of a terrible situation.

"If you have never been in a crash, you would have difficulty understanding what the experience is like. As soon as the wing tip hit the ground, the plane started to cartwheel, from wing tip to nose, to the other wing tip, to the tail, to wing tip, to nose . . . For two city blocks, the Fokker jolted, spun, whirled and crashed, rolling itself up into a ball of twisted metal and tattered fabric. I was the centre of the ball.

"There wasn't time to be scared, but I can remember vividly that I had a face mask on, against the cold in the open cockpit, and with the first big impact as the plane wheeled onto its nose, my head went right through the 'shatterproof' windscreen. Then, each time we bounced there was another pain someplace . . . and I couldn't do a thing about it but try to cover my face as best I could and wait for it all to end.

"Finally, the crashing and cartwheeling stopped, and there was an almost eerie silence. Then I began to take stock of the situation. I opened my eyes and got a terrible shock. There was just a white blankness. I couldn't see a thing. I was blind!

"I was also worried about fire because I had taken off with full tanks of gas in the wings, and I imagined, with all the friction sparks and spewing fuel, we would be going up in flames any second. I was also concerned about my mechanic back in the cabin with a loose drum of oil. He'd be dead, crushed by the heavy drum! He had to be!

"I was tightly jammed into this cage of fractured and twisted steel tubing and could hardly move, but I managed to get one hand up to my face and push off my goggles. Then, I could see! This was the first good news I had had that day!

"The glass lenses of my goggles had cracked into opaque

discs during the crash and this was what had made me think I was blind.

"At about this time a lot of people came running over from the airport and near-by houses. Someone started cutting at the tubing with a hacksaw because I was wedged into this tangle of metal and crumpled fuel tanks.

"I saw someone else rush up to the chap with the hacksaw and knock him right off his feet with a blow to the jaw. It was Limey Green, my mechanic. By some miracle he had survived, and pretty well, too—just two front teeth broken. When he pried his way out and saw someone making sparks with a hacksaw near all that spilled gasoline, he went after him. Wham!

"By this time I had a chance to size up my predicament in a little more detail, and decided the situation was not at all good. The Fokker cockpit is separate from the cabin and sits right up behind the engine.

"The crash had driven the engine right back into my lap and, as I was to discover, had broken my legs in seventeen places. Both hips, as well as some fingers and ribs, were fractured. One knee-cap had been driven up my thigh and shattered.

"One reason I had difficulty in moving was that a rod had pierced right through my arm, so I was really nailed in there. When I looked down I was astonished to see the bottom of a foot facing me, for a moment I wondered whose foot that could be. Then I realised my leg was broken so completely at the ankle that this was my own foot twisted right around 180 degrees.

"Now, by this time I had come to the conclusion it had been quite a crash! I didn't feel much pain yet, except in my knee, but it didn't take me long to realise that I should be dead.

"This all happened pretty close to my home in Calder so it wasn't long before Doc Cameron, our family doctor, turned up and peered at me through the wreckage. When he asked me how I was, I said I felt fine but suspected I wasn't in the best of health.

"Doc Cameron thrust a half-size bottle, which I would call a mickey, of brandy in to me and said, 'Drink this.' Well, up to this time in my life I only knew that alcohol was for rubdowns. But I figured this was medicine, and not knowing any better I gulped down the whole thirteen ounces of brandy straight.

"By the time they had cut me out of the wreck I was feeling so good I thought I was ready to fly again right then, and when they got me to the hospital I thought everything was just wonderful. Here I am going to have a great rest in the hospital, with all these good-looking nurses, I thought.

"One thing was nagging at my mind, however, and even as they wheeled me into the hospital I realised that I knew the reason for my crash. While they were pulling me out of the scrambled cockpit I had seen a slab of ice slide off a propeller blade and fall to the ground.

"Nobody knew too much about it in those days, but it didn't take a wizard to realise what had happened.

"While I was in the flight office chatting with Uncle Harry the engine had been running. Conditions in that ground fog had been just right for a coating of ice to build up on the whirling prop. If I had taken off right away, of course, I would have been up into the sunshine before any amount of ice could accumulate, so everything would have been normal.

"By the time I was ready to go, however, those propeller blades were so deformed with ice they wouldn't bite into the air properly, and that's why I couldn't get real flying speed. And that was why I didn't fly fish that winter."

During two months in the hospital, Grant McConachie had plenty of time to reflect on the crash, but there were new concerns to occupy his attention. The doctor was afraid of peritonitis (or gangrene as it was then known) in the badly-mangled left leg. He wanted to amputate it above the knee. McConachie disagreed. The doctor decided to wait and see. The poisoning did not develop.

When he finally emerged from the hip-length cast McConachie was thunderstruck to find his left leg from hip to ankle was as stiff as a plank. Some slight improvement might be expected from exercise of the muscles and stretching of the tendons, the doctors said, but he would always be lame. He would never fly an airplane again.

McConachie, with the cockiness of twenty-three, refused to believe that his air career was over. He had a strong faith in his own destiny. For a few weeks in Edmonton he persistently exercised his stiff leg with long pain-racked hikes in the deep snow. The sensational publicity attending his mercy flight and the crash had made him a local hero. Everywhere he went he was overwhelmed with attention and sympathy. People wanted to help him on and off street-cars. He was embarrassed, frustrated and sometimes angry. He was also very concerned about the fish-haul operation which would be falling behind schedule without the help of the second Fokker which was a pile of junk. He decided to leave the city for the fish-flying base on the bleak shoreline of Lesser Slave Lake. Anything would be better than sitting around doing nothing.

Still on crutches, he moved into the town's bachelor cabin and proceeded to direct the fish-flying operation. The doctor had bound the shattered knee-cap of his rigid left leg with kangaroo tendon and assured him there was no fear of its coming apart. He advised plenty of exercise.

In the deep snow and on the steep incline from the cabin down to the lake, McConachie found the crutches useless so he discarded them in favor of an ice axe which he used to drag himself along through the drifts. Despite many hours of painful snow-crawling, however, his stiff leg seemed to show no improvement.

Then McConachie was struck with an idea he was later to refer to as the drastic cure:

"My pilots, Lionel Vines and Charlie Tweed, were doing the best they could with the Fokker and Puss Moth, but we were getting further behind all the time on the contract. I decided a little extra incentive was in order. I said, 'Boys, if you fly in enough fish to finish up this carload by tomorrow night, I'll put on a party for you at the quarters.' You see, I could do this because once the car was loaded there would be two days' lay-off until another express car came in for loading.

"Well, it meant flying ten hours the next day, but they made it. So on the Saturday night I got hold of a few bottles of gin and the party got started. I had only had a drink once in my life—in the crash when they fed me brandy—but that had seemed like a pretty good idea so I decided I might as well join the boys in trying out the gin.

"After I had a few drinks there didn't seem to be any problems at all, not even my stiff leg. I was sitting on the edge of a bunk and I started thinking out loud about this leg that was going to louse me up for the rest of my life.

"I said, 'You know, I think that if I were to lie on that table with the stiff leg sticking out, from the knee down, out over the end, then if someone jumped on it hard they would break those adhesions that are holding it rigid. The doc said with those kangaroo tendons I can't break the knee-cap, so what harm can be done in giving it a try?'

"The others were dead against the notion, but the more I thought about it and nourished the idea with a few more sips of the gin, the more logical it seemed to me.

"Finally I convinced Lewt Veweger, one of the mechanics, that it could work and he agreed to jump on the leg. Since he weighed over two hundred pounds at the time, he was well equipped for such delicate surgery.

"So I said, 'I'll lie on the table with my leg sticking out and you, Lewt, get a good run across the room and jump on that leg with all your weight. Whatever happens it can't be less useful to me than it is now!'

"So they all stood back to watch. Some of the guys had doubts, but there wasn't any doubt in my mind. This was going to work. I lay on the table waiting with that leg out over the end, and Lewt took a run and jumped on it. With great gusto.

"Well, it just lifted me right off that table like a cart wheel and hurled me up in the air and on to the floor—which was quite a leverage because I weighed two hundred and twenty pounds at the time. And there I was on the floor, writhing around in pain. And now completely sober, too!

"By this time I was convinced the operation by 'Doc' Lewt Veweger had *not* been a success. I couldn't move my leg at all. The pain was so bad that it almost made me pass out. And my whole leg began to swell up so fast they couldn't pull my pants off and had to cut them away.

"The party was over. Everybody was feeling pretty badly about the failure of the drastic cure and what the consequences might be. Anyway, they put me to bed, which was the best they could do.

"I was in bed all the next day and barely able to move, but two days later the swelling started to go down and the terrible pain went away. A couple of days after that I was able to get up and move around. To my delight and astonishment, as they say, I found I had about three-quarters movement in the stiff knee. The adhesions had been partially broken loose and the bones were moving again in the knee-cap.

"It was very sore and tender for a while, but improved rapidly. So what the hell, I climbed into the Puss Moth and found I could work the rudder pedals fine. I took off and flew without the slightest difficulty and before long I was back in the air on the fish haul.

"A month and a half later when I was straining to lift a heavy fuel barrel, my good leg suddenly broke through the snow crust, putting the full weight on my left leg. The bad one. This bent the knee under great pressure and broke the rest of the adhesions. So once again I was in great pain, and there was the swelling for a few days. But when it was all over, my leg had full movement. I could walk without a limp, and from that time on I have never had the slightest trouble with it."

11. THE HIGH GRANITE WILDERNESS

In the deep interior of British Columbia, well up on the Pacific shoulder of North America, is a strange, forbidding and little-known land. The region is flanked by two mountain ranges, the Coast to the west, the Rockies to the east, with a third granite spine, the Stikine, writhing through it.

For nearly two hundred years, white men have known and travelled the Coast range and moved through the relatively easy passes of the Rockies. But it is the Stikine, the central barricade running south from the high ramparts of Alaska and the Yukon, where the adventurer has consistently run out of luck. Indians say the Stikines are bad country and avoid their more forbidding regions . . . sheer granite peaks, deep and desolate canyons, high mountain deserts.

But even hostile territory will lure men if there are furs to be taken and gold to be found, and there were fur animals and game in the lower valleys of the Stikines, and granules of free gold in the gravel beds of the mountain creeks, so there had been a few white trappers and prospectors dribbling through the more accessible parts of this bleak land. Mostly, however, it was still unexplored, larger than half of Europe but so isolated it might almost as well have existed on another planet. Huge fires could burn through forests all summer and no one would know of them. It was a great, silent, lonely land whose mysteries conveyed an implicit warning to the intruder: Trespass at your peril.

And then came the bush plane, a buzzing dot against the high blue sky.

It was the easy access offered by the bush plane that lured the professional gold-seekers like Barney Phillips to the Stikine country. And it was Phillips who placed a mysterious phone call late in February 1933 inviting Grant McConachie to a late-night rendezvous in the tiny Independent Airways office in Edmonton. It was a strange way of doing business, but the young president of the world's most rickety flying operation scented adventure and revenue. Now that he was back in shape he was ready for adventure. And Independent Airways was certainly ready for revenue. With one of the Fokkers wrecked and the other unable to keep up with the fish-haul contract, the company seemed to be staggering towards a financial crack-up.

In the privacy of the small office that night, Barney Phillips revealed part of his secret to McConachie.

"I've got a gold creek, a rich one." They were alone but he spoke in hushed, almost furtive tones. "It's away up in the Takla Lake area of the Stikine country, next to hopeless to get at except by plane. That's why I've come to you. I need to bust in there with a work party, supplies, equipment. It's got to be done soon before the spring break-up because I want my gang there ready to work the sluice boxes on the creek as soon as the ice goes."

"But why me?" McConachie asked. "All I can put on the job right now is a Puss Moth."

"That's just it. You're a small outfit. I don't trust Mackenzie or Canadian Airways because they fly for some of the big mining companies. They've got too many contacts, and they might talk. I need somebody who'll keep his yap shut till I get my claims staked."

The deal was made. Phillips unfolded a large map of

British Columbia on the desk, stabbed it with a forefinger and said, "Prince George." Another stab, "Takla Lake, one hundred sixty miles northwest of George. When we leave George we leak the word we're heading for Finlay Forks country, but of course we're going the other way. That'll fool the bastards."

McConachie nodded but didn't reply. He was frowning at the map of the Takla area, noting the closely-spaced brown contour lines depicting near-vertical landscape and the black numbers denoting peak elevations. High granite . . . the Stikine range. All of McConachie's 720 air hours had been flown over undulating bush or flat prairie. Mountain flying in the underpowered Moth, in strange territory, and on a mission so secret there could be no hope of search and rescue, well . . . it would not be a dull assignment, he decided.

"It sounds great, Mr. Phillips, but if you've never been in to this fabulous gold creek, how do you know for sure there's actually any pay dirt there?" the young pilot queried.

It was a fair question and Phillips, a gold-hunter for most of his life, was only too pleased to answer it at some length. Some years back, in 1925, "Black Mike" McLaren had spent a summer in the Stikine range and come back to Seattle with $17,000 in his poke. The next year Black Mike had gone in with his wife and had just as much luck, but then had lost everything when his raft was wrecked. The next year Black Mike went in with a partner, and neither of them ever came out. His widow was flown around the area by Black Mike's friends but was unable to recognize the creek where the gold was.

It seemed that Black Mike's secret had died with him. Then Thomas Thomas, known to all as Dirty Tom, decided to take a hand. He figured that the Indians of the area would know where McLaren had camped. For two years Dirty Tom lived with the Indians there until, finally, he persuaded one of his Indian friends to show him the creek where Black Mike had struck it rich.

But winter was moving in fast and Tom just made it out of the mountains before snow choked off the passes. He got to Edmonton where he told the story and gave the map to his grubstakers, the McLelland brothers. Then he died.

Barney Phillips, in turn, had purchased the treasure map from the McLellands. Grant would be shown the secret map once they got to Takla Lake.

The fuel would have to be cached at Takla, Phillips explained. From there, he and his crew and their supplies would be air-shuttled in to the secret strike deeper in the mountains.

Setting course northwest out of Edmonton with Phillips in the Puss Moth, McConachie crossed the snowy monotony of the farmlands of the Peace River Block and flew through the rock-walled pass of the Rockies to emerge into the heavily-forested valley of the upper reaches of the Fraser watershed. They refuelled at the thriving logging community of Prince George.

Westward again, he followed the twin ribbons of the Canadian National Railroad tracks, and at Burns Lake, Phillips arranged for fuel and provisions for the air-supply shuttle. But he was still far from the gold strike. Fuel (in forty-five-gallon steel drums) and supplies would have to be air-staged ninety miles north into the mountains to Takla Lake.

The first task was to get Phillips and the first load of supplies up to the gold site so he could set up camp and prepare for the spring sluicing while McConachie ferried in the miners and their supplies. It was a huge job for a tiny plane and an inexperienced youth.

The ninety-mile flight north was uneventful, through broad passes, but as the red Puss Moth sloped down towards the narrow strip of lake ice at Takla Landing the rugged sentinels of the Stikine range towered more than a mile high. To the north the pilot could see nothing but a sheer and solid phalanx, rank on rank, of mountain peaks. To the prairie pilot, it was full of mystery and menace.

The Stikine country in winter! He had no experience in the complexities of mountain flying. He had heard reports of violent turbulence in the narrow valleys, of strange savage whirlpools of air, and of sudden down-drafts that could slam a small plane against the wall of a gorge like a slapped mosquito.

The country was so poorly mapped that a flatlands pilot could easily get confused and lost in the labyrinths. A wrong turn could end in disaster. There were many dead-end canyons that, in poor visibility, would be certain death.

He left his mechanic at Takla, to make more room for supplies. As he took off into the unknown with Phillips, he knew that the slightest mechanical failure would strand them in that rock-bound wilderness without hope of rescue. Once their tiny monoplane vanished over the first ramparts, they would lose all contact with the outside. Their mission was so secret nobody would know where to search for them. The snow in the narrow valleys was shoulder-deep. Walking out would be hopeless. They would die of slow starvation before the melting of the snows.

McConachie's inexperience was bolstered, however, by the brash self-confidence of youth. He never seriously doubted that his own resourcefulness and flying skill would get him through any dangers awaiting him in the high mountains. And whatever misgivings he might have had were brushed aside in the excitement of this new adventure.

But he did have two reservations: Could Phillips find his way in to the secret gold mine, and would he himself be able to thread his way back out through the awesome mountain maze alone?

The route took them deeper and deeper into the mountains, through terrible chasms, past eternal glaciers, sometimes almost brushing the naked rock of towering peaks with the wing tips, northwest over Bear Lake, up Sustut Pass flanked by seven-thousand-foot pinnacles, over the middle-high ice plateau of Thutade Lake, then along the frozen water course of the Injenica to Toboggan Creek. Finally, Phillips pointed down. There lay a small lake blanketed with deep snow, a mile above sea level in a cradle between the twin peaks of Two Brothers Mountain. Here goes, Grant thought, and slanted the Puss Moth into a steep glide towards Two Brothers Lake.

He levelled into a long power approach and his wings swished over the tree-tops so low that he could see the tracery of animal tracks in the snow. Then he was down, where no aircraft had ever been before.

As the skis settled into the deep powder, a white cascade spumed up over the cockpit to be swept away in the wake of the slip stream. There was an abrupt jolt of deceleration as the skis went under and the Moth slewed to a stop, almost buried in the snow.

Sunk to the wing struts, the Moth could not even be taxied. With the engine snarling at full power, the small plane lurched and wallowed like a cow in a quagmire, sinking deeper with every effort to extricate itself.

This was an alarming situation for the prairie pilot, who knew nothing of the peculiarities of high-mountain snow fields. He had counted on taxiing to the shore, off-loading Phillips and supplies, and taking off without shutting down the engine. He didn't *dare* shut down because of a temperamental magneto. Without his mechanic he might not be able to get the balky engine started again. Then it would freeze and he would be in real, deep, hopeless trouble.

There was only one chance—leave the engine idling, dump the cargo, get on snow shoes and tramp out a runway long enough to get the Moth airborne. It meant what seemed like hours of the most exhausting toil, but with their lives at stake the men had no choice. They plodded back and forth on their webbed feet until the snow had been compressed into the semblance of runway. For McConachie the ordeal was a nightmare for he still had knee adhesions in his injured leg. Every step was agonizing. But it was a race against the slow but steady consumption of fuel in the running engine. Would there still be enough fuel left in the tanks for the journey back? Or would it be engine failure over the Stikines—which meant certain death?

The job was done. Under full power, the Moth lurched along the makeshift runway, gathered speed and planed up over the forest to wheel in a wide arc and head back along the tortuous route to Takla Landing. After the brutal labour, the take-off turned out to be simple. And the gas held out.

In all, McConachie was able to complete seven flights in to Two Brothers, enough to deposit the members of Phillips' three-man work crew and a load of supplies to last them until the middle of June.

Despite the success of the most difficult flying assignment of his young career, Grant McConachie's return to his Edmonton base was anything but triumphant. As he taxied the red Puss Moth up to the hangar and shut off the engine, the airport manager, Jimmy Bell, stepped forward in the company of a middle-aged stranger with a look of no-nonsense efficiency. He *was* efficient, too.

Before McConachie had time to manoeuvre his lank frame out of the cabin, the stranger had pasted a large white sticker across the windscreen of the Moth, seizing it on behalf of the creditors. In the hangar McConachie found that the sheriff had already got to the remaining Independent Airways Fokker, plastering it with a bankruptcy sticker.

Things were desperate. But McConachie could still talk: "I got the more important creditors together and explained the situation. If they would just release the Fokker, I pleaded, we could earn money barnstorming, then as soon as the northern lakes were open, haul freight for the northern mines. We got the Fokker out of hock."

Teen-aged Grant McConachie in the football uniform of Victoria High School, Edmonton.

Young Grant McConachie was reared in an atmosphere of steam, soot and cinders in the small railway settlement of Calder on the outskirts of Edmonton. Here the high school youth, in snappy plus fours, visits the scene of a spur-line train wreck.

High school graduate Grant McConachie enjoys a rare moment of relaxation in the back garden of the family home in Calder.

Edmonton's airfield was a quagmire on June 30, 1931, when the famous Wiley Post landed his white Lockheed there on a world-circling solo flight. The event made a vivid impression on young Grant McConachie.

Grant McConachie's first commercial passengers were 200 yellow-tailed crows, subject of a migration theory experiment of Professor Archibald Rowan, shown at left with the five crates of birds. Others are: Jimmy Bell, Edmonton airport manager; McConachie; Uncle Harry; and Bert Haddow, Edmonton city engineer.

Bush mechanic Lewt Veweger, left, struggles to repair the broken undercarriage of a small plane he built himself while twenty-three-year-old bush pilot Grant McConachie stands by.

One of McConachie's early fish-hauling planes, the Puss Moth, at right, was contributed to the Independent Airways partnership by Princess Galizine, an American heiress married to a Russian prince. The other craft is a Fairchild KR 34 biplane.

Standing in the cockpit of his fish-packing Fokker, Grant McConachie in winter flying gear adjusts the heavy canvas cover used to protect the engine overnight.

After a hard winter of hauling fish from northern lakes in his blue Fokker, McConachie enjoys a respite back in civilization. As a congenial bachelor, he found plenty of ladies to ride in his Model A Ford.

Grant McConachie poised for take-off — or posed for a photograph.

When the metal undercarriage strut of his fish-hauling plane snapped, Grant McConachie was stranded at a remote lake in northern Saskatchewan until the local Indians made emergency repairs. As shown here, they fitted a birch sapling trunk to the shaft as a splint, which they bound with wet caribou thongs.

For winter flying north of Edmonton in the thirties, pilot and plane were fitted out to resist the cold. When flying in open cockpits McConachie, shown here in his air togs, also wore a leather face mask. At dawn the long-suffering bush mechanic would wriggle under the canvas hood to warm up the engine with a blowtorch.

So far so good. But then his luck ran out. The pilot he hired to share the barnstorming chores somersaulted the Fokker on a sand bar in Gull Lake, south of Edmonton, while hopping passengers at the beach resort on a Sunday afternoon. No one was hurt but the aircraft was wrecked beyond repair, never to fly again.

Uncle Harry and Princess Galizine, the two backers of McConachie's enterprise, were engaged in a bitter feud, and each refused to invest another cent. And thus, with its overload of misfortune, Independent Airways sank without even causing a ripple in the business community. But for young McConachie it caused a tidal wave of anxiety.

"There I was," he later recalled with a grin, "a failure at twenty-three, finished as an airline executive, career in ruins. And what could be done to get supplies to the Two Brothers miners? I was the only man who knew where they were. Their lives depended on me."

After several weeks of frantic effort to line up a plane, and disturbed nights fretting over the fate of the Phillips' camp, McConachie finally got lucky again. A friend, Charlie Elliot, who had a Junkers low-wing monoplane based at Vancouver, agreed to meet Grant at Burns Lake and fly a load of groceries in to the gold creek. The problem appeared to be solved. The Junkers was a rugged plane skinned with corrugated aluminum, with a dual open cockpit and a roomy cabin.

As they took off with their load from Takla Landing for the mining camp, McConachie, thoroughly familiar with the 160-mile route to Two Brothers, was relaxed and confident because he knew that Charlie Elliot was an experienced and skillful mountain pilot, one of the best.

They were still climbing over the serpentine northern reaches of Takla Lake, with visibility diminished in heavy rain, when loud explosions shook him out of his complacency. The aircraft shuddered as the engine bucked and backfired. The plane began to lose height. They were on the way down. As they broke into clearer visibility McConachie was alarmed to see the lake choked with deadfall logs.

But Elliot was unperturbed. Calmly the pilot banked the Junkers into a final approach, snapped off the ignition of the faltering engine and stalled the heavily-loaded plane on to the log-filled water. There was a series of sharp jolts as the floats bounced off the timbers, then a swish as they settled into the water without serious damage. To McConachie it was an astounding demonstration of cool piloting, as well as a tribute to the ruggedness of the Junkers.

Elliot discovered he could repair the battered floats easily enough; but the engine was another matter. A metal roller on a rocker arm responsible for opening and closing the valve on one of the cylinders had shattered. It was an essential part. The engine wouldn't run without it. More than a hundred miles of tough and mean wilderness was between the stranded aviators and the nearest outpost with a radio. And the mid-June date of the supply flight essential to the survival of the Phillips' party had long since passed.

Meanwhile, at the mining camp at Two Brothers Lake, all pretense of digging for gold had been abandoned as the hope of survival diminished. The energy of the men was replaced by a listless inertia. The miners, Mulvanie, Smith and Johnson, had in early June been so confident of McConachie's return with supplies they had given away surplus stocks of moose meat and flour to a passing band of Indians.

When mid-June passed with no sign of the supply plane, annoyance had become concern and then alarm. They hunted, but shot no game. Their meagre rations disappeared and hunger became acute. Endlessly each day the men searched the sky and listened. Finally, the fear of the stranded men turned to resignation as they became convinced that McConachie had crashed in the mountains. He was dead, and no one else knew of their predicament or of their location. It was impossible to walk out. They were in a wilderness prison. Hopeless dejection took command. They waited for death.

But the downed aviators on Takla Lake had a plan. They had found an Indian dugout canoe beached at the mouth of a creek. McConachie would paddle twenty miles back down the lake to Takla Landing. He would hire a boat for the hundred-mile journey down the Middle River and along Stuart Lake to Fort St. James where he could get out a radio message for help. Elliot would repair the floats and tinker with the engine.

This plausible scheme quickly foundered on the remarkable instability of the dugout canoe. McConachie was no more than twenty feet on his journey when the round-bottomed vessel suddenly turned turtle, dumping the surprised pilot into the glacier-fed waters of the lake. After five dunkings in as many minutes, he was forced to conclude that the dugout was not for any white man and most certainly would never carry him to the Landing.

Walking out was impossible. To survive, the pilots had to rely entirely on their own resources. They were able to devise makeshift patches for the damaged floats. Then Elliot, who was a natural mechanic as well as a fine pilot, had the idea that he might improvise a tappit roller by drilling and filing to size the socket from one of his wrenches. He devoted five full days to drilling and filing the hard steel of the socket until it achieved the dimensions of the missing part. Then he reassembled the engine.

A shift in the wind had cleared the log jam and soon, miraculously, the sturdy Junkers was in the air. But, obviously, neither floats nor engine were in shape to venture deeper into the mountains. The best that Elliot could do was drop his companion at Burns Lake, then set course for Vancouver where the plane could be properly repaired.

"I saw Charlie disappear down the lake, and I walked back to the town and I was sure I was going out of my mind. Here I was, with nothing, and there were four men up there at that damned lake depending on me, but I was getting nowhere while they were starving to death," McConachie recalled.

Every plane in the area was working and there was no air-sea rescue system to call in. By the time McConachie's desperate efforts to locate a relief aircraft were at last rewarded, it was the end of July. The supply mission was more than six weeks overdue when Ken Dewar, a staff pilot for Consolidated Mining & Smelting Company, agreed to pick up McConachie and the provisions at Burns Lake and fly them in to the gold camp.

As their float-plane landed on the open water of Two Brothers Lake and taxied to shore, McConachie was horrified to see only one man, Barney Phillips, on the shoreline to greet them. The tents stood like mute sentinels in the forest. The camp betrayed no sign of life.

"The tents were there, but there was nobody around. I thought, God, they're dead!

"Well, Barney looked bad. He looked like a skeleton with skin! He lifted up his hand and let it drop. We jumped on to the shore and ran to the first tent. It was empty. In the second I saw Smith, Johnson and Mulvanie. It was hard to recognise them. They were sitting like a row of skeletons on a camp cot, emaciated dummies. When I said, 'Hello, boys, I finally made it,' I knew they didn't believe me. They thought I was a ghost."

They were suffering not only from malnutrition but from the shock of hopes deferred and disappointed until they no longer believed even the reality of their salvation. During the endless empty hours, stretching into days and weeks of waiting, of listening, of scanning the skies, they had begun to hear the drone of the motor they so fervently wished to hear. They began hearing planes every day, phantom planes that never appeared, until finally, weak with hunger, past caring, they had taken to their tent. And there they sat, unable to rejoice or even to comprehend the fact of their rescue. To them the sudden appearance of the pilots was just another mirage conjured up by their desperation and hunger.

Days later, after hospital care and nourishment had restored their strength and rationality, the miners were able to work up a raging fury over their abandonment. They cursed McConachie with the full range and colour of their long-nurtured profanity. Only after giving release to this hoarded bitterness were the miners content to listen calmly, and with understanding, to the story of his frustrated efforts to reach them.

The reaction of Barney Phillips was quite different. He was able to remain casual and unperturbed throughout the ordeal and his recovery. At no time did he blame McConachie for his terrible experience. He took a friendly and practical interest in the plight of the young man, regarding him as a congenial and enterprising youth plagued with misfortune. Why not, he proposed, organize a new flying company? He needed air service for his mining venture and would find the financing to set up the operation. McConachie could provide the flying ability and the operating experience.

It was in this fashion that United Air Transport came into existence, with G. W. G. McConachie its twenty-four-year-old president and general manager.

12. FLYING FOR GOLD

Barney Phillips' decision to get into business with young Mc-
Conachie was not unexpected to those who knew him. In 1900
Barney had come west at the age of eighteen to make his
fortune. He promptly fell in love with the country and was
soon active all over the north prospecting and staking claims,
revelling in the rough life of the shack settlements and shanty
towns of the gold-seekers. But he was more than an ordinary
prospector. For several years he deserted the wilderness to
lead and inspire the campaign of the desperate home owners of
Battleford, Saskatchewan, whose lands were threatened with
confiscation. His successful legal battle was described by the
press of the day as "an epic of western history."

With this background it is hardly surprising that young
McConachie's starry-eyed dreams of opening up the West by
plane should have appealed to him. But there was more than
sentiment behind his backing. Barney now had a lot of city
money from Calgary behind him and his Two Brothers Valley
Gold Mines. And now that prospecting at Two Brothers was
going ahead, there were tons of equipment to be hoisted there.
Bush plane was the only way. To set up a flying company with
young McConachie that would work for Two Brothers in the
summer and haul fish in the winter was a sound business move.

The deal was that if McConachie could find some cheap

planes, Barney would get the money for them. McConachie knew where to look. He went to James McKinnon, the man who had become the receiver for McConachie's late-lamented Independent Airways.

"I figured he'd have the finger on other bankrupts, and I was right. An air prospecting outfit, Northern Exploration, had folded, leaving two planes in McKinnon's charge. He was quite sympathetic to me. A great booster of Edmonton and aviation, he was anxious to help me get started again. Besides, the market for beat-up bush planes wasn't that great in thirty-three."

The new partnership of McConachie and Phillips soon acquired two Fokkers with "Northern Exploration" emblazoned on their flanks. They paid nothing down and ten cents on the dollar based on a depreciated evaluation. Both were sold "as is, where is." And that was the joker.

One of the planes, "HJ," was in the Edmonton airport hangar ready to fly north as soon as its skis were exchanged for pontoons. But the other, "HE," was in the bush near Prince George in central British Columbia.

In the middle of the previous winter, Louis Leigh, then chief pilot for Northern Exploration, had landed HE on a lake near Prince George, taxied ashore, then walked away from the plane and the bankrupt owners. It had sat there on its skis in the forest beside the lake for the rest of the winter and on into the early summer.

When McConachie and Green took possession, the deserted Fokker was a sad spectacle. The skin was floppy and faded. What was worse, much of the engine had disappeared. Souvenir hunters from Prince George had stripped it of every removable part. The cylinder heads were serving as ash trays in living rooms around town. Valve stems, rocker arms, spark plugs and pistons were missing. The "as is" engine could only be described as a heap of junk.

At this early stage of his career, McConachie showed the

instinct for publicity that was later to enhance his reputation. He promptly called on the editor of the Prince George weekly newspaper, explained his plight, and dwelt at eloquent length on the importance of air services to the future prosperity of the community. An editorial appeared in the next issue appealing to the fine people of Prince George to return the souvenirs. The response was so generous that the resourceful Limey Green soon had recovered all the missing parts and was able to rebuild the Wright engine. And it ran, too. It would still need a lot of work to be dependable, but would probably hold out long enough for the flight to Edmonton.

The next problem was to remove the skis, fit wheels and trundle HE to a take-off strip. They recruited local labour to help clear a path for three miles through the trees, then to haul the Fokker out to a road and along it to a field long enough for a take-off run.

McConachie knew this aircraft had no right to be in the air, so from take-off he flew it with a gingerly respect for its decrepit condition. He climbed up to cruise in the smooth cold air 7,500 feet above sea level, close to the plane's ceiling, and followed the big loop of the Fraser Valley rather than risk the turbulence and the jagged terrain of a more direct route. The engine was running rough between spasms of coughing and shuddering. It had to hold out for five hours to Edmonton.

He inspected the leading edges of the wings with some misgivings. After spending most of the winter and all spring abandoned in the woods, the Fokker's plywood skin was wrinkled and warped. He knew, too, that the fabric covering the steel-tube skeleton of the fuselage, which should be drum-tight, was so loose that it billowed in the vortex of the slip stream. He did not relish crossing the Rockies in this beat-up monoplane with its sputtering engine.

But he felt confident that he could deal with whatever emergency might arise. In any case, there was little choice but to face the risk since he had to get the aircraft into the shops and out on the job for Two Brothers Gold without delay.

In the clear afternoon air McConachie was admiring the craggy 12,000-foot majesty of Mount Robson at close range when he was startled by something prodding him in the back. He twisted in the cockpit to see a gloved hand protruding from the small port that was the only means of communication with the cabin of the Fokker. The hand was shivering and the index finger was pointing down, gesturing emphatically.

McConachie had been so preoccupied with nursing the plane through the mountains that he had completely forgotten about the doctor. Too bad about Doc—that had been the word around Prince George. A fine man and a first-rate physician until his misfortune. His wife had run off with the butcher, and the tragedy had robbed the young man of all incentive. He found he could only tolerate his world when he viewed it through the bottom of a glass. Grant had met him just two days before in a pub and the doc was a bum . . . unshaven, seedy, sodden.

In a rare interval of coherence, the doctor had unburdened his troubles into the sympathetic ear of young McConachie. If he could only get away to a new environment and make a fresh start . . .

McConachie had spontaneously offered him a ride to Edmonton in the Fokker but had warned him it would be a cold flight at high altitude over the mountains, and with no heat in the cabin. Bundled in his fleece-lined flying gear and warmed some by the radiations of the engine, he had forgotten about his passenger in thin street clothes. Now the doc was signalling frantically through the peep-hole and shouting that he had to get down. He was freezing to death. McConachie bellowed through the aperture that as soon as they had crossed the Rockies he could get down to a lower altitude where it would be warmer.

As the pilot returned his attention to the cockpit he happened to glance at another aperture which formed a tunnel to the hollow interior of the plane's wing.

There, to his astonishment, he saw a rat peering out of the wing interior into the cockpit. Like the doctor, the rat too was shivering, and as it crouched there facing the pilot, eye to eye, it also seemed to be pleading for him to go down to the warmth of the earth.

When the aircraft reached Edmonton for major overhaul, the mechanics made a thorough search for the flying rat. But it was never found and the hangar staff decided it was just another McConachie yarn.

Grant took the dissipated doctor home, somewhat to Mrs. McConachie's surprise. The religiously non-alcoholic domesticity of the McConachie home in Calder proved to be the right prescription for the doctor. He recovered his self-respect and his interest in his career. For years after he became a highly successful physician in Montreal he continued to correspond with the young pilot who had helped to salvage him from the scrap-heap.

The two Fokkers salvaged from the collapse of Northern Exploration were teamed with a third purchased in Calgary to make up a fish-flying fleet to operate a fairly successful haul from Peter Pond Lake in northern Alberta to the railhead at Cheecham during the winter of 1933–34.

As soon as the spring thaw had freed the wilderness lakes of ice, the planes were fitted with pontoons and the big freight-lift to the remote Two Brothers gold site was on.

The first heavy machinery that Grant flew into Two Brothers Valley was a portable sawmill and a caterpillar tractor for power to cut timber to build the sluice boxes. Next was a power-driven placer-mining machine for working the gold-bearing sands and gravels. There followed drag lines, hoists, engines—a total of more than one hundred tons of equipment and supplies, in addition to personnel.

The Calgary *Albertan* did a feature story on one group of miners travelling to Two Brothers. The reporter was impressed by the air shuttle between Takla Lake and Two Brothers. "Although the route is over as rough and rugged a mountainous country as a pilot ever flew, not a man of the crew showed any signs of nervousness in taking the trip. They looked at the 6 feet 2 inches of energy which is Pilot McConachie and at the same confident smile he has displayed piloting his plane over thousands of miles of rugged peaks in northern British Columbia and at his giant Fokker Universal, then they stepped confidently into the plane and in a few moments they were on their way . . . the skyway to Two Brothers. . . ."

In May of 1934, McConachie was shocked by the news that his sponsor, Barney Phillips had died suddenly in Calgary of a heart attack at the age of fifty-one. The youthful pilot flew to Edmonton where he worked out a plan to keep United Air Transport airborne despite the tragedy. He formed a new partnership with Phillips' eighteen-year-old son, "young Barney," who had been working as a cook at the Two Brothers gold camp. Young Barney inherited one of the Fokkers, McConachie got the other.

But the ambitious young aviator had learned to be canny as a result of Independent Airways' demise at the hands of the creditors. United Air Transport, which had been nothing more than a casual working arrangement, was incorporated by the youthful partners, but the company owned no assets of interest to the bailiff. The two Fokkers were registered in the names of the boys' mothers, who leased them to UAT for a monthly rental.

The two UAT-leased planes, HE and HJ, joined the Calgary-based Fokker BJ flown by Gil McLaren for an active summer of freighting deep in the interior mountains.

But the young man described as "6 foot 2 inches of energy" was not content with the routine of flying. Hence the Great

McConachie Experiment, which might easily have wiped out the Two Brothers fleet and the pilots of the three Fokkers.

The Experiment was triggered by McConachie's chagrin because the Fokkers were under-powered. Their Wright J-5's, which had a sea-level rating of only 225 horse-power, were less than efficient at seven-thousand-feet altitude over the Sustut Pass. The lack in performance had limited the pay load to eight hundred pounds on the Takla–Two Brothers airfreight run. Since they were being paid by the pound, this limitation was a money problem to McConachie.

One evening he was watching Limey Green at work on HJ's engine. The mechanic had removed the serpentine tubing that piped the exhaust from the outlet ports around the circumference of the engine mounting and discharged it under the fuselage. This "collector ring" lay on the dock, where it formed a useless-looking heap of plumbing. McConachie studied the engine. It looked trimmer, more streamlined with just the short stub exhaust stacks protruding behind the cylinders.

"Leave that ring off," he told the mechanic. "I'm going to see how this crate performs without all that damn tubing." The Great Experiment was underway.

Minutes later he was skimming across the lake and lifting the Fokker into the twilight for a test flight. Floating in to the dock twenty minutes later, he yelled, "From now on, we can forget the collector ring. I've just discovered how to get the power and the performance out of this machine. I've never seen anything like it . . . takes off like a homesick angel! First thing in the morning let's give her a load test. We'll see just how much she'll carry with that extra power."

The trial runs proved that without the back-pressure and the weight of the cumbersome tubing, the Fokker would climb out easily with 1,200 pounds of load instead of the eight-hundred-pound limit. (Grant didn't realize it until years later, but part of the increased power was contributed by the jet effect of the hot gasses spurting back from the open exhaust ports.)

"That was a great day in my life," McConachie later told friends. "By this simple change I had been able to increase the pay load of the Fokker by fifty per cent. Think what it meant to our profits. I figured I had made an important aviation discovery and couldn't wait to get the other two aircraft stripped of that useless piping."

The next day McConachie took off for Two Brothers with a 1,200-pound load. Without the muffling effect of the exhaust plumbing, the J-5 roared thunderously. In his open cockpit the pilot could feel against his cheeks the heat-blast of the vapors spewing from the outlet ports of the top cylinders. But apart from the noise and the heat it was a routine flight.

Then as he crossed Thutade Lake and eased back the throttle for a slanting descent into the valley of Two Brothers he became conscious of a feeling of nausea and a headache which increased in intensity so that he was barely able to land before becoming violently ill.

While HJ was being unloaded, the pilot lay on the dock, sick, dizzy and puzzled. He had never been ill this way before. Certainly it couldn't have been the turbulence. Air sickness had never bothered him. He decided it must have been something he had eaten, perhaps a bad tin of beans from the store.

When the aircraft had been unloaded and was ready to go again, McConachie was feeling considerably better and had decided he would be able to fly the return trip. But after the first sixty miles he was again nauseous, a headache was pounding with the beat of the engine and some new and frightening symptoms were evident. His face seemed to be paralyzed. He was unable to blink his eyes. His hands and wrists were becoming numb. He could not move his fingers. He decided he would have to land while he still could.

Thutade Lake extended for several miles ahead, making a straightforward descent possible. When he tried to close the throttle he found that his fingers were paralyzed. He managed to hook his left wrist around the throttle knob to reduce the power for descent, at the same time forcing the control column forward with his forearm. He had become so skillful in flying the Fokker that he was able to set the aircraft down on the water even though his vision was blurring, his head was aching painfully and he had to wrap both wrists around the control stick to level out from the glide. When the plane stopped, McConachie managed to hoist himself over the rim of the cockpit and slide down the undercarriage strut. He sprawled along the deck of the portside float, feeling like death. He wondered what was happening to him.

He tried to scoop up cold water to soothe his throbbing forehead but was so helpless that he slipped off the float and would have drowned except that one arm was hooked around the strut. He was so sick he had little interest in survival, but he looked up to see the wind driving his plane towards the rocky shore. The starboard wing and the tail assembly soon would be crumpled against the rocks.

The danger revived his energy. He pulled himself up into the cockpit, started the engine and taxied back into the middle of the lake. After half an hour there, his sight began to clear. His headache disappeared. Gradually he recovered the use of his fingers and found he could blink again. He manoeuvred the Fokker into wind and took off to home base and bed.

He got another forty miles south and was over Bear Lake when the clammy sickness overcame him again. This time he did not hesitate but put his aircraft into a steep glide and landed. Some Indians who had seen the strange landing were able to catch the tail of the plane as it drifted ashore and they helped the semi-conscious pilot from the cockpit. They anchored the plane and McConachie, thoroughly sick and bewildered, crawled into his sleeping bag and slept for several hours. He awakened refreshed and ready to fly again. On the final leg from Bear into Takla, however, sickness hit him again and once more there was the struggle to fight off oblivion, to cling to his senses long enough to get his aircraft safely down at Takla.

Next morning, McConachie was fit as ever, but the sickness worried him. Perhaps he had developed an ulcer. In any case, he thought it would be wise to consult a doctor. Some gear had to be taken to Burns Lake, where he knew there was a doctor's office, so he decided to fly the load over in his stub-exhaust Fokker. It was only a short flight, but again he felt ill and had developed another violent headache.

He described the symptoms to the puzzled doctor. He hadn't been doing anything unusual lately, except perhaps eating quite a lot of canned food and whooping it up at the occasional party at Takla.

In the casual discussion, McConachie mentioned his experiment with the exhausts, and the doctor stopped him: "Is there any possibility you could be inhaling the occasional whiff of those exhaust fumes when you are flying?"

"The occasional whiff?" McConachie snorted. "All the time I'm in the air I can feel those hot fumes blowing against my face."

"Good God, man!" the doctor exclaimed. "Do you realize you've been breathing a strong dose of carbon-monoxide gas? You might just as well be drinking poison. I don't wonder you were sick. I am only surprised that you are here in my office today. By all odds you should be dead!"

That was the end of The Great Experiment. McConachie was thankful that in his exuberance he had not immediately stripped all three of the Fokkers and sent them into the air to pour their deadly exhaust fumes into the cockpits.

"Just think, Doc," he said later. "My big idea could have killed all of us; wiped out our whole deal. I guess those aircraft designers knew what they were doing after all."

13. FORD WITH THREE ENGINES

Everyone knew Harry Oakes.

He had been an ink salesman in Massachusetts who chucked security for the Klondyke rush of 1898, and although he lucked out in the Yukon, the gold bug had bitten him severely.

For thirteen years, he had roamed the globe in search of gold, usually penniless, usually ill-fed, forced on by the devil-dreams of the big bonanza. And in 1912 he found it, his Lakeshore Mine on Kirkland Lake in northern Ontario, and now he was rich, as rich as any maharaja. His mine was hailed as "the richest half mile in the world" and every year Harry Oakes became richer.

He also became tougher, meaner, more cantankerous, more anti-social and more thoroughly convinced that everyone was conspiring to grab away his riches.

Grant McConachie didn't know Harry Oakes except by reputation, and he didn't want his gold. But Oakes had something that McConachie wanted, and badly.

Sitting on the Fort Erie airport near Niagara Falls was a huge three-engined Ford aircraft owned by Harry Oakes. It was ruggedly built. It had the safety margin of three engines. It could operate on skis or on wheels. Above all, it could carry a terrific load. In fact, it was the biggest thing that flew. Grant McConachie was convinced that with the huge all-metal aircraft he could introduce a new era to bush flying. What was just as important, he was sure that the Ford could make the winter fish haul and the summer barnstorming pay off.

This prospect appealed to Barney Phillips, who was uncomfortably aware that United Air Transport's finances were far from sound. He agreed that Grant should visit Oakes at his estate. Phillips and McConachie both knew that the Ford had cost $55,000 just two years previously; to United Air Transport that might as well have been fifty-five *million*. But Grant had heard through the pilot's pipe-line that the huge aircraft was tethered most of the time, gobbling up overhead and depreciation. So he travelled east to try his luck.

On his first visit, McConachie quickly saw that Oakes's legendary cheapness didn't apply to his Niagara Falls estate, Oakes Hall, for it was huge in acreage and incredibly lavish. Few homes in North America could come anywhere near to matching his baronial pile.

But the multi-millionaire did measure up to his reputation for meanness. He was even more objectionable than McConachie expected.

"I paid fifty-five thousand dollars for the Goddamned machine, so why should I get a dime less," he snarled at their first meeting in the great oak-panelled living room.

That first interview got him nowhere, nor did the second, nor the third. But McConachie's youthful enthusiasm and determination may have been getting through to the short, squat old prospector-cum-mine-owner. Somehow, on McConachie's visits the old prospector found that the conversation was steered around to the north and to the hard but happy days Oakes had spent in the wilderness areas before money turned him sour on the world.

On his fourth visit, McConachie knew it was his final play of the wheel. Time was important. He was badly needed in Edmonton. He would put everything on the last spin.

Playing it smoothly, he prompted Oakes once again to reminisce about the long hard years, the sweat, hunger, loneliness and frustrations of his many years as a prospector, always seeking, never finding. The old man agreed with McConachie that the Canadian prospector was the forgotten man, the guy at the bottom of the pile, kicked about, stomped upon, cheated and then tossed aside. Both agreed the prospector deserved a far better deal.

Then McConachie went into his act, explaining how the bush plane had opened up the north for the prospector.

"It's a great new day for the north. You yourself can realize what it means. Entire new areas being opened up, the people no longer cut off.

"But there's just one catch, as far as the prospector is concerned. The present bush planes are too small, and they don't have enough range. They fly the prospector in to some remote region and put him down at the base of his summer's work, but the single-engined bush plane can't carry enough supplies to last out the season.

"This means the poor guy is off there hundreds of miles from nowhere and soon he's running short of grub, and he's wondering what's happened to the pilot who's supposed to be back with more supplies. Maybe the pilot's got sick, or he's been sent off to another part of the country, or perhaps his plane's gone haywire. So there is the prospector, slowly starving to death.

"Mr. Oakes, you have the biggest airplane in Canada today. If I had an aircraft like that it would mean I could fly in five prospectors with all equipment and supplies for the whole season. Just one trip. Think of it! What's more, your Ford could fly deeper into the north than we've ever gone before. That aircraft is the key to a whole new deal for the prospector. It's up to you. You know what it's all about. The only trouble is, I'm just trying to get started and I can't pay you anything like your fifty-five thousand dollar price."

Harry Oakes was silent. Then he looked hard at McConachie. The habitual scowl remained, betraying no hint of encouragement.

"How much can you pay?" he gruffed.

This was it.

"Twenty-five hundred dollars is all I've got."

Harry Oakes did not hesitate an instant. He had already made up his mind.

"Sold!"

McConachie thought he saw the faint flicker of a smile as Oakes barked out the single word, but he couldn't be sure.

(Not long after the sale of the Ford, Oakes quit Canada and its taxes forever to live in the Bahamas. He dabbled in real estate but sometimes would don tattered clothes to work full shifts on a road gang. On July 8, 1943, at the age of sixty-eight, Oakes was murdered in his bed by an unknown assailant wielding a miner's pick. The murder of the millionaire prospector saddened Grant McConachie, and he thought of the rare moment of generosity in the bitter life of Harry Oakes, the sale of the Ford, and he remembered that faint flicker of a smile.)

On the trip back west in the Ford the exultant McConachie was accompanied by ten friends who, one way or another, had contrived an invitation to ride back to Edmonton on this ferry flight. It was four days to Edmonton by train, three by air, but for these hitch-hikers the time saving was incidental to the thrills of a cross-country adventure in this three-engined super-plane. They were in for more excitement than any of them had counted on.

Putting in at the Chicago airport to refuel proved to be a bewildering adventure for the young bush pilot, accustomed as he was to the solitude of the northern skies. Air traffic seemed to be milling all around him as he skirted the perimeter of the big field at the regulation circuit altitude of one thousand feet. He had no radio. The control tower opera-

tor flashed a white light signal from the aldous gun. Not
knowing what this was supposed to mean, McConachie held
his altitude and stayed in the circuit. He stuck to this flight
pattern through a sequence of equally puzzling orange and
red flashes from the tower, where the controllers were turning
purple. Finally, as he was starting to worry about running out
of gas, he was given a green signal. He knew what *that* meant.
With relief he retarded the throttle levers and sloped the big
Ford down to the hard-surfaced runway.

After refuelling at Chicago, the Ford began bucking blizzard
head-winds, and for five hours the cold seeped into cockpit
and cabin. Then the welcome lights of Minneapolis appeared
in the wintry landscape below. As they taxied along the
runway after landing the number one engine coughed, spluttered
and died. Strange! From his cockpit Grant could see right
into the interior of the wing where a glass U-tube attached to
the fuel tanks showed that each tank was still a quarter full.

The following day as they approached the end of the next
leg, Minneapolis to Miles City, Montana, trouble brewed.
The Ford was fighting strong westerly gales and Grant had
let down to low altitude, but still their progress was agonizingly
slow. He wondered if they could make it to Miles City before
the tanks ran dry.

The fuel level indicator tubes in the wings showed both
tanks nearly a quarter full when the Ford suddenly lurched
to the left. The number one engine, on the left wing, had
conked!

"There goes number one," McConachie muttered to his
mechanic. "You'll have to check it in Miles City. We can make
it on the other two."

There was a short series of blurps, a cough, and number
three engine quit. Without waiting for instructions, Green was
scrambling down the aisle for the comparative safety of the
tail section. He knew they were on the way down—fast. They
had been flying only three hundred feet above the trees.

Before Green had time to reach the tail, number two, the nose engine, sputtered, caught on again, roared briefly, then died with an asthmatic wheeze. After hours of muffled thunder from three engines, the silence was eerie. The high-pitched moan of the airstream filtered into the silent cockpit and cabin.

McConachie instinctively put the wheel forward, tilting the plane into a steep glide to maintain essential airspeed, and desperately looked around for an emergency landing area. He had precious little height and only seconds to make a decision. But this sort of crisis was more familiar to him than landing at an airport like Chicago. He banked the Ford towards the leeward edge of a small clearing. It was a pocket-handkerchief of a meadow, snow-covered, too small for a safe landing with the big plane. But he had no choice.

Two things were working for him. The stiff head-wind would slow the approach ground speed and shorten the landing roll, and the far end of the meadow was an upslope that should help to break the heavy plane before it smashed into the trees.

While still a hundred feet up, he rolled the Ford into a side-slip to the right, then to the left, skidding off surplus height, then levelled with sure precision to skim in so low that the wheels almost grazed the top strand of the barbed-wire fence.

As the wheels scuffed the snow McConachie pitched forward against his seat belt. The Ford lurched to a stop in less than half the length of the small field. The nose was high. The aircraft was resting in the normal tail-down attitude. A miracle! It was just as if the big bird had somehow been snatched out of the air and pinned to the ground. Landing roll less than a hundred yards! But why that strong jolt at touching down?

It didn't take long to solve the riddle. He saw a long snarl of barbed wire looped around the tail of the aircraft and trailing far back across the snow in a distorted vee.

Normally, the Ford would have cleared the fence but with

the mechanic prudently crouched far back in the tail the plane had mushed in nose-high. The tail wheel had snagged the top strand, uprooting nearly a quarter-mile of fence. Like an arrester gear, it had dragged the plane to an abrupt halt.

The dip-stick confirmed the suspicion that the three engines had failed because both wing tanks were empty. Not a squirt of gas. But the U-shaped glass-tube fuel level indicators in the wing roots on either side of the cockpit were still registering a quarter full. You could see the gasoline right there inside the glass.

Limey Green knew better. That was water condensation from the tanks that had drained to the bottom of the U where it had frozen, cutting off the gas and fooling the pilot at the same time.

At this point the frozen group around the plane were surprised to see a dirty grey panel truck heave through the white haze of the blizzard, bouncing and swaying across the frozen landscape towards the winged intruder. In it rode a farmer wearing a faded-blue mackinaw coat, a tattered peaked cap with fur ear flaps and an expression of extreme displeasure.

"You saved our lives with that fence of yours," McConachie shouted, with a grin, before the farmer could utter a word. He was soon deeply engrossed in McConachie's account of the lying gauges, the engine failures, and the escape from flaming disaster.

"It's a small field for a big plane like this," McConachie observed, "but if we can get some gas in a hurry we've a chance of getting off against this wind. If that wind dies, we may be here forever."

After introductions to Green and the passengers, the farmer had forgotten about the damages to his fence in the excitement. At Grant's suggestion, he cheerfully cranked up the Overland and chugged off into the snowstorm to fetch a supply of gas for the big plane.

Waiting for the farmer's return, McConachie and the other

stranded wayfarers huddled in the unheated cabin while the blizzard increased. In the grip of the gale the aircraft shuddered, fish-tailed frantically and seemed about to rise into the air of its own accord. When the truck returned, Limey Green had the unwelcome chore of lugging the cans of gas up an aluminum ladder and sprawling across the corrugated metal wing to avoid being blown off as he funnelled fuel into the tanks. Finally the expedition was ready to go. With the farmer's truck hitched to its tail, the Ford was hauled through the gap in the fence to the very edge of the forest, to allow the maximum take-off run. With the passengers loaded and belted in, McConachie tested both magnetos on each of the three engines then advanced the throttles to full take-off power before releasing the brakes.

The big aircraft lumbered clumsily over the field for no more than two hundred yards then rose majestically into the gale and disappeared from the farmer's view. Only then did he realize that he had forgotten to get paid for the fence. Ah well, it made a good story.

Next morning at Miles City's airport, the weather was perfect for a lift-off at 70 miles per hour on the hard-packed, 2,500-foot strip. At 70, McConachie eased back, the tail lowered—but the Ford did not lift. Funny, he thought. At 80 mph he tried again. The plane shivered, the wheels skipped on the hard snow, but no lift. It was now too late to abort the take-off, and with the speed needle up to 100 there was very little runway left. Dead ahead was a green barn and a row of tall elms. This is it, thought McConachie.

In his mind's eye, he saw the smash, crumpled fuselage, ruptured tanks, geysers of gas, tortured metal, showers of sparks, flames. The end.

With the needle past 100, he pulled back on the stick. The plane shuddered, the nose came up, and straining, it mushed slowly up. The wheels cleared the roof top by a few feet and brushed through the bare branches of the elms. Then, as if exhausted by its effort, the Ford slumped downward. Directly ahead was Celestial Haven, Miles City's cemetery, and the Ford, with McConachie's luck still running, was heading directly for a patch of lawn beyond which a narrow corridor ran between two rows of tombstones.

McConachie jockeyed the plane down, working the rudder-bar brake pedals in a frenzied attempt to dodge Celestial Haven's tombstones. Inside the cabin all was chaos. Splintering glass sprayed the passengers as the Ford wrenched and jolted through the graveyard, its struts and undercarriage toppling the stone monuments.

McConachie jumped down, and he and the mechanic made a quick survey as the passengers filed out, badly shaken and scared witless.

Miraculously, the Ford had survived nearly intact. There was no glass left, of course, and there were a few dents here and there. But the wings and propellers were fine. The Ford was still airworthy.

Examining the wing, McConachie came on the cause of the crash. There was a thin frosting of ice on the wing surface. It was his Edmonton air crash story all over again! Fortunately, Grant didn't have time to dwell on his mistake—he was too busy fending off questions from passengers who wanted to know how many more crash landings he had in the flight plan for the trip to Edmonton.

Grant's jokes managed to mollify the passengers. But he and Green knew just how close they had been to feeding a pillar of black smoke, attracting spectators from miles around to the funeral pyre.

But the spectators came anyway, on foot, bicycle, horseback and by car. Grant soon had them helping to turn the tri-motor around and guide it down the aisle between markers, through the cemetery fence (which they obligingly pulled down), around the line of trees and on to the airport.

McConachie polished the wing surfaces free of all frost,

and this time the Ford slanted gracefully into the winter sky and was gone. After fuel stops at Great Falls and Calgary, Canada's biggest commercial aircraft landed at Edmonton.

Grant McConachie was home with another story to add to his growing legend.

14. THE FISHPACKER

When the three-engined Ford landed at Edmonton a large crowd lined the airport perimeter to goggle at "the biggest commercial aircraft in Canada." McConachie, always aware of the value of publicity, had wired airport manager Jimmy Bell his time of arrival, knowing that Bell would relay the news to press and radio in the aviation-conscious community.

Grant gave the press their money's worth at an impromptu press conference beside the huge plane.

"This is the beginning of a new age of northern flying," he told them. "No more worries about engine failure. This aircraft will fly easily on two engines. Why, it will even stay up on one. They're J-5 Wright Cyclones, 225 horses each. Same engine Lindbergh used to fly across the Atlantic. There's no better reliability than that.

"Not only safe, she's got the size . . . carries more than twice the load of any bush plane in history," and he kicked a wheel. "A great piece of equipment."

How about starting up three engines in sub-zero temperatures? McConachie expressed confidence.

"In the bush, up there, we can get three or more single-engined planes started within a short time, so there should be

no problem in warming up the three engines on one aircraft."
His mechanic was not asked for an opinion.

To the bush pilots of the high Arctic, the popular heroes
of the day, the fishpackers were a smelly crew. The top bush
pilots considered them airborne garbagemen, certainly no credit
to the winged fraternity. It was unfair, but if this concerned
McConachie, he never showed that he gave a damn. His
only interest during the five fish-hauling winter seasons between
the fall of 1931 and the spring of 1936 was economic survival.

His first winter shuttle, Cold Lake to Bonnyville, had been
a pioneering venture, a token enterprise with one pilot, one
Fokker and a mechanic. But it showed that McConachie's
idea would work. The fish companies became interested and
so did a lot of job-hungry pilots.

The second winter, at Faust, had been plain unlucky, starting with McConachie's crash that wrote off the blue Fokker
and came within an ace of killing him. It put him out of action
for most of that season. One of the remaining aircraft, the
Puss Moth, could carry only half a load. Sub-contracting plane
owners had given up in mid-season. The haul had been dismally
small. Grant's high hospital bills were deducted from revenues.
It meant the ruin of Independent Airways.

But now the young pilot's hopes were high as he took off
from the snow-covered Edmonton airport early in February
1935 and tilted the broad wings of his ski-shod Ford on to a
northeasterly course for the 250-mile flight to the new fish-
hauling base. The fish haul had started on January 2. Now,
with the big Ford in the fleet, this was his chance to recoup.
His fish contract had been signed with MacInnes Products of
Edmonton. The rate was three and a half cents a pound for
fish flown over the hundred-mile shuttle from Peter Pond Lake
in Saskatchewan to the Northern Alberta Railways loading
yards at Cheecham.

The Peter Pond camp was in the middle of nowhere. It consisted of the fishermen's bunk-house, the cook-house, the fish-house where the day's catch was stored overnight for the next day's air haul, and "the roost" as the fishermen termed the bunk-house of the pilots. The roost had neither elegance nor charm.

The floor was worn planking, the peeled poplar walls were dust-grimed, blending with the dung colour of the dried moss crammed into the chinks. The horizontal roof poles supported a foot-thick pack of dried mud. This insulation was so effective that with the oil-drum stove roaring, the door had to be kept open, even with outside temperatures far below zero. The curse of the mud roof was that anyone walking on the floor would set up vibrations that would loose a rain of dust.

One end of the rectangular cabin could be considered the living room since it had a calendar featuring "Chorus Cuties of 1935," a small table of apple-box wood, a threadbare grey sofa that leaked stuffing from several ruptures, a litter of old magazines and a kerosene lamp suspended from the ceiling.

This was home, office and social club for McConachie and his fish-flying colleagues. Now there were four aircraft with a pilot and a mechanic for each. The president and his mechanic Red Rose had the Ford. Ted Field, the pilot, and Red Gray were assigned to one of the Fokkers. Ernie Kubicek flew the second Fokker with Ralph Marshall his spanner-man. Gil McLaren was flying a leased Curtiss Robin with Frank Kelly of the "black gang" with him. North Sawle came in for a while to fly the Puss Moth. Under McConachie these men worked harder than any other air team in the north. He cajoled, wheedled, threatened and appealed. And they worked. They worked a steady six hours a day (in seven hours' daylight) six days a week. They would have flown seven, but the fishermen rested on Sundays. While most northern pilots got base pay plus a nominal bonus per hour flown, McConachie paid his pilots by the poundage of fish delivered to the rail-head.

With the nearest air regulation inspector 250 miles south in Edmonton, the pay-eager pilots cheerfully ignored the legal load limits and crammed into the cabins every pound they figured the aircraft could lift. While the rule book set the top allowable load of the Puss Moth at five hundred pounds, it staggered off the lake with ten sacks of fish—eight hundred pounds. The Fokker flew fifteen sacks weighing 1,200 pounds, double its regulation limit. McConachie coaxed the thundering "tin goose" over the tree line, its cabin oozing with forty-five sacks of fish, a load of 3,600 pounds. This was 1,600 pounds over the air regulation top weight. He would have liked to pile more in, but the cabin was stuffed full.

Red Rose, the Ford's mechanic, began work at the Peter Pond fish camp long before daylight. His alarm clock was the thump of Ernie Kubicek dropping from his bunk to light the drum stove. Ernie paid for his determination to sleep with the cabin door wide open, even at 50° below, by being fireman, and as "the roost's" temperature crept up, Rose inched his lank frame out of the sleeping bag, took the three pails of oil labelled "CARC," the Ford's registration, and set them on the stove to thaw and heat. The oil had been drained, still warm, from the Ford's engines at the end of the previous day's flying and kept indoors.

Before first light he had donned his gear (three suits of long woollen underwear, two pairs of heavy socks, double-weight coveralls tucked into calf-length buckskin moccasins, fur-lined mitts, and a brown fur cap pulled over his red thatch), and with his "black gang" mates was stumbling down the bank to the aircraft stake-out.

"Most mornings," Rose recalled, "the engines were so cold you could have chinned yourself on the propellers without budging them. You had to crawl under the tarpaulin tent covering the engine and light up the gas blow-pot. Normally,

you just sat there for about an hour sucking in the stink of the
fumes, sweating in the heat, and watching for fire."

McConachie's confident press statement back in Edmonton
that the Ford's three engines could be started in sub-zero as
easily as three single-engined planes had overlooked a significant
item. Three planes had three mechanics. The Ford had only
Rose.

With his triple portion of woe, Red had no time for the
dubious pleasure of sweating out the warm-up under a tarp
tent. As soon as he had the first torch burning right he would
burrow under number two engine tent and get a flame going,
and then on to number three. His fire watch consisted of
scurrying between the three tents until he judged it was time
to retrieve the first pail of hot oil from the cabin stove, mount
the ladder and pour the lubricant into the number one engine.

As if to pile grief on woe, the J-5 engine had an inertia
starter and the mechanic had to mount the ladder, insert a
crank and rotate it vigorously. At the right moment, the pilot
at the controls would then engage the starter.

"It worked most of the time," Red reported. "The Ford
certainly put in its share of air time. But the real agony hit
me every so often when I'd have two engines running nicely,
then the third would get balky. Just refuse to catch. After a
few tries, of course, it would start to cool out and then it was
hopeless. All you could do was shut the other two down, put
the tarp hoods back on, drain the oil, get out the blow-pots
and start the dreary business all over again."

The winter weather in the Peter Pond region was normally
clear and very cold with only an occasional ice-crystal fog
to mar the visibility for flying. Forty below zero was routine,
but it sometimes dipped to 50° and 60° below. Rose remembers
starting up the Ford's engines at 68 degrees below zero, exactly
100 degrees of freezing.

"It was so frosty that morning you had to breathe real
shallow or you'd sear your lungs. Your spit would freeze

solid in mid-air. Any exposed flesh, a cheek, an ear, your nose, would go white and numb, frozen without you even knowing it. It was the very devil thawing out later, too, painful! The ice boomed and twanged along the pressure ridges out on the lake and the air was dead still. You had to warm the gasoline before it would light up. The engines were a bloody long time getting warm that day."

It wasn't just infuriating, freezing, miserable work. It was dangerous too. Rose vividly recalls one occasion. "I must have been half asleep. The engines were all running up but the skis were stuck, so I ran over to one of them and started the usual pulling and jerking, not paying much attention to anything else. Then I heard this peculiar noise . . . tick/tick/tick/tick/ tick. A funny sound, I thought. I backed away and straightened up to get my breath. Then I discovered that the whole peak of my fur cap had disappeared. That funny ticking was the blade of the propeller chewing up my cap!"

Meantime, in the cockpit, rigid with horror, McConachie had watched helplessly as his mechanic missed death by an inch. He hadn't dared to cut the engine for fear this would cause Rose to look up, which would have been fatal.

"When I realized how close it had been, I had the shakes for about half an hour," Red said.

There were damn few breaks in the drab routine. Meals were served at the fish company's cook-house. Good food, lots of meat. Nobody ate fish. The pilots did the cabin house-keeping, which meant sweeping the plank floor once a week. They hauled cordwood from the cook-house woodpile and melted snow in a tub on the stove for drinking, bathing and brewing coffee. In the evening, the crews played bridge or read in the flickering yellow light of the kerosene lamps.

On Mondays, the day off, the mechanics might strip the cylinders off an engine, grind the valves, and then put it all back together again, just for something to do. Or, if the fish haul had been going particularly well, McConachie would herd

the entire gang into the Ford and fly the 160 miles to Mc-
Murray, the end of steel, the jump-off for northern flying, but
more important, the locale of the nearest beer parlor. When
the fishpackers trooped into the pub, the bush pilots made a
show of holding their noses. Someone would yell, "Who let
them stinkers in?"

This social ostracism had no apparent effect on McConachie,
however, for he knew all the bush pilots and most of their
"black gang" and exchanged banter with the other tables. On
one of the McMurray nights out, he climbed on to a table and
used a beer bottle as a model to demonstrate to the rowdy
bunch how he had performed an upward side-slip in a Gypsy
Moth at the Edmonton air show.

At the camp the fiendish ingenuity of Ted Field—"the joker"
—was appreciated, even by the victims of his schemes. Field's
prank program could be relied on as a source of group en-
tertainment. During the first days at the roost there was some
puzzlement when Field volunteered to help the others to build
their bunks. The mystery was soon solved as he used this opportunity to build into the bunks certain trick devices that
enabled him to collapse an entire bed, upper and lower, occupants and all, by pulling a single pin.

"There's one thing I'll say for Ted," Red Rose said, "he was
always considerate. If he set up a stunt to dump a pail of water
on a man, he always did it when the chap was coming into
the cabin, never when he was going out into the cold.

"All this sort of thing could drive a fella crazy, but we all
thought it was great fun."

Either despite Ted Field's cheery jokes or because of them,
the first winter haul at Peter Pond was a success for Mc-
Conachie's new company, United Air Transport. During the
three-month winter season of 1934–35, UAT hauled more than
a million pounds of fish.

15. FORD OVER THE ROCKIES

The first commercial flight over the Canadian Rockies began to take on substance one morning in mid-May in 1935 when Gil McLaren, one of McConachie's fish pilots, picked up the phone and heard a strong and confident voice say, "Captain McLaren, this is Robert Wilkinson. Can you find a big airplane to fly me over the mountains to Vancouver?"

McLaren had met Wilkinson, and knew him to be a very wealthy man and also a man of unpredictable ideas, but one who always came up with the money.

McLaren kney where there was such a plane, but he had just returned from a long winter of hauling fish for McConachie, and was counting on spending a week or so of bliss in Calgary with his bride of the previous autumn.

He hesitated to risk getting involved and bringing on bride trouble. But he also knew McConachie's yen for the spectacular, so he put through the call to Edmonton.

"I've got a chance for a charter Calgary–Vancouver," he told the boss. "Chap named Wilkinson, a big-time broker and oil tycoon down here, wants to go to the coast in a hurry and in style. Asking if I know of an aircraft big enough to make it."

McConachie bellowed into the phone. "The Ford!"

"That's what I figured. Wilkinson's not worried about the cost, willing to pay a thousand bucks to get there by air. Says he's got some real estate deals to close. The flying's a whim, I guess. That's the kind of guy he is. He can afford to be whimsical."

McConachie liked the smell of cash, which his airline sadly needed. But even more, with his sharp instinct for publicity he saw the chance of scoring a first. No commercial flight had yet crossed the Rockies from the prairies to the west coast. He didn't hesitate.

"It's a deal, Gil, provided you'll co-pilot. I'll fly the big bird down tomorrow. Meet me at the field around two o'clock. We're practically on our way," and McConachie hung up.

In 1935 long-distance flights caused the same widespread excitement that trips to the moon do today. The public's taste had been whetted by a series of pioneering air spectaculars beginning with Lindbergh's solo crossing of the Atlantic in May 1927. More recently, Lindbergh and his wife had completed a 29,000-mile air tour of Europe, Africa and South America. In January 1935 Amelia Earhart Putnam had been the first to fly from Hawaii to California. The front pages of every newspaper on the continent had been enlivened with many such air adventures, every one loaded with suspense.

So it was hardly surprising that on May 16, 1935, the Canadian Press flashed the following news around the world:

"Under sunny skies, a Ford tri-motored plane piloted by Grant McConachie took off from the Calgary airport at 9:30 this morning for the first commercial flight over the mountains to Vancouver."

Prior to the departure, McConachie had been astounded at the huge crowd, alerted by radio reports, that had thronged to the Calgary field to witness his take-off. Press and radio interviewers demanded details of the flight. Aware as he was of the publicity angle, he wasn't all that prepared with details. It was really to be seat-of-the-pants flying, but he bluffed his way through with cheery confidence.

For all his cheerful talk ("Not a chance of getting lost. I

can always use the pilot's friend, the 'iron compass,' the railroad—as long as I'm careful not to fly into a tunnel"), McConachie realized that his blind flying skill could be tested to the utmost in clouds over the Rockies. But, of course, he didn't mention this. Confidence was the word.

When the news of the Ford's departure reached Vancouver, the excitement stirred by yet another pioneering flight was intensified by a report that McConachie was actually inaugurating a scheduled air service to the coast. He had nothing to do with the report. It was nothing more than a rumour. But the rumour was to cause him trouble.

As the big Ford climbed westward over the arid slopes of the foothills, Gil McLaren occupied the bucket seat on McConachie's right. He had as much flying time as Grant, but was not planning to handle the controls on this trip since he had no experience on the Ford. Nor did he have instrument training. This was McConachie's show.

Back in the cabin, Bob Wilkinson, the charter passenger, had settled back to make the most of his thousand-dollar whim. Glancing over his shoulder, McConachie was amused to note that the stocky, fair-haired broker was already very much at home in his unaccustomed environment. Immaculate in a pinstripe blue suit with pale grey cravat, he puffed contentedly on a long black cheroot and sipped Drambuie, replenished regularly from the squat bottle he had provided himself with to ease whatever discomforts his historic journey might entail. The cabin still stank of fish, but Wilkinson certainly was travelling first class. He always did. After all, he was a big oil man.

Over Banff, the sunshine was suddenly turned off as the Ford bored into dense cloud at 14,000 feet.

After twenty minutes, McLaren began to regard the grey world with real concern. All his experience had been seat-of-the-pants flying, which meant ground visibility. This business of racing on blind, relying on the indifferent dials, was something else again. He mentioned his concern, and was only slightly reassured by McConachie's apparent nonchalance. He was worried. Unknown skies, unknown hazards.

"Nothing to worry about, Gil," Grant answered breezily. "I just have to keep my eye on these four little pals, the turn needle, which tells me I'm flying straight, the spirit level, which assures me I'm not side-slipping left or right, the airspeed and the altimeter. That doesn't come as news to you. But for sure, though, you better believe those instruments. Flying blind like this, your physical sensations betray you and you'd swear the instruments are wrong. When you stop believing your dials under conditions like this, you're dead."

They were still in heavy cloud some time later when Grant realized that something was wrong. The aircraft was not responding properly to the controls. Its movements were sluggish. The altimeter needle kept creeping down and he had to keep nudging the throttle knobs forward to maintain height. How much more could they be nudged?

He leaned forward and peered through the side windscreen. The thick leading edge of the wing was coated white! My God! Ice! McConachie felt a shiver of doubt. This was something they hadn't taught him at the flying school at Borden. What do you do when you start to pick up ice? He had a dread of the white menace ever since his Fokker crash at the Edmonton airport three years ago. Then it had been ice on the propeller. After that, the crash landing in the Miles City graveyard had been caused by frost on the wing.

Now the controls were becoming slushier by the minute. "I've had enough of this," McConachie yelled as he pointed to the white sheath of ice now extending the entire length of the wing's leading edge. "It'll be building up on the tail surfaces, too, and on the propellers. We've got to get the hell out of this."

He was already banking into a careful 180-degree turn by

the compass, his eyes steady on the turn needle, using the rudder to keep the ball centred, nursing on more power to hold airspeed and altitude steady.

Back home to Calgary. But where was Calgary?

By the time the big aircraft finally broke out of the grey shroud into clear skies the accumulation of ice had made the plane almost unmanageable. The engines were roaring at near take-off power, and he had to fight the rudder and ailerons to get any response.

Losing altitude now to shed ice, McConachie could feel the tension drain away. That had been another close one! If he had flown another twenty, perhaps even ten, minutes deeper into that cloud, they never would have made it back out. The Ford would have been sunk by the ice—it would have gone down like a rock. He thought of the jagged peaks of the Rockies below.

Gil, obviously thinking along the same lines, summed up his relief with a grim jest: "One thing I don't like about those clouds, Grant. They look like cotton candy, but in this country some of them have rock centres."

As the Ford descended in the sunshine, the ice flaked off its wings. Full control returned.

Back in the cabin, the air-pioneering Wilkinson, oblivious to the danger they had passed through, had removed his shoes and propped up his feet. He had just fired up a fresh cheroot, and he nursed a half-empty bottle.

Below them they could see Calgary. They had to land somewhere to get enough gas to take them to Vancouver. But Grant had no relish for landing in disgrace back at Calgary. And he didn't want to risk losing his thousand-dollar passenger. He decided to cut southwest to Grand Forks.

About noon, the startling sight of a three-engined aircraft circling overhead sent almost the entire population of the small mountain community of Grand Forks scurrying to the crude airstrip. As the plane stopped at the gas pumps on the perimeter of the weedy field, the mayor of the town stepped forward to extend formal greetings. Howdy, he said, inviting the air adventurers to be honored guests of the community at an impromptu civic luncheon. It was noon, so the hotel staff was ready anyway.

For McConachie, the congeniality of the occasion was diminished only by the necessity of making a speech when called upon by the mayor. He wasn't a practiced public speaker but managed to utter a few words about the importance of air services, particularly to such isolated communities as Grand Forks.

It was three in the afternoon when the civic delegation escorted McConachie and his companions back to the airport where the Ford had been refuelled ready for flight. On an impulse at the luncheon, a typical McConachie impulse, Grant had invited Mayor Love and his wife to join the flight to Vancouver. Swell, thanks! Mr. Wilkinson didn't mind the extra company in the cabin. He was well supplied with black cigars and Drambuie for the second stage of his pioneering journey. So off they went.

But unknown to the happy voyagers, alarm was spreading in Vancouver where the radio stations were interrupting regular programs with bulletins announcing that the Ford was unreported and overdue. It had been expected to arrive at 2:30 P.M. Pacific Standard Time. And the rest of the nation listened, too. Where was the Ford tri-motor?

At Grand Forks the sky had been sunny but they soon encountered cloud again. Not wishing to match his meagre instrument flying against the elements again, McConachie kept low, threading the valleys and mountain passes in a turbulent but uneventful passage.

At 6 P.M. the Ford droned out of the Coquihalla pass over the town of Hope and into the broadening expanse of the Fraser Valley. Since nobody in Grand Falls had thought to phone Calgary about the diversion, the radio bulletins had by now declared the Rockies' flight a certain disaster, since they knew that the Ford's fuel tanks would long since be empty, and the flight path traversed terrain as rugged as any in the world. The only speculation now was as to where in the mountain jungle the tri-motor had gone down. Another pioneering air tragedy!

Meantime, the Ford's passengers were enjoying the panorama of rich green farmland as they skimmed low over the town of Chilliwack in a light drizzle. The countryside back in Alberta was still drab, awaiting real spring. The soft air wafting in from the Pacific and the fresh colouring of the dairy farms were a treat, especially for the two winter-weary fish pilots.

An excited farmer who had been listening to the radio reports heard the big monoplane roar overhead. He phoned in the news to a Vancouver station. Within minutes the public was hearing the electrifying news: "The Ford plane on its historic flight across the Rockies has been reported still in the air! It is expected to land at the airport within half an hour."

As might be expected, the news reports contained puzzled speculation as to how the aircraft had been able to remain in the air more than three hours after its fuel tanks should have run dry.

"When I sighted Sea Island airport, I was astonished to see that there were hundreds, maybe a few thousand, cars parked along the edge of the landing area," Grant recalled later. "I remember thinking, this must be the busiest airport in North America, and it struck me that such an enormous crowd must be out to greet an ocean-crossing flight."

Finally, the airport manager, William Templeton, came running over to the Ford.

"Come on, Captain McConachie," he shouted, "the mayor is waiting to greet you."

"Greet me?" the pilot yelled back. "Why?"

Mayor Gerry McGeer, always the crowd-pleaser, was not the man to neglect such a well-publicized event as the arrival of a historic flight that had been given up for lost. McConachie, McLaren, Mayor and Mrs. Love of Grand Forks, and an astounded Mr. Wilkinson—still clutching the dregs of his Drambuie—were shown to open convertibles for a police-escorted parade to the Hotel Vancouver.

At the Hotel Vancouver the pilot heroes were conducted personally by the mayor and the hotel manager to a luxury suite and invited as guests of honor to a civic banquet that had been hastily planned for the following evening, a banquet to honour the first commercial flight from Calgary.

"I had never been in a hotel suite before in my life," McConachie said later. "This was *real* luxury, especially coming from our cabin at Peter Pond with the dirt falling in our faces when anybody slammed the door and having our Saturday night baths in a tub of melted snow."

But Gil was worried. He kept pleading for Grant to clear up the misunderstanding and explain to the officials planning the banquet that he was not, as they obviously had assumed, starting a regular air service across the mountains.

The flamboyant mayor, Gerry McGeer, presided at the celebrity event the next evening, delivering an eloquent tribute to the flight, which he described as the prelude to the new air service over the Rockies. The president of the board of trade followed, elaborating on the significance of the new service to the business community, and then D. R. McLaren, a distinguished war ace and manager of the western region for Canadian Airways, introduced the guest of honour.

As McConachie rose awkwardly he was greeted with a standing ovation and upset a glass of water fumbling toward the lectern. He then blurted out a few remarks about the flight being routine. It was not really the inaugural of a new air service, he said, but at least had demonstrated that such a service was feasible.

The demonstration following his short speech was considerably more restrained than the preceding one, but Grant was sufficiently flustered by this time that he joined in his own applause.

"It wasn't exactly a disaster," Gil McLaren reflected later, "but nobody was about to carry McConachie around the room on their shoulders either. I guess the way it turned out was a break for us. The officials dropped us like hot pennies and we were on our own for the rest of the week in Vancouver."

When it was time to check out of the hotel, however, the heroes discovered that the mayor's gesture in providing the suite had not extended to the cashier's desk. The bill was more than they could raise. (Wilkinson's thousand-dollar cheque was made out to United Air Transport.) Grant persuaded Gil to wire his bride for a hundred dollars, but it was still not enough for fuel back to Calgary and Edmonton after the hotel accounts were paid.

"Guess we'll just have to put the tin goose to work," Grant grinned. He phoned friends in the interior community of Kelowna to line up sight-seeing flights in "the biggest aircraft in Canada." The barnstorming venture provided enough revenue to buy gas.

When the Ford finally came to roost back at the Calgary airport, McConachie was ready with a statement for the reporters about the significance of the flight . . . age of the air . . . scheduled service soon . . . bigger, faster planes coming . . . shrinking distances. . . . But when he turned to McLaren for confirmation he got no more than an incoherent mumble. It was obvious the co-pilot did not share the captain's enthusiasm for the mountain-hopping exploit.

Gil could find only two sources of consolation in the flight. He had helped McConachie to inscribe a short paragraph, if not a chapter, in the annals of air history. And he had come out of it alive.

For Grant McConachie the Rockies flight had yielded yards of the kind of front-page publicity on which his career was to thrive. But more significantly, the encounter with wing ice had been another knuckle-rapping lesson he was never to forget. Three times now he could easily have paid with his life for failure to heed the unforgiving laws of flight.

He recalled all too vividly the crash of his blue Fokker at Calder with an iced propeller, his pancake landing of the Ford in the Miles City graveyard, caused by frost on the wings, and now the close squeak with ice accumulation over the Rockies. Once again Grant was able to reflect that old pilots are the ones who have survived the follies of their own ignorance. Scores of the early U. S. Airmail pilots and not a few Canadian bush pilots had died learning. But out of their experiences were to emerge new devices, such as wing and prop de-icers, in the long and often tragic progression towards safety in the air.

16. FARMERS
AND SNAKE CHARMERS

The tin-goose Ford was great for packing fish or hopping Rockies but useless for summer bush flying because it could fly only on wheels or skis, since there were no pontoons to match its jumbo size. So in the spring of 1935 McConachie took the big bird barnstorming on the country-fair carnival circuit. The hulk of "The Largest Aircraft in Canada," as it was heralded on the advance posters, became familiar in the skies over such prairie hamlets as Ponoka, Red Deer, Moose Jaw, Cardston, Okotoks and Olds. Rides in "The Flying Boxcar" were bally-hooed at the sensational rate of "a cent a pound."

It was late Sunday afternoon as the winged boxcar banked lazily in a cloudless sky over Pincher Creek, Alberta. Grant McConachie chuckled as he swivelled at the controls to peer back into the dim cavern of the big plane's cabin. He had a full load of farmers. Despite the steep tilt of the plane, most of them had left their seats and were crowding to the windows. They were enjoying the celebrated "THRILL RIDE." By pay-ing an extra premium these customers had been privileged to ride in the same cabin with the parachute jumper and to watch him leap through the open door into space. Now they were watching excitedly as the white canopy blossomed below them.

McConachie pulled back the cluster of throttle knobs. The

thunder of the three engines diminished and the Ford spiralled down towards the crowd that filled the fair grounds and over-flowed on to the adjoining patch of meadow that was serving as a landing strip for the flying circus.

The broad-winged monoplane swished low over the fence and flattened its glide as the wheels scuffed the tall grass. As the weight of the freighter eased almost imperceptibly from the wings to the wheels, the pilot jockeyed the rudder pedals gently to maintain a straight landing run between the lines of spectators pressing in on either side of his makeshift runway. He was too preoccupied to notice that back in the cabin the farmers were already out of their seats and crowding to the open door as they were accustomed to do when the train con-ductor called their station.

There was a loud report from the region of the undercar-riage and McConachie felt the big plane lurch. The right tire had blown! The Ford was swerving into the line of spectators! The plane continued to veer even as he applied full left brake and rudder to offset the drag of the crippled wheel. The metal blades of the three propellers were slicing towards the crowd on the right. This could be a massacre!

Realizing he could not stop the lethal swing, McConachie suddenly released the left brake and at the same time tramped hard on the right brake pedal. The swerve became a tight turn as the steel rim of the right wheel tore through rubber and gouged into the soft turf. The aircraft ground-looped on its own axis like a giant pin-wheel, smothering the spectators in a shower of black dirt and spewing its passengers through the open door of the cabin. Farmers rolled and bounced for twenty yards across the meadow. Some were propelled slap through the fence into the crowd.

McConachie relaxed his white-knuckled grip on the control wheel, settled back into his seat, and slid open the side window to admit some cool air. Through the dust cloud settling around the aircraft he was astonished to see his passengers picking themselves up off the ground, slapping the dirt from their overalls and chortling in evident glee.

"By cracky, that was a fancy landing if I ever saw one!" one of the farmers shouted. "I'll say!" rejoined another. "I'd like to take that one again. What a thrill ride!"

The big Ford transport plane was the carnival's star attraction the day it joined the prairie circuit of Ringling Brothers early in that spring of 1935, and its popularity continued throughout the season. At first the carnies resented the competition of the spectacular intruder and the passenger flights selling for a-cent-a-pound. Nothing on the midway compared with it. But McConachie soon had them convinced that the presence of his super-plane would prove to be such a crowd magnet that the whole carnival stood to benefit. Furthermore, he assured them, he was prepared to pay generous commissions on the sale of plane-ride tickets at the midway booths.

McConachie thrived in the atmosphere of the carnival. When he wasn't working, at the controls of the Ford tri-motor, he never lost an opportunity to mingle with the crowds and inhale the exciting aromas of the midway. He was entranced by the persuasive skills of the barkers and the pitchmen. Some observers of his career were later to claim that his own promotional talents were three parts Ringling.

Since Grant had to be in the air much of the time, however, the carnival liaison duties fell to Bud Sutherland, his one-legged mechanic. Bud relished the chance to exercise his personality and his banjo on this special assignment as "carnival sales representative" for the McConachie barnstorming enterprise. The new title carried no extra salary but Bud was delighted to be pitchman for the sky-ride. He was able to cajole some of the barkers into shouting up the flights when they weren't busy with the girlie shows, the half-man-half-woman, or the chamber of horrors. Sometimes Bud managed to take over a temporarily-vacant platform to harangue the crowd himself.

To increase Bud's influence with the carnies, McConachie had authorised him to invite a select few to ride in the big monoplane each time the carnival moved on to a new location. For them the plane ride was a delightful relief from the tedium of the long hot train journey, and it soon became a much-coveted prize. Thus, McConachie was surprised to note that on every move the same bright-eyed little brunette turned up in the select company of air commuters. It seemed she was a dancer, who performed with pet snakes in one of the midway shows.

Bud was evasive at first but finally confessed to his boss that he had fallen in love and was engaged to the shapely little snake dancer. Her stage name was "Bella Medusa," but to the carnies, and to Bud, she was simply "Bitsy."

When the news of Bud's approaching marriage to Bitsy reached his boardinghouse in Calder, Mrs. Bell, his landlady, immediately started making plans for a wedding party to honour her favourite boarder and his bride. The preparations for the great event involved quite a few of the neighbours. No detail was neglected. There were offers of extra chairs, dishes, silverware, glasses and many suggestions. Mrs. Howell, from next door, helped carve a huge punch bowl from a solid block of ice, using instructions she had clipped from a party supplement of the *Ladies' Home Journal*. The punch, from a recipe in the same periodical, was a special blend of fruit juices sparkled with ginger ale, which was only right and proper for a party given by the vice-president of the local Women's Christian Temperance Union.

In all their planning, however, the good ladies of Calder had not reckoned with Ted Field, McConachie's co-pilot, and one of the numerous guests invited to the party. Mrs. Bell knew him only as a shy and diffident young man who seldom spoke, and then only in a whisper. She had no reason to suspect that he was possessed of a devilish sense of humour, and that he was an infamous practical joker.

Ted was one of the early arrivals at the Bell boarding-house on the evening of the party. He carried three flasks of pure alcohol camouflaged in gift-wrapping. The hostess was busy in the front hall as the guests continued to arrive, a legion of Bud's airport cronies plus a colourful group from the carnival. So it was easy for Field to stealthily dribble the contents of his three flasks into the carved-ice punch bowl.

Early in the evening the Bells' party had already become the jolliest in the history of 112th Street. The hostess glowed. She was delighted with the evident success of her soiree and happily surprised at the popularity of her fruit punch.

"It just goes to prove what I've always said," she triumphed to her husband. "If a party is well planned, people can have more fun *without* the abomination of liquor."

Some time well after midnight Mrs. Howell, who had a strong voice, managed to command the attention of the guests and called on the hostess for a presentation on behalf of Bud's fellow-boarders. Mrs. Bell's preliminary remarks were a little vague and rambling. Then she unveiled the gift, a cut-glass bowl in the shape of an Indian canoe.

"And this," she announced, exuding geniality and fruit punch, "is a token of our esteem, to show how much we think of our Bud." She thrust the crystal canoe, somewhat unsteadily, in the general direction of the bridegroom.

"Whaddyamean *our Bud?*" It was Bitsy. Shrill with indignation, her voice pierced the wave of applause that had greeted the hostess's presentation. Obviously, the bride had devoted much of her attention to the *Ladies' Home Journal* punch bowl during the long evening. As she tottered forward a lock of raven hair straggled down her forehead and her dark eyes flashed.

"Aren't you forgetting somebody?" She slurred. "What about *'our Bitsy'*? You may think I'm some kind of a circus freak, but I'm just as good as you are, Mrs. Stuck-up, and I'll show you what I think of your stupid present."

The snake dancer made a sudden grab, snatched the glass canoe from her bewildered hostess, and crashed it to the living-room floor. In the stunned silence that followed there was only the tinkle of cut-glass fragments exploding to all parts of the room. Then confusion. Mrs. Bell and Bitsy were staggering about the room, locked in a hair-pulling, screaming scuffle. Bud was struggling without success to insert himself between the combatants. The guests milled aimlessly about in various stages of befuddlement.

Moments later, the melee was punctuated by another violent crash. Bud's right leg had broken through the metal grill of the cold-air register in the corner of the living-room floor. Horrified witnesses saw that the poor man's limb had plunged through the grating almost to the knee. Spears of torn metal had pierced his leg and, like enormous fish hooks, were gouging deeper as he pulled and struggled to extricate himself. At any moment they expected to see blood spurting from the mangled limb. "Call a doctor!" someone shouted.

But to almost everyone's astonishment, the victim of this strange accident showed no sign of suffering. No blood flowed as he continued the vain struggle to extricate his leg from the cold-air shaft. Meantime, Barney Phillips, a close friend of the victim, had run downstairs to the basement where he took a grip on the protruding boot and ankle.

"Okay, Bud." His voice boomed up through the ventilator shaft. "Undo the straps and I'll pull 'er down through." Crimson with mortification, Sutherland unfastened his belt, reached down his thigh inside the pant leg, and undid some complicated fastenings. From below, Phillips was then able to pull the wooden leg through the tangle of shattered grating. Moments later he appeared in the living room to present Bud with his right leg.

"Say, what in blazes goes on here?" It was Bitsy again,

Takla Lake, the jump-off for the great air-freight supply feeding the Two Brothers Gold placer-mining operation at Thutade Lake. The three Fokker bush planes represented the entire fleet of the bush-flying enterprise launched by Grant McConachie and Barney Phillips, Sr., in the summer of 1934.

"HJ," the Fokker bush plane that nearly killed McConachie when the young pilot tried to fly without the exhaust collector ring to give more power. Pilot Ted Field is at right, on the shore of Takla Lake.

This was home for Grant McConachie in the summers of 1933 and 1934 at Takla Lake.

McConachie with his Fokker in idyllic summer weather.

A midwinter scene with the famous Ford with three engines, and a dog-team.

Two Fokkers of the United Air Transport fleet on the frozen margin of Thutade Lake, deep in the Stikine mountain range of interior British Columbia. This was the site of the Two Brothers Gold placer-mining development.

Bush flying in central and northern British Columbia in the mid-thirties, an air base was where you found it, usually a lake or a farmer's field.

In November 1934 Grant McConachie was selected to take an instrument-flying course with the RCAF at Camp Borden. He is shown at left with two of his colleagues during the special training, with the open cockpit biplane in the background.

There was nothing ritzy about the accommodation at the Peter Pond Lake fish camp where the fishermen hauled whitefish from under the ice and McConachie's bush planes flew them to the railhead. Here Grant McConachie stands in the cookhouse doorway with the camp cook and a fisherman.

The settlement on Takla Lake in the wilds of British Columbia where Grant McConachie brought his city bride. Their new home was the third cabin from the right.

After surviving a comic-opera "first commercial flight over the Canadian Rockies" from Edmonton to Calgary in United Air Transport's tri-motored Ford, Grant McConachie, left, and his co-pilot, Gil McLaren, were acclaimed at a civic banquet in Vancouver. Here, in non-flying garb, they chat with Vancouverites under the wing of their rock-hopping "tin goose."

this time bug-eyed with astonishment. She confronted the red-faced groom, her temper once again flaring. "You never told me you had a wooden leg!" she stormed. "What else haven't you told me? Can you do any other tricks?" She tossed her head disdainfully, surveyed the circle of onlookers, then returned her attention to her new husband.

"Well, Mr. Tricky," she spat, "you're quite a performer, aren't you. We'll just see about that. Perhaps I can do a few tricks you don't know about. How about the flying splits? You'll be happy to know that your wife is one of the few women in the world who can do the flying splits." She surveyed the audience with disdain. "Stand back, everybody, this performance is going to be absolutely free to one and all."

Bitsy backed to the living-room wall, took several quick steps, and leaped high in the air, her legs extended horizontally, fore and aft. She thumped on to the floor in the full-splits position. Perhaps the fruit punch had affected her timing or her balance. In any case, it was soon apparent that her execution of the flying splits this time had not been a total success. She couldn't move. Apparently the crash landing had dislocated her hips so that she was locked in the full-splits position. After a further interval of confusion someone phoned Dr. Millbank, who lived down the street. He stirred out of bed to study the problem, to no avail. Finally, several of the men carried the bride, still in her fully extended pose, to one of the cars for the trip to the Miseracordia Hospital, which was to be the scene of her solitary wedding night.

"It was a strange ride and certainly a weird ending to the wedding spree," Barney Phillips recalls. "Grant was driving his dad's Buick. I was in the right front seat. Bud was in the back trying to balance Bitsy, who had one foot on the shelf against the back window of the car and the other resting on my shoulder in the front seat. Nobody was doing any talking. It didn't even seem very funny at the time."

The marriage of Bud Sutherland to the pretty snake dancer seemed to be ill-fated from the very beginning. She persuaded him to give up aviation in favor of a more settled life, insisting she had always lived like a gypsy and now wanted to settle down in one place. Against the advice of his friends, he quit his job as McConachie's mechanic, drew his entire life pension from the railway in a lump sum, and bought a garage in the small town of Stettler, Alberta. The business itself did well enough, but Bud discovered too late that the restive Bitsy had been syphoning off cash from the till into the neighbourhood beer parlor. After several turbulent years with Bitsy, Bud finally regained his freedom and returned to work as a mechanic for McConachie for the rest of his days.

17. BUSH PILOT'S BRIDE

When he wasn't poisoning himself with carbon monoxide or *Ladies' Home Journal* punch, Grant McConachie's energy was always remarkable. Even back in the days when he was grounded in the Edmonton hospital after his crash he had been surprisingly active.

While an attractive nurse named Margaret MacLean was hurrying to get an emergency case for the operating room, a large dark-haired young man zipping around a corner in his wheel chair nearly ran her down. Then, a few minutes later, when she was wheeling the patient to the elevator, there was the same young man, this time in animated conversation with a fellow-patient, blocking her way with his wheel chair.

"Do you mind," she snapped, "moving that clumsy chariot of yours, sir?"

Although she had heard about the young bush pilot brought in with multiple fractures, she was not to discover the identity of the hospital charioteer until some weeks later, after he was released and was travelling on crutches. She was asked to a party by another nurse who was going with a pilot friend called Grant McConachie.

It was a noisy party. Margaret remembered thinking they were a horribly rowdy bunch, especially Grant McConachie. But a week after the party, Grant phoned Margaret MacLean for a date, which she accepted, and they went dancing at the Cave.

It took nearly two years for the friendship of the pilot and the nurse to become an engagement. Miraculously, the engagement survived a holiday at Takla Lake where Margaret went with a girl friend. It was Grant's idea, since he thought it only fair to introduce her to his world before they got married. Unfortunately, the girls were nervous about Indians. Their nervousness was not allayed when a drunken pilot friend of Grant's stumbled over their tent while chivalrously checking that they were all right.

But Margaret MacLean was the descendant of hardy Scots from the Isle of Skye. Her own father had left Prince Edward Island to farm a chunk of raw territory in the Peace River Country. Margaret had grown up on the homestead with three sisters and four brothers. For all her blue-eyed willowy good looks, she was tough. So even Takla Lake was not enough to destroy her romance with Grant McConachie.

The day after their marriage, on July 6, 1935, the bush pilot and his bride drove two hundred miles in his father's blue Buick over the gravel-surfaced road from Edmonton to Calgary in southern Alberta. Their honeymoon destination was Banff, in the Rockies west of Calgary. But the Calgary Stampede was on, and Grant insisted on staying over in the city the next day to see Uncle Harry, who had a midway concession at the Stampede.

"I'll never forget, as long as I live, my first sight of the famous Uncle Harry, Grant had told me so much about," the bride later confided to friends. Uncle Harry was standing on an open-air platform, brandishing a bottle of liquid and extolling its virtues to an open-mouthed crowd. His pale-pink face was surmounted by a black derby hat pulled well down to rest on the tips of his ears, even though it was a hot summer day. He wore a pale yellow shirt, a broad silk tie in several shades of lavender, a scarlet vest, and a black-and-white checked suit with eighteen small buttons on the jacket. The buttons fascinated her. She counted them again. And that black derby! It seemed so incongruous in that heat, and in the land of the cowboy stetson.

Incongruous or not, it performed a useful function for Uncle Harry. For the bottles he was selling were full of "Sur-Gro— the miracle hair tonic." Only when the tonic had sold out and they had returned to the privacy of his tent did Uncle Harry take off the black derby to reveal a shining bald scalp.

Since that midway encounter, the bride had taken to wondering what sort of a clan she had married into. She got a pretty clear idea of that when their two-week honeymoon at Banff was cut short after two days. The groom dumped her on his surprised parents back in Calder while he flew north to help in the search for a missing fellow-pilot.

Now, a week after the wedding, the air-sick bride sat on an oil-stained duffle bag on the floor of a freight-plane as it wallowed in air turbulence over the Rockies. She squirmed in discomfort and viewed her surroundings with distaste. She must remember to speak to Grant about the condition of this aircraft, she decided. The cabin was simply filthy. Floor, walls, windows, all needed a good scrub. And it smelled. Enough to make a person sick, even without bouncing around like a rowboat at sea. It reeked of its many cargoes, of tools, of tractor parts, of grub, gas drums, oil kegs, of hay, horses and dogs. There was even the stink of raw fish from the winter haul. A good disinfectant was needed, that was sure.

As Grant piloted the shuddering Fokker through the storm, Margaret McConachie tried to take her mind off her present unhappy situation by thinking about Takla. Last year's holiday there in the tent had not been an unqualified success.

But Grant had promised it would be altogether different now, with a fine new home on the shore of the lake, just like a summer resort as he had described it. The log residence had been built by the Indians under his direction, and he himself had installed shelves and cupboards. It would be as comfortable as any home in the city, he had assured her. The furniture and household effects had been forwarded to Fort St. James by train and from there by lake barge to Takla Landing. It would be installed for their arrival. While he was away flying she would have the company of Vi McLaren, the other pilot's wife, who would be up in a few weeks, and, of course, Mrs. Aitken, the Indian agent who ran the general store at the Landing.

Up front in the cockpit of the Fokker, Grant McConachie worked hard with the stick and rudder to fly through the storm as non-violently as possible. He was acutely aware of his bride alone back in the cabin with no seat belt—in fact, without even a seat to protect her from the plane's escalations. He wondered what she would have to say when they landed. The storm had slowed the plane's ground speed to a crawl. They were already more than an hour overdue at Takla. The shadows of dusk were deepening in the mountain valleys and creeping up the slopes. McConachie knew he would have to find his destination and land on Takla Lake in the darkness of night.

He wasn't worried about getting lost in the maze of mountains and valleys. He had traversed the skies of this wild country many times and could recognize its craggy features like a familiar face. He adjusted his goggles to peer over the side. Heavy rain continued to sluice around the cowl of the windscreen and stream in horizontal ribbons past the open cockpit, but he could make out below his wings the wormish contours of Great Beaver Lake. There was no way he would make it to Takla before nightfall.

It was black as midnight when the Fokker finally flew low over the waters of the Middle River where they broadened into Takla Lake. But the pilot's experienced eyes could detect the slight change in the texture or the shade of the darkness that distinguished water and shore. It was a trick he had learned on the fish haul, and it served him well in the present circumstance. When he sensed that he was close to the tiny settlement he dropped to fifty feet and began to circle. After five minutes of orbiting in the darkness, he finally saw what he had been waiting for. White discs had appeared further down the shoreline, shining out of the black black sky-line like homing beacons. Alerted by the roar of the Fokker, the Hudson's Bay factor, his wife and his son were in the yard of the trading post shining their flashlights against the white wall of the building. McConachie completed another half-circle then throttled back to put the Fokker into a nose-high power glide in the direction of the lights.

He realized that letting down blind onto a choppy lake might be a lot rougher than the night ski landings on snow with which he was familiar. It was. The steps of the pontoons took the impact of a wave and the Fokker bounced twenty feet in the air as McConachie closed the throttle and pulled the control stick into his stomach to stall the wings. The impact of the second touch-down shook the entire aircraft so violently McConachie wondered if it might have buckled the undergear struts. Then they were wallowing in the waves. Before the Fokker could weathercock into the wind, McConachie lowered the water rudders, advanced the throttle, and steered for the lights on the shore. They had made it. But he knew his troubles were just beginning. He still had to face a very shaken-up bride.

As she emerged from the plane, however, his wife was too glad to be alive to think of complaining. Now she was occupied with the task of backing down the metal ladder from the cabin to the deck of the plane's pontoon, then leaping across to the rain-slick planking of the dock. Even with her husband's help, it was tricky in high heels, silk stockings, girdle, and the close-fitting sheath of her dress. She was already regretting her stubborn refusal, back in Edmonton, to put on the bush boots, blue jeans, sweater

and windbreaker Grant had advised. With so many of her
friends at the airport to see her off, she would have felt
ridiculous in such outlandish garb.

When Grant finally loomed out of the darkness of the
trading post compound he was accompanied by the trader's
boy, Luke, who had volunteered to help carry the supplies.
Both were burdened with shoulder packs, bedrolls and duffle
bags. He was terribly sorry, Grant told his bride, but there
was no choice, they would have to hike along the shore trail
to the cabin, not very far, just a couple of miles. He would
come back for the plane the next day, when the storm had
subsided.

It started to pour again as they set out in single file along
the bush path, and the raindrops glistened in the beams from
their electric torches. Grant was in the lead and Margaret,
followed by Luke, struggled to keep up with his long-legged
stride. Her spike heels sank into the mush and finally she
had to carry her shoes and walk in stocking feet. The tight
skirt hobbled her legs. She stumbled on roots and rocks that
tore her silk stockings to shreds and bruised her feet. When
she concentrated her attention on the trail, to avoid a sprained
ankle, her face was whip-lashed by unseen branches spring-
ing back from her husband's broad-shouldered passage. Her hair
was soon streaming down her cheeks and she was soaked to
the skin. She knew she must look a fright, but was too miserable to care any more. Her one concern was to reach the
end of this wretched journey, to find refuge in the comfort
and security of her new home. She thought gratefully of a
roaring fire, of clean dry sheets, the comfort of a warm bed in
the snug lodge her husband had described so enthusiastically.
She hoped Mrs. Aitken had thought to arrange the new furniture and make up the beds ready for their arrival.

The night trek dragged on in silence. There was only the
rhythmic squish of their footsteps and, all around them in
the darkness, the soft rustle of the rain on the leaves and

branches of the forest. Finally, the bush trail widened into a clearing and their flashlights played on ugly humps of cardboard, rusted tin, wood and canvas. The Indian village. Then the trail veered towards the shore of the lake, and a few minutes later they had arrived.

As they approached the door of the new cabin, however, Grant stopped, put his arm around his bride, and drew her aside.

"I'm afraid I've got some bad news for you, Peg." He spoke quietly. "Joe Farley told me about it back at the dock. There was a big storm on the lake. The freight barge went to the bottom, and all our new furniture was lost."

He opened the door. Their flashlights probed the dark interior of the cabin. It was empty. Absolutely empty.

The bride stumbled across the threshold of her new home, dropped her wet shoes to the floor, and looked around her in a daze at the white spruce planking of the floor, the skinned logs of the walls, the naked windows. She was too dumbfounded for words. She looked helplessly at her husband, her blue eyes glistening with tears. He drew her close.

"You must be very tired, darling," he whispered tenderly. Then he grinned reassuringly. "I'll have a fire going in no time and we can get dried out. Then we'll roll out the sleeping bags and turn in. You'll feel fine in the morning, after a good sleep."

Bright sun shining through the curtainless windows of the cabin awakened the newlyweds. The storm had passed and it was a cloudless day. With the resilience of youth, Margaret had already recovered from the ordeal of the previous day and not even the sight of the empty cabin could depress her spirits. She rustled utensils and provisions out of the duffle bags and soon had a good breakfast of bacon and eggs sizzling on the stove. This stone-age style of housekeeping was going to be awkward for a while, but she would make out, she told her husband.

Grant assured her he would send out a message to order
new furniture from Edmonton. In the meantime, he reminded
her, their trunks would be arriving on the next barge, in a
couple of weeks, and she would at least have materials for
carpets and drapes. They could buy other needs at Aitken's
store and the trading post.

And thus, for nearly six weeks, until the new furniture
ultimately floated in on the Takla Transport barge, the
McConachies bivouacked on the floor of their cabin.

Despite the isolation of the Takla cabin, Margaret was
surprised to discover that she wasn't lonely when her husband
was away flying. There seemed to be so much to do, and it
was all an exciting change from the city life she had got used
to. She chopped and hauled wood for the stove, baked her
own bread, and hauled water from the lake. Grant joked
about the "running water" . . . you took a pail down to
the lake and ran back with it. Enormous wild strawberries and
huckleberries grew abundantly in the woods behind the cabin.
Berry-picking was fun, and the fresh fruit was a welcome
change from the canned food and preserves, but you had to use
mosquito netting and insect repellant to fight off the black flies,
scourge of the north woods in summer.

Occasionally Grant was able to take an afternoon off from
airfreighting to the mine, and like any other young couple,
the McConachies would take off on a trip to the store—150
miles away! Burns Lake was on the rail line from Edmonton,
which meant that it was supplied with fresh meat and vege-
tables. These were a welcome change from the food available
at the Takla store.

But even after the furniture arrived, Margaret McConachie
found that there were drawbacks to life at Takla. The Indian
neighbours for one thing. They were very curious about the
new whites and used to take turns peering into the cabin
windows. What was almost as bad, they used to come to the
door with moose meat for sale, oblivious of the fact that the

meat was crawling with big blue flies. They were surprised by Registered Nurse McConachie's reaction to the proposed sale.

But despite the Indian neighbours and the tiresome visits of the other white resident, Mrs. Aitken, the storekeeper ("a wonderful woman—but even when I made tea for her she would tell me how it should be made"), Mrs. McConachie was happy at Takla. She and her husband were never to forget the rugged beauty of those first two summers of their married life, in the cabin on Takla Lake.

18. WHITE WATER

That first summer together at Takla was almost the McConachies' last summer on earth, thanks to Jack Hammel's horses.

Hammel had been prospecting in the area, using a string of horses he had flown in as colts. Now the animals had grown too big to be flown out by bush plane for winter. And already by the end of September the passes out were choked by snow. Unless feed—loads of it—could be flown in, the horses would never last the winter.

When Hammel turned up at Takla, McConachie's fellow-pilots had already flown out to Edmonton where they would sit out the period "between seasons" until the lakes and rivers had frozen solidly enough for ski landings. McConachie himself was all set to leave when Hammel offered to pay double the air-cargo rate if he would fly in a winter's supply of feed. Even if the hay were double-compressed to reduce the bulk, Grant figured that it would take a month's flying to do the job. It would mean float flying off Takla right up to the first of November. It didn't seem possible—but he made the deal with Hammel.

Freezing spray was the menace that closed the flying season on Takla at the end of September and made the Hammel deal seem impossible. Like other deep-water mountain lakes, Takla did not freeze over till mid-winter. But during the run-up of the engine and on the take-off run, the whirling propeller of the bush plane would send up spray, which froze on the metal blades of the propeller and lashed back in the slip stream to coat the wings and the struts. As young McConachie had learned in his near-fatal crash at Edmonton, even a small build-up of ice on the propeller could be murder.

McConachie and Red Gray, his mechanic, set about solving the problem. Before the first barge-load of double-compressed hay from Fort St. James arrived at Takla Landing, they had found a way to beat the menace of the freezing spray. At the edge of the lake they built a sloping platform of logs. Its surface was slicked with ice, its lower edge lapped by the water of the lake. They hauled the Fokker tail-first up on to the platform. The tail-skid of the plane was then hitched to a tree with a length of rope secured by a slip-knot. The mechanic and an Indian helper used blow torches to heat the metal blades of the propeller and the wing struts. As his mechanic tumbled aboard, McConachie advanced the throttle to full take-off power, then signalled the Indian to yank the slip-knot. The released Fokker slithered down the skidway at full power, skimmed the water and slanted into the air before spray-ice could accumulate on the wings or on the pre-heated blades of the propeller.

The crazy system worked beautifully and became a routine performance during the hay shuttle. Delivery at the Hammel mine was simple. McConachie simply circled low over the property as Red Gray pushed the bales of hay through the open door of the Fokker's cabin. Thus the hay haul was completed by the end of October, the Hammel horses were assured of survival, and Grant McConachie, with a fat wad of Hammel money, was ready to take off for his between-season base at Edmonton.

The young pilot was in a thoughtful mood early on the morning of November 2, 1935, as he and Red Gray checked the emergency supplies and loaded extra cans of gas into the

cabin of the Fokker as it perched on the skidway ready for the
final departure of the year. With the temperature at zero he
knew that they were leaving not a minute too soon. And already he regretted assuring his wife that this would be just
a routine flight of a few hours to Edmonton. Thus encouraged
she had happily shed her Takla costume of boots, sweater
and men's pants, and prepared for a stately arrival in Edmonton in her city shoes, brown gabardine city suit and her
Persian lamb coat.

It just *might* be a routine flight, Grant conceded to himself, except for the small problem of landing at the snow-
covered Edmonton airport on floats. Ah well, something would
turn up.

Something did. The number-three cylinder of the Fokker's
Whirlwind engine blew its top soon after the take-off from
Takla. There was a violent explosion and a cascade of black
oil spewed back in the slip stream to smear the windscreen
and splatter the fuselage of the plane. The engine seemed
to be shaking itself apart and the aircraft was shuddering so
violently the instrument panel was a blur.

In the open cockpit up forward McConachie reacted with
instinctive speed. He closed the throttle, snapped off the ignition
switches and pushed the control stick forward to put the Fokker into a powerless glide back towards Takla. With the skilled
ease of long experience, he selected a landing area close-in
by the shore, tilted the plane into a side-slip, levelled off a few
feet above the lake, and set the plane smoothly on to the water.
Red Gray slid out of the cabin, detached a paddle from the
pontoon, and guided the bush plane back to the ramp from
which it had so recently departed.

One look at the shattered, oil-drenched wreck of the Fokker's engine convinced the mechanic that nothing short of a
return to the factory could get it working again. The plane
would have to be abandoned there on the shore until after

Christmas when a ski-plane from Edmonton could land on the ice with a replacement engine.

Grant had no intention of being isolated for two months at the outpost awaiting rescue. He decided that he and Red would hire a boat and an Indian guide and make the 140-mile river journey to Fort St. James, where they could get a ride to Edmonton. It was a rough, dangerous trip—too rough for Margaret, of course, who would be left behind with Mrs. Aitken —but it was better than sitting doing nothing in Takla.

There were only two drawbacks. First, the local Indians were greatly enjoying the conviviality of a potlatch ceremony and could not be persuaded to lend a guide or a boat except at extortionate rates. Secondly, his wife announced that she had no intention of staying; if they could go by boat, she could go by boat. So they bundled her up in several layers of men's clothes and set out to try their luck against the rapids, without a guide.

It was late in the afternoon and the sun had long since disappeared behind the western mountains when the McConachie expedition set out in a white boat from Takla Landing. Their craft, a twenty-foot freighter with a Seahorse outboard bolted to its stern and *Alice* printed in black script on the prow, had been borrowed from Mrs. Aitken. Provisions were stowed in a waterproof bag under one of the seats.

They formed a strange and inept little group of mariners. Grant McConachie, huddled in his fleece-lined flying suit, with leather helmet and goggles to combat the freezing spray, was at the helm in the stern of the boat. Red Gray, facing backward, crouched in the shelter of a heavy blanket in the prow. Margaret McConachie lay on the ice-flecked slats of the boat's floor, enveloped in a sleeping bag. Only her white toque and her blue eyes were visible above the rough brown quilting of the eiderdown.

It was dark and bitterly cold when McConachie finally steered the freight boat into the shore of the lake to announce they would make camp for the night. As they pulled the boat up, hoisted the outboard clear of the water, and built a fire, the voyagers noted with some discouragement that in the clear night air they could still see the winking lights of Takla Landing. They had been travelling for hours, yet their point of departure was still visible along the darkened shore. Accustomed to the hundred-mile-an-hour pace of the bush plane, McConachie was having difficulty adjusting to the eight-miles-an-hour all-out speed of the power boat.

While Red beached the white boat and pulled the engine from the water, Grant made a twig fire, Indian style, with a green-branch tripod over it to support a billycan in which the coffee was brewed. Dinner was half-frozen meat from a tin, chunks of rye bread and hot black coffee.

With clear skies overhead, the temperature dropped to 20° below zero during the night as the three travellers sought the warmth of their sleeping bags. They slept around a log fire which the men took turns at replenishing during the long hours of darkness. They dozed fitfully, startled into wakefulness at intervals by the howling of timber wolves deep in the woods, dozing again, then waking to look at the stars and to wait for the dawn that never seemed to arrive.

Finally, with the first bleak light of day Red and Grant were up checking the boat and stowing the gear as the girl from the city struggled to prepare a hot breakfast over the embers of the night fire. The fare was simple enough: fried sausages, bread and black coffee.

Mrs. McConachie later remembered the occasion very vividly, "If you can imagine crouching in the snow trying to open tins and cooking over an open campfire while bundled in heavy clothes and wearing fur mittens, you'll have some idea what kind of a breakfast it was. But at least we didn't starve. Believe me, we were hungry enough to eat our leather shoelaces!"

After spending an annoying hour thawing out the engine

over the fire, the travellers shoved off for the second day of their journey. The lake narrowed as they cruised south and soon they were chugging downstream on the Middle River. After several hours, the river widened again into the broad and turbulent expanse of Trembler Lake.

"Flying over this lake I had often wondered how it got its name," McConachie later remembered. "Now, crossing it in the motorboat, I realized it was so named because it was never still. It was located in a draw or channel between high mountains and there was always a wind rushing through there. It didn't take us long to cross Trembler but it was scary for a while, with those icy waves breaking right over the prow of our boat."

The crucial test was still to come, however, for they were now nosing into the Tachcie rapids, a twenty-mile stretch of turbulent white water. The travellers did not know it at the time, but the Tachcie had taken many lives.

Nor did they know that at this time of year, the season of shallow water, the Tachcie was avoided even by the Indians, except for a few who were familiar with its treacherous shoals. Now the water foamed wildly over the exposed rocks and swirled across the gravel bars in midstream. Grant was an inexperienced helmsman, and he had the unfortunate notion that he would find the deepest water, and thus the safest passage, in midstream. Actually, he should have been hugging the shore, where the flow was deeper and less turbulent.

"It was a violent nightmare from the moment our boat was caught in the white water of the rapids," McConachie later remembered. "We hadn't gone a hundred yards into that twenty-mile torrent when the propeller hit a rock and tore off the shear pin, which meant we had lost all power and steering control."

The heavy freight boat bucked and wallowed in the roaring spume of the waves. Black rocks swept by in the foam as the boat swirled helplessly along in the surging stream. Now it was hurtling down sideways, completely out of control. Grant McConachie knew a terror he had never experienced in the air. He wasn't so much afraid for himself as he was for his wife who couldn't swim a stroke and who was encased in the heavy eiderdown sleeping bag. If the boat went over, or was disembowelled on one of the rocks, she was doomed. There could be no chance of saving her, he realized.

Suddenly the water was deeper and the white foam subsided into a smooth-flowing current as they came to a quieter section of the rapids. The two men stroked furiously with the paddles, which had been useless in the white water. They perspired freely despite the cold, aware that the lives of all of them depended on getting the boat to shore before they were swept on down to the turbulent waters below.

"You fools. Why did you ride in the white water? Do you want to get yourselves killed?" The shout came from an Indian on the far bank of the stream. He had observed their perilous journey in the out-of-control boat swirling down the middle of the rapids; now he spoke as they grasped the anchor of over-hanging willows on the opposite shore.

A shouted palaver across the fast-flowing waters of the Tachcie elicited the information that the Indian could not guide them through the rest of the rapids since his family awaited him upstream. He advised them, however, that Dave Hoy, the bargeman, had a camp just around the next bend and could probably supply an Indian guide, as well as fix their propeller.

When they found the Indian guide at Hoy's camp he proved to be much more reasonable in his demands than the potlatch Indians of Takla. He agreed to pilot them down the twenty miles of rapids and hike back home for five dollars. With his expert knowledge of the river, the Indian had no difficulty in manoeuvering the *Alice* downstream, hugging the shore, avoiding the white water, dodging rocks and gravel bars, seeking out the deeper channels. Finally, in the early dusk of approaching winter they reached the end of the rapids at a tiny settlement of three log cabins where the river flowed into the broad sweep of Stuart Lake.

After the wild terror of the Tachcie, the three voyagers welcomed the placid waters of the big lake, even though they were cold, cramped and utterly miserable. After paying off the Indian guide at the settlement, McConachie again took over the helm of the freight boat *Alice*. Sixty miles of open water lay between the settlement at the mouth of the Tachcie and the haven of Fort St. James, but the leader of the expedition had decided that come what may he would not expose his party to another night of camping out. They would chug on. He advanced the outboard throttle to full speed to propel the boat through the water at a steady eight-miles-an-hour.

At long last, after a journey that did not reflect well on Grant's navigation skill, the winking lights of Fort St. James could be discerned through the mist and the gloom. McConachie breathed a great sigh of relief. The ordeal was almost over now, and it was full speed ahead on a straight course to the warmth and comfort of the settlement.

Crash! The occupants of the *Alice* were jolted out of their reveries as the boat ground to a sudden halt against some unseen obstruction. Instinctively, Grant cut the motor. In the sudden silence, his wife's voice was edged with exasperation, "What have we hit this time?"

Investigation quickly disclosed that this time the *Alice* had grounded on neither an island nor the shore line but had come up against a shelf of shore ice that extended out more than a mile from shore. The men were able to pull the heavy boat up on to the ice, whereupon the three travellers gathered their few possessions and set out on the weary trudge across the ice to the shore. Not sure of the ice thickness, Grant insisted that his wife carry an oar from the boat in a horizontal position so that if the ice gave way underneath her she would have something to hold on to.

"By this time," she recalled later, "I was so cold and miserable I was almost hoping I *would* go through the ice and put an end to the ordeal."

Finally, they were climbing the snow-covered slope of the shore. It was three in the morning as they banged on the door of Forsythe's, the only stopping place in the small settlement of Fort St. James.

Mrs. Forsythe, still half-asleep, opened the door to greet the threesome with utter astonishment. They had apparently just walked out of the night from nowhere. The two men carried sleeping bags, and the half-frozen-looking woman in the red jacket and white toque was clutching a boat oar. Before the men had time to speak, the woman addressed Mrs. Forsythe. It was more a plea than a question.

"Can I get a hot bath?" she asked.

"Why, yes, just as soon as I can heat the water," Mrs. Forsythe responded. Then she looked dubious. "We'll have to charge you $1.50. It's our regular rate."

That bath, Mrs. McConachie later told friends, was the one thing in life she coveted above all else at that moment. "Even if it had taken every cent Grant had from the haylift, I would have cheerfully paid it out for the heaven of that hot bath."

19. "THE McCONACHIE DEAL"

As it turned out, Grant McConachie's "steal" of Harry Oakes's $55,000 Ford for $2,500 was no more than a try-out for a succession of such notorious performances. Some of these episodes were close to incredible, though all were abundantly verified. In each instance they were to eke out for a little longer McConachie's financial survival as a bush air-service operator. Together they were to create in local aviation circles the legend of "The McConachie Deal."

One such deal involved the disposal of the Ford. Though he had billed the tri-motored plane on barnstorming posters and in the press as "the largest commercial aircraft in Canada," the big bird could not fly off water. Thus it was a flop as a bush-country money-maker. McConachie decided to unload it.

Rugged though it was, the Ford had been designed for smooth runways and civilized flying. Its creators had never anticipated the cruel sledge-hammering of overloaded take-offs and landings on ice-humped northern lakes. Two winters on the northern fish haul had so strained the skeleton and sinews of the cumbersome craft that the aspirin-and-band-aid treatment of routine maintenance no longer were enough. The surgery of complete overhaul was needed. Red Rose, the oil-stained mechanic responsible for keeping it in the air, had become so alarmed that he would ride in G-CARC only under protest. Red flew with his fingers permanently crossed.

So he was not happy at the end of the 1936 fish-lift, when he was told to fly with the Ford on a mine-equipment haul out of Takla Lake. On the return flight pilots Ted Field and Len Wagen had strict instructions from McConachie to fly straight through to Edmonton. Don't land at Prince George! McConachie knew his gang.

And a strange combination of events began!

"In those days," Red explained, "Prince George was a boisterous frontier community and to all of us in bush flying it spelled only one thing. A big party. Nobody knew this better than McConachie himself. Once he threw a lot of bedroom furniture out of the Imperial Hotel window in an uproarious mood.

"Unfortunately the weather closed down on us and we *had* to land at Prince. No choice. Sure we had a bit of a party. What else was there to do with the weather duff? But we took off as soon as it lifted the next day. The trouble was, we hadn't dared to wire McConachie that we were squatted down at Prince. So as far as he was concerned we were just unreported. Then our weather trouble began."

The roundabout route north to Fort St. John to refuel had taken the Ford between the walls of a deep canyon which formed a granite funnel for the storm winds.

"We were right down in Devil's Canyon when the blow hit us," Red recalled with a shudder. "Man, was that a rough one! All hell bust loose! The plane shook so hard the ski cables broke and I'll bet half the rivets popped. Then the wind suddenly flipped us right upside down. A spare engine in the cabin broke its lashings and crashed down to the roof, twisting the frame so much that it broke all the windows. It was murder! I honestly don't know how we stayed in the air."

The crippled plane jolted on through the turbulence to Fort St. John where for two days the crew waited for the storm to abate. Red made baling-wire repairs to hold the Ford together for the homing flight south to Edmonton.

Meantime, a very worried McConachie had been sending out tracers. When he discovered that the missing crew had put in overnight at Prince George before proceeding to Fort St. John, he crackled off a wire to chief pilot Field: LAND AT FAUST STOP FERRYING PLANE UP AND WILL MEET YOU THERE STOP YOU ARE ALL FIRED STOP MCCONACHIE.

"Of course getting fired didn't bother us," Rose said. "We were used to that. But we were anxious to get home with that creaky plane and weren't happy about landing at Faust."

When the Ford eventually settled on to the ice of Lesser Slave Lake and skittered up to the Faust air base on the shore the day was dying. The boss was there to confront the offenders.

Field got in the first words,

"Okay, Grant, we know we're all fired. So let's get some sleep, and we'll fly on down to Edmonton tomorrow," he yelled.

"Sleep, hell!" McConachie retorted. "I *bet* you characters need some sleep after your caper in Prince, but you can forget it. We're taking off for Edmonton tonight. Right now. Get some gas pumped into The Goose."

"But, Grant," Rose protested. "Let's be sensible. It'll be pitch dark before we get half way there. You know they ain't got lights at Edmonton, and there's no snow on the field for our skis either."

"You just let me worry about that," McConachie replied. "I'm flying the aircraft. You guys don't work for the company any more. You're just cargo."

And, half an hour later, off they went.

Circling over the dark airfield at Edmonton, McConachie took his bearings from the lights of the adjoining city to manoeuvre the Ford on to a powered-approach descent. As he neared the edge of the field he eased back the side window.

Operating the controls with his right hand, he thrust a flash-light out into the slip stream, aiming its beam ahead to pick up the surface of the field so that he could judge the flare-out and landing.

"None of us was too happy with the boss at the time, but we sure had to give him credit for that landing," Rose commented. "There was no snow, but he slicked those skis on to the grass so smooth you hardly knew you were down, and then we skidded right up to the hangar. It was beautiful!

"Then he stomps out of the aircraft and says to us, 'Okay, you guys, get wheels under those skis and roll this can into the hangar.'

"But we're fired," Red reminded him.

"'You're fired tomorrow morning,' he replies, and marches off, so of course we stowed the Ford for him before we went home."

Red Rose, now an unemployed mechanic, ran into Mc-Conachie three nights later. It was in the dim grotto-like Cave, Edmonton's only night club, where Grant with his wife was pouring from a table bottle of rye. He flashed his big grin, waved Red over and boomed:

"Sit down and have one, Red. You're back on the staff as of right now. Say when on the water," and splashed rye generously into an extra tumbler.

Red's initial reaction was caution.

"Grant always poured them deep, but when I saw how the rye was flowing I knew he was after something. Still, what the hell. Grant was always such good company you couldn't stay mad at him. Besides, it was a free drink, which meant something in those days."

McConachie soon disclosed he had sold the Ford to George Simmons of Northern Airways based at Carcross, up in the Yukon. He was exultant. Simmons would trade for the Ford a Fairchild FC2W2 float-plane valued at about ten thousand dollars plus eight thousand cash. Since McConachie had paid

Harry Oakes only twenty-five hundred dollars for the Ford and had battered it up fish hauling, barnstorming and freighting, he rated this a very good deal indeed. And, indeed, it was a very good deal. A McConachie deal.

After more slugs of rye, McConachie announced that he, Len Wagen and Red would be taking off the next day to deliver the Ford to the Yukon buyer.

"Hold it right there, Grant," Red broke in. "Just hold it. This time don't fire me because I just quit. I'm sure as hell not riding to the Yukon in that beat-up bucket!"

"Have another drink. Relax, Red. You take life too seriously." He sloshed more rye into his mechanic's tumbler and draped a friendly arm across his shoulders.

The night teetered along. Little more was said about the flight. But somehow the delivery trip took off from Edmonton next morning with Rose aboard. They spent the night at Takla Lake and then pressed on the next day for Finlay Forks, a trading post in the Rocky Mountain Trench. Simmons was to pick up the aircraft at the tiny locked-in settlement.

"I was surprised and relieved the Ford held together through the mountains, but how could I ever know what would happen next," Rose recalls. "As we approached Finlay Forks, McConachie held cruising height, about seven thousand feet, then he looks back at me, sort of grinned and says, 'Simmons is down there. Guess we better put on a show for him.'

"Then he tilts the Ford right over on its back and down into a screaming spiral, power still on, everything shuddering and rattling something awful. I don't think I was ever so scared in my life. All I could think of was if we ever get this flying nightmare down in one piece, at least we'll be rid of it."

The grandstand power dive had played to an empty house. Simmons had been and gone. When they landed, there was a message that Simmons would meet them in Whitehorse, far to the northwest.

At Whitehorse the next day, Simmons appeared dubious

about the beaten-up appearance of the plane and wondered about its capabilities. McConachie immediately volunteered to stage a demonstration flight to Dawson City with the plane overloaded at thirty-five hundred pounds. The pay load included diamond drills, pumps, groceries, dynamite, two trappers, a deacon of the Anglican church, and four crewmen from a paddle-wheel boat.

The overweight Ford took off easily from the snow plateau of the Whitehorse field, circled over the small settlement, then levelled to follow the north-flowing watercourse of the Lewes to its confluence with the Yukon and then on past the gold creeks of the Klondyke. McConachie could pick out gold-bearing gravel benches beneath the snow. Along the river shore he could see the decaying hulks of paddle-wheel steamers that had had their glory days during the Great Gold Rush of 1898. He thought of the legions of gold-seekers who had swarmed for weeks and even months down the rivers, through the valleys and over the mountain passes to reach the Klondyke; and he marvelled once again at the wonder of air transportation. He thought of the isolation of these people of the Yukon who, more than thirty years after the trail of '98, were still almost entirely dependent on surface transportation to the outside world.

So, as he piloted the Ford between Whitehorse and Dawson, McConachie's thoughts crystallized into a determination that he would provide the air link to the Yukon.

After the Ford's return to Whitehorse, George Simmons still was not entirely satisfied. He wanted a demonstration under more rugged bush-flying conditions. What more did the man want? He proposed a haul over the tractor-train route from Atlin to Carcross. McConachie was most happy to oblige. He had to clinch this deal. It meant a lot. So they flew down to the tiny settlement of Atlin.

The Ford's cabin-load for the return Atlin-Carcross hop was a mixed bag, part of a delivery originally consigned to one of the tractor sleigh-trains that lumbered over the bush trails. In addition there were ten passengers—two trappers and eight Malamutes, those half-wolf partly-wild sleigh dogs of the north.

As the three engines roared and the big plane accelerated on the take-off run across the ice of Atlin Lake, the Malamutes panicked. All hell broke loose. One of them snapped his leather leash with his teeth and scrambled to the back of the cabin and on through the open door of the washroom. He then scrambled through a small inspection port in the bulkhead right into the extreme rear of the plane amongst the wires and pulleys that operated the rudder and tail-plane control surfaces. The other Malamutes tore loose, too, yelping and snarling in the full fury of their wolfishness. They raced after their mate.

In the cockpit, McConachie had the control wheel full forward to raise the tail ski off the ice. But why should the plane be so tail-heavy? Sluggishly, the Ford lifted into the air and over the tree line.

At this critical moment, the two trappers stumbled to the back of the cabin to untangle their dogs. The shift of weight— with two men and eight dogs in the tail—unbalanced the plane's centre of gravity, teetering the Ford into an increasingly precarious nose-up attitude. The angle of climb was impossible. Airspeed was falling off. McConachie was dumbfounded. Why? Why? Something had to be done or the Ford would stall and go out of control. At such low altitude a stall would be fatal. But he couldn't figure out what was wrong.

He jammed all three throttles forward against the stops, cranked the tail-trim control to the full "nose-down" setting and forced the wheel forward with all his great strength. From a cruising 90 mph, the airspeed needle was still falling—70 . . . 65 . . . 60. He watched the needle with horror, and over the roar of the three engines he heard the shouting, thumping and yelping from the melee in the tail. Trouble with those Goddamned passengers—but what?

The Ford was beginning to buck and shudder. The controls

were mushy as the wing and tail surfaces rode in a slackening airflow. The airspeed needle was flickering on 55. If it went to 50 they were all dead, pilots, trappers and dogs, too. With a flick of his head McConachie ordered Simmons back into the cabin to do something. Anything. Simmons acted fast, grabbed the trappers by the necks and pushed them forward.

McConachie felt someone lurch against the back of his seat, as Simmons shoved the two bewildered trappers into the cockpit. They were crammed against the starboard windscreen, Simmons squeezed in behind them. The dogfight continued back in the tail, but the weight of the four men up front slowly brought the nose down. The airspeed needle began swinging the other way—65 . . . 70 . . . 80 . . . 90. The crisis was over. McConachie relaxed his wet grip on the control wheel. He managed a grin, and slowly said, "Keerist Almighty!"

But he still had a deal to make.

"The Ford performs pretty good in low-speed flight, eh, George?" he suggested.

Simmons' face was grim. And pale. He made no reply. They continued the uncomfortable flight to Carcross with the pilots and trappers jammed into the cockpit. Nobody spoke. The fear-crazed brutes snarled and snapped in the tail until the aircraft was on the ground.

It was a flight like no other. It was a flight to be talked about later.

"If you're planning any more demonstrations like that, forget it," Simmons told McConachie over a drink. "You've sold me. It's a deal. Shake."

It was *quite* a deal. When the government inspector checked Northern Airways' recently-acquired Ford, he grounded the plane for the entire summer season while extensive repairs and a major overhaul were completed. McConachie's outfit moved aircraft north to take over the freight contracts originally assigned to the Simmons Ford.

To add insult to injury, McConachie proceeded to buy another Ford: one that *could* fly on pontoons. Now he was almost ready to start the service north to the Yukon that had flashed into his mind as he had flown north to complete his deal with Simmons.

But before he could start there were a few problems to be faced. Like money. With the 1936 winter fish haul over, United Air Transport was flying hungry again. To stand a chance of surviving, Grant McConachie had to get mail contracts.

United Air Transport's canary-yellow Fairchild FC2W2 weathercocked into the wind far out from shore at Cooking Lake where McConachie had taxied to take-off position. Crouched in the single-seat cockpit he was intent on the study of his maps as the bush plane drifted, its motor warming.

In the cabin of the yellow Fairchild, buckled into the only passenger seat, sat Walter Hale, the district postal inspector who had been assigned to make an airmail appraisal of the route between Fort St. John and Fort Nelson. His report to Ottawa would determine the success or failure of the UAT application for an airmail contract on the run.

McConachie also had a full load of eggs and oranges, because, as he later explained, "We were setting out on a thousand-mile return trip deadhead. The post office wasn't paying for it. Running a plane that far costs a lot of money, so I decided I might as well take on a pay load. The people up at Fort Nelson were really isolated, hardly ever saw a fresh orange or an egg, so why not fly some in and sell them at fabulous prices?"

As McConachie stowed the maps to return his attention to the oil temp. dial he was astounded to see water trickling in over the sill of the cockpit. He squirmed around to open the door of the cabin section. My God! Floating oranges! The cabin was gurgling with lake water. The plane, the eggs, the oranges and the postal inspector were going under! The Fairchild was sinking tail first.

It was only later that McConachie had time to reconstruct the disaster. As he was taxiing out on to the lake, the tail ends of the overloaded pontoons were riding under water. The stream force had lifted off the inspection caps from the rear float compartments and the water poured in. This added weight then sunk the tail deeper, raising the next set of caps, and so on. Studying his maps, the pilot had been unaware of this progressive catastrophe. The rumbling of the engine had smothered the desperate shouts of the postal inspector.

Now only the engine, the tips of the floats and the cockpit were out of the water. The Fairchild was pointing skyward. Had the inspector drowned?

"Fortunately," as McConachie explained to the press later, "there was a very powerful engine in the Fairchild. I didn't have a second to spare. I poured on full throttle, right to the stops—it was almost like a helicopter, lifting the plane out of the water, at least enough. I figured we now had the inspector's head out of the water, if not the eggs and oranges. Of course with the tail still deep under, the rudder was useless. I couldn't steer so I just went straight ahead, boring across the lake with the engine roaring wide open until we crunched right up on to the gravel beach on the far shore.

"That performance did not impress the postal inspector with our flying operation, but I guess he was happy enough just to have survived. In any case we got him dried out there on the beach, repacked the eggs and oranges, pumped out the floats and put the compartment caps back on, *very* securely. Then we took off for Fort Nelson."

During the long flight, Grant McConachie was able to restore Inspector Walter Hale's dampened sense of humour so that before their first landing the Cooking Lake episode had become the subject of good-natured joshing.

"You have the unique distinction," McConachie told Hale,

"of being the first . . . and I hope-to-God the last . . . passenger we've submerged. Oh, we've bent lots of planes, one way and another, but we've never injured a passenger or lost any cargo."

On his return to Edmonton, Inspector Hale's favourable report resulted in the award of a government contract for UAT to carry the mail between Fort St. John and Fort Nelson ten return trips a year, which was monthly minus freeze-up and break-up.

The airmail was not lucrative enough to oust the eggs, the oranges or even the fish dog-food as revenue fillers on the northbound runs, but it did yield some desperately needed regular cash. And later the same year, on the further recommendation of the dunked postal inspector, UAT got another mail contract: Peace River–Dawson Creek–Fort St. John.

While McConachie was thus devoting his energies to flying and promoting traffic, his partner, Barney Phillips, at headquarters in Edmonton, was fending off creditors and bankers while trying to scrounge money or more credit for parts, supplies and pay-days.

He said: "With our reputation, all our supplies came C.O.D., of course—most of it CNR Express. They wouldn't accept anything but a certified cheque. For us, cash was out of the question, but we had to get those supplies to keep flying. So I had to go to the bank and talk the accountant or the manager into certifying a cheque to cover an amount that wasn't in the account. Believe me, it was no easy chore."

Then there were the bailiff stickers.

"The sheriff would arrange for Jimmy Bell, the airport manager, to put these bailiff stickers on our planes that grounded us. We couldn't stand for that. We had to have those planes working if we were ever to pay off the debts. It was my job to persuade Jimmy to take off the stickers and release the planes. This usually took a couple of days' talking."

McConachie's precarious financial position was shared by

his employees. But, somehow, they always seemed to get caught up in his enthusiasm. Leo McKinnon, now an Edmonton businessman, relates his first experience as an employee of United Air Transport.

"When Dick Fisher and I joined the company, Grant picked us up in the Waco at Fort St. John for the flight to Edmonton where we were to sign on. Instead of going to Grande Prairie, the usual refuelling stop, he diverted to Peace River. He'd got the word that Imperial Oil had cut off his credit at Grande Prairie. We landed at Peace with not enough fuel to reach Edmonton.

"Grant tried to get some gas on credit but the word had beat us there, too. No credit. Great airline, I decided. So Grant came around to each of us and collected whatever money we had in our pockets and bought a couple of drums of gas. That got us in to Edmonton.

"By this time, Dick and I realized we had joined a pretty shaky outfit, but somehow it didn't bother us too much. Grant seemed so confident. It wasn't hard to believe in Grant McConachie because he believed so sincerely in himself and in the ultimate success of the flying business."

Stan Emery, an underpaid mechanic, during this flying-hungry era once stormed into UAT's Edmonton headquarters, yelling, "This is a show-down. Either I get a raise or I quit."

After half an hour in the president's office he emerged smiling, and then said seriously, "I agreed to a ten-dollar cut for the time being because things are pretty tough right now. But I think it's worth sticking around. This flying business is going places and I'm in on the ground floor. Grant says we'll be flying around the world some day."

Eventually Emery was to retire as a $25,000-a-year captain still working for McConachie.

Ralph Marshall, another early mechanic who later did well with the airline, actually started working for no salary. He fed himself on the customers' left-over sandwiches he found in the cabins of incoming planes and slept in the hangar.

New mechanics brought their own tools, worked six months as apprentices for no pay, and then became qualified specialists at forty dollars a month. When there was money in the bank.

20. AIR ROUTE TO THE YUKON

As the Ford floated free of the wooden dock at Cooking Lake, Edmonton's sea-plane base, Grant McConachie jotted in his log book "July 5, 1937, 0815 hours."

He ruddered the sea-plane into the breeze and advanced the throttles. Morning sun bounced off the metal flanks of CF-BEP as the tri-motor lifted off the slick, banked in farewell salute over the cluster of dignitaries below and levelled on a northwesterly course for Whitehorse in the Yukon, over 1,200 miles of farmland and mountain wilds.

To the Edmonton *Journal* editors and their air-minded readers, this was to be no routine flight but a Pioneering Epic written large in page-one superlatives. It would be a Space-Conquering Feat, recorded for posterity as The Aerial Conquest of the fabled "Trail of '98" over which gold-fevered sour-doughs had toiled four decades before. The dawn-to-dusk flight would weld a Historic Link of Communication between the Yukon and the rest of North America. The new weekly air service being inaugurated this day would Shrink to Hours the days of sea and rail travel to the Yukon and Alaska from the Outside.

The flying shuttle to the Yukon, moreover, was destined to be more than a first-ever link between Alberta and the Yukon. It would soon be extended, the newspaper reported, northwest over the Aleutians to China and at the other end, from Edmonton south to link up with the United States airline network as well as to Eastern Canada via the anticipated cross-Canada air service. Thanks to the irrepressible McConachie, optimism rode high.

In a series of gee-whiz news features, the *Journal*'s aviation reporter wrote that the Giant Three-engined Airliner that would inaugurate the Yukon air service was the most powerful aircraft in Canada flying on pontoons. Its floats were the Largest in the World. With a wingspan of seventy-five feet and a length of forty-five feet, the Ford could take off with an all-up weight of ten tons, carry twelve passengers, mail and cargo, and cruise at one hundred miles an hour. Readers learned that the Ford's cabin had been decorated in tasteful colors, and on this new service for the first time in the history of northern flying, passengers would enjoy the convenience of a flying biffy, coyly identified in the *Journal* as "indoor plumbing." (Traditionally, northern passengers had waited till the plane landed or used empty beer bottles, when appropriate.)

To mark this historic moment in Edmonton's history, Mayor Clarke and a cavalcade of prominent businessmen had jounced over the eighteen miles of rutted side road to Cooking Lake for the departure ceremonies. In his send-off speech, the mayor said he had trekked the gold trail from Edmonton to the Yukon in 1897 and had not come out until 1902, so he could testify to the benefits of the air service over what he envisaged as "one of the great air routes of the world."

There were a number of invited guests on the flight, armed with a bouquet of fifty Edmonton-grown roses to be presented to Yukon dignitaries. McConachie had found only one revenue passenger, an Indian returning to his trap line in the Fort Nelson area. The Ford also carried four hundred pounds of mail, which was the real pay load.

The flight plan provided for fuel stops at Fort St. John, Fort Nelson and Lower Post. ETA (estimated time of arrival)

Whitehorse: 10 P.M., Edmonton time (8 P.M., Yukon time);
Ground time en route: 1 hour 45 minutes; Air time 12 hours;
Total elapsed time: 13 hours 45 minutes.

Forty minutes out, McConachie peered through a break in
the cloud cover and knew he was in trouble. The hamlet he
spotted and pinpointed on his flight map was only forty-five
miles from the air base! Head-winds buffeting the Ford since
take-off had reduced ground speed to a mere 67 mph, compared with the planned and ballyhooed 100 mph. Unless
things improved, the total time to Whitehorse would be twenty
hours—even more. The much-publicized one-day, dawn-to-dusk
flight could be a real fiasco. The anti-climax of an overnight
stop at Fort Nelson seemed certain.

McConachie glanced at the empty co-pilot's seat. Another
vexing problem! Minutes after take-off, co-pilot Ted Field had
been hit hard by an attack of sunstroke, the result of the
previous day's exposure to the sun while lake-fishing. Poor
Ted lay on his back in the aisle of the passenger cabin.

Two hours out of Edmonton, the flight was still bucking
vigorous head-winds. There would not be enough fuel to reach
Fort St. John, 350 miles from Edmonton, the first planned
fuel stop. McConachie called his Grande Prairie radio operator
and arranged for four barrels of fuel to be hauled, pronto to
Bear Lake. There the air pioneers were greeted by Grande
Prairie mayor Percy Tooley (who was also the UAT agent)
and about a hundred citizens, virtually the entire population
with access to transportation. They applauded and laughed as
their mayor grew weary hand-pumping gas from the red steel
drums into the Ford.

They liked their mayor, despite his eccentric disregard for
clean clothes and regular shaves and haircuts. McConachie
liked him too—he had turned Percy into an evangelist for air
transport in the north. He had once even allowed Percy a
free flight so that he could record the event on his 8-mm
movie camera. Percy later showed this movie to local church

groups and the like. Then Ted Field got hold of the film and, with a projectionist friend, spliced in a number of nude sequences. The effect of these erotic scenes bursting in on the mayor's air expedition to the Yukon touched off unbelievable repercussions. But it also enhanced His Worship's fame as a public speaker and did his popularity no harm.

Fortunately the early head-winds eased off. As the sea-plane nudged into the dock at Whitehorse McConachie's watch showed 10:55 P.M. In the long northern twilight, the crew and passengers of the trail-blazing craft were puzzled to observe that only four people met them on the dock. One was a preacher. He introduced himself as the Reverend Gordon Cross, the local Anglican rector, and escorted the party of pioneers to their lodging at the Whitehorse Inn. Strolling the high boardwalk of the main street, McConachie wondered aloud why there wasn't a crowd at the dock.

The young president learned soon enough.

"You must know, Mr. McConachie, that Whitehorse is a company town; Whitepass and Yukon owns it. They were here before the gold rush a long time ago. They own the railroad to Skagway on the ocean, they run the river boats to Dawson, they operate the stage line. So they own the town.

"By, 'they,'" he explained, "I mean H. J. Wheeler. He runs Whitepass. He *rules* Whitehorse. There's the Territorial Council, yes, but Wheeler's the king of the Yukon. He resents your air service barging into his kingdom. He put out the word. So you're being ignored. You'll have trouble getting gas. They won't throw you a rope, tie you up at the dock or even give you the time of day. I would suggest you call on Mr. Wheeler in the morning."

Next morning as he climbed the creaky wooden staircase of the Whitepass depot to Wheeler's office, young McConachie thought over his hearsay impressions of "Old One-eye." The black-thatched Irishman had a fearsome reputation, a fighting loyalty to the company, and a heavy-duty-sandpaper vocabulary for anyone who crossed him. God help the outsider who stuck his nose into Whitepass affairs!

He had once snatched a cigar from the mouth of an American millionaire who struck a match against a company no-smoking sign. It was tough-nut Wheeler, then running the stage line from Whitehorse to Dawson, who had blocked a laudable plan to widen the Dawson trail, since a decent road would invite the competition of trucks and cars.

"So you're McConachie!" and it was an accusation. The man was in his late fifties, silver streaking the dark hair, pallid complexion, strong features, conservative clothes. One eye bored in on the visitor in cold hostility, the other stared over his shoulder.

"I want to tell you something, young man. I'm going to run you out of this country! How about that?"

"That might prove to be rather difficult. But why would you want to run me out?" said McConachie coolly.

"You know damn well why. We came in here. There was nothing. Whitepass built this country, from nothing. Lost a few fortunes doing it. Mail, passenger, cargo; it's our business here. There's no place for an upstart like you. None. Savvy?"

"I'm sorry you feel that way about it," said McConachie and he smiled. "But we've signed a two-year contract with the Government of Canada to carry the mail between Edmonton and Whitehorse. We intend to fulfill that contract."

"I'll tell you one thing, McConachie," rasped Wheeler. "If you have any sneaky ideas of running your planes between here and Dawson, forget it! Whitepass has just about everything up here, supplies and services. Figure that one out. Neither you nor anybody else is going to steal the passengers off our river boats. Got that straight? Savvy?"

Until that moment, the president of United Air Transport had not even considered an extension to Dawson. So here was a challenge. Why not? It was a four-day boat trip. The Ford could do it in less than four hours and charge the same fare.

He resented this tough guy's arrogance. He picked up the challenge.

"It's still a free country, Mr. Wheeler," McConachie said carefully, but with quiet assurance. "I would prefer not to displease you and your company, but we are planning to operate a weekly air service between Whitehorse and Dawson. It starts tomorrow morning. Why don't you join us? See it from the air. It's pretty country. You'd enjoy it."

H. J. Wheeler flushed, making a futile effort to hold his temper.

"Get the hell out of my office!" he roared.

(In the months to come, United Air Transport was to feel the impact of Wheeler's power. Barrels of aviation fuel consigned to UAT at Dawson on the Whitepass river boats always seemed to get mislaid. It was difficult to find help. Passive resistance to UAT seemed to be the new Code of the Yukon. Whitepass bought a fleet of planes to compete with UAT on the Dawson run. In time, however, McConachie contrived to thaw the permafrost of Herb Wheeler's antagonism. Whitepass and United worked out a co-operative arrangement. Wheeler and McConachie eventually became friends.)

After two days in the Yukon, the inaugural party took off from Dawson in the first light of mid-summer dawn, 2:30 in the morning, Thursday, July 8. The big Ford splashed down on Cooking Lake to complete the 1,600-mile home-bound journey in 14 hours 35 minutes flying time, 19 hours elapsed time. The airline to the Yukon was open for business.

Inauguration of the weekly airmail service to the Yukon did not transform United Air Transport into an airline. McConachie, the realist, knew his air service was still bush league. It was beset with all the hazards, the whimsicalities and the economic head-winds of a float-ski, fly-by-night, seat-of-the-pants flying circus.

He called in Jack Moar for advice. Moar was not just a

pilot; he had airline operations experience and was a friend of some of the really big wheels south of the border—Pan Am's Juan Trippe, TWA's Jack Frye, Phil Johnson of United. Moar had been around. McConachie showed him his operation then asked for his impressions. He got a terse reply: "Grant, it's the slap-happiest excuse for an airline I've ever seen or heard of. You can never hope to go anywhere as long as you're on floats and skis. You've got just one choice. You go wheels or you go bust."

McConachie knew that Moar was right. Line squalls, blizzards, warm fronts, cold fronts, darkness, freeze-up, break-up —even smoke from forest fires downed his planes.

"The trouble," he told Moar, "is that we're a blue-sky airline without enough blue to keep us in the air."

Then to Moar's astonishment McConachie began to talk about Moar joining them. He painted a great picture of the airline's future. To his horror, Moar found his misgivings (based on sound judgement) yielding to stirrings of excitement and enthusiasm. When McConachie wound up his pitch with, "Are you with us?" Moar's reply was cautious. "The future may be as bright as you paint it, but I can't eat prospects. What kind of a salary are we talking about?"

"I had in mind about four fifty a month," McConachie said, but as he spoke a door near by was loudly slammed. Moar was momentarily distracted by the noise.

"How much did you say?" he asked.

"Five hundred. I was thinking of five hundred a month," McConachie replied. He chortled, "I'm afraid that's as high as I can go, Jack, because that's the salary I'm drawing as president. I can't afford to give myself a raise, and I could hardly pay you more than the president of the airline, now could I?"

So Jack Moar became operations manager of United Air Transport. His job was to transform the flying circus into an airline.

Soon the pilots were wearing natty blue uniforms—officially. McConachie's pilots had been flying around the north for so long in sweaters and windbreakers that they hated blue serge and brass buttons. On every flight after twenty minutes, Alec Dane shucked his uniform and happily donned his old chewed baseball cap, his washed-out mackinaw and brown running shoes. Charlie Tweed hated "the monkey suit" as he called it; whenever he had the chance he reverted to his beloved old brown pith helmet. It was a slow business introducing uniforms to the airline.

Getting the airline on wheels was even slower. The trick was to find level patches of land along the Yukon route, take out the trees, flatten the humps, and spread a little gravel. It sounded easy. But it took time. The first of these "airports" was constructed on sand-bar islands on the Liard River north of Fort Nelson, and it played a part in a history-making run later, in November 1938. The sand bar provided an emergency landing spot (unnecessary, as it happened) for McConachie's tri-Ford on its non-stop flight on wheels from Fort St. John to Whitehorse. The non-stop six-hundred-mile flight was made possible only by a strange arrangement involving seven forty-five-gallon fuel drums in the cabin. As they flew the long-suffering Red Gray wobble-pumped the fuel from the drums into the tanks. It was unorthodox, but it worked. Grant McConachie had the satisfaction of beating the freeze-up for the first time in northern history.

But for the next few years almost all his runways were still lakes and rivers. In summer the planes rode pontoons, and skis in winter. At best, it was a ten-month flying year, with all the planes grounded for at least a month in the spring and again in the fall as the runways melted and froze. During the in-between seasons, the rivulets of the company's revenues were dust-dry. Thus, economic incentive, combined with the service demands of the isolated communities on the airmail route, pressured the pilots to stretch the flying season at both

ends—to chance the odds for that extra flight—as the ice
thinned in spring or thickened in the fall. UAT flew on thin
ice, literally. With the arrival of the spring, as regularly as the
blooming of the wild flowers would come the news of a
float-plane cracking through the ice. Freeze-up often meant
that a late-roaming pontoon craft would be trapped by the
ice floes bobbing down a river or that an early-venturing
ski-plane would dunk into one of the half-frozen lakes.

A twin-engined Barkley-Grow southbound with the Yukon
mail early in April of 1939 crunched through the rotting ice
of Charlie Lake, the Fort St. John base. The silver monoplane
was partly submerged, its wings supported by the ice. But
spring sunshine blazed from a clear sky, and it was obvious
the valuable airplane would soon slip to the bottom as the
ice weakened.

Under the direction of Glen Fenby, the other mechanics
slid two-by-eight planks beneath the wings to distribute the
weight of the aircraft. This didn't work. The sun heated the
timbers and they began to sink through the ice. So Fenby set
up a bucket brigade from the near-by sawmill to spread a
four-inch blanket of sawdust over the wings of the plane and
the surrounding ice. This protected the ice from the sun's
heat. It halted the melt. The rescue squad then wielded picks,
axes and ice saws to clear a fifty-yard channel of open water
to shore. Using the ice-pan on which it sat as a raft, they
attached ropes to the aircraft and hauled it along the water
channel to dry land. After the ice on Charlie Lake had
melted, the Barkley-Grow was changed over to pontoons and
continued its disrupted journey to Edmonton. It was a very,
very tough way to run an airline.

Scotty Moir dunked a Bellanca air freighter through the
spring ice at Isle à La Crosse with a load of liquor for the
government store. The cargo was salvaged, but all the labels
had soaked off. The customers bought that booze blind, but
it was still booze.

Ice was no worry for Joe Morris as he circled Watson Lake, losing altitude for a float landing. It was a hot, clear July morning and the air was so still that the lake surface was a mirror reflecting sky and shoreline. As the young pilot eased back the control column to flatten his glide before flaring out for the touchdown, he was shocked by a jolt so violent his forehead cracked forward against the instrument panel.

The plane had smacked the water in the glide; the impact buckled the struts, popped the pontoon rivets and sent the plane bouncing high in the air.

The dazed pilot recovered quickly enough to jam the throttle forward, gain flying control and settle his crippled plane back on to the water.

He had been booby-trapped by another float-flying hazard —glassy water. In these flat, calm conditions, the surface of the water appears to the approaching pilot either higher or lower than it actually is. Many pilots, like the inexperienced Morris, had "flown in," some wrecking their aircraft. Others had made a perfect landing thirty feet in the air, which was followed by a terrific, gut-wrenching splash as they plopped in. Very embarrassing—and very rough on the hardware. Pilots beat glassy water by tossing a seat cushion out into the lake to cause ripples which showed the surface of the water. Again, a tough way to earn the groceries.

There were no prepared runways, no windsocks, no control towers. The pilot learned to judge wind strength and direction from riffles on the water. The survival-conscious veteran always checked unfamiliar water carefully before landing or taking off. A sand bar screened by rippling water, a dead-head log, or a rock just beneath the surface could mean a lot of embarrassment—sometimes even death.

Some years later Charlie Tweed found out in the very worst way about sun-glare blindness. He was at the controls of the Fairchild FC2W2 float-plane, the aircraft McConachie had acquired in trade for his original Ford tri-motor. He had just taken on a full cabin-load of gasoline in small ten-gallon drums, and with his mechanic, Cece Pickell, aboard he was to fly from the harbor of Juneau, Alaska, to a mining camp just over the Yukon border. It was late afternoon, and the sun was blazing from a clear horizon as Tweed idled the engine, allowing the float-plane to weathercock into the wind.

As the Fairchild gathered speed and rose on to the step of the floats in its take-off run, the pilot was blinded by the glare of the sun across the water. But he was able to judge the take-off easily by looking through the side window. Then the crash! The fuselage of the Fairchild crumpled like a squashed toy. Raw gasoline sprayed from the ruptured wing tanks.

Floundering in the cold water, Cece Pickell took in the situation with one horrified glance. The Fairchild had rocketed head-on into one of the huge log pylons planted in the harbor for ship anchorage. Already flames had started to lap at the spewed gasoline saturating the wreckage. Realizing that Tweed must be trapped in the cockpit, Pickell swam desperately to the nearest pontoon. He struggled on to the float, set his foot on the rung of the cockpit ladder and tugged violently at the cabin door. It was jammed!

At that moment the gas drums inside the plane's cabin exploded. The percussion threw Pickell thirty feet through the air, back into the water. Dazed and hardly conscious, he was rescued by one of the tugs speeding to the scene.

Pickell's legs and lower body were seared with the flames and pocked with the shrapnel of the explosion, but he recovered after three weeks in the hospital. Tweed had died, either in the crash or in the explosion.

21. BUYING GAS WITH HOT AIR

McConachie's expansion into the Yukon didn't resolve his financial problems. On the contrary, United Air Transport continued to fly deeper into the red. The summer of 1938 was the toughest time of all financially. At that point, McConachie had run out of backers, yet nothing short of a very hefty infusion of new capital could save the company from the bailiff. The Nesbitt Thompson investment house had ventured far more than was reasonable for them. The Royal Bank of Canada held notes for $250,000. McConachie donned his business suit to make calls on financial houses in Pittsburgh, in New York, in Montreal, in Toronto. Somehow he couldn't get the money men to raise their eyes from the red ink of his ledgers to catch his vision of the airline's future.

"I knocked on more doors than I like to remember. Got nothing but calluses on my knuckles," he related. "I was getting so desperate I was almost ready to face the prospect of going out of business."

Then he thought of Imperial Oil. Why the hell not? He had been a steady customer for gas and oil since the start of his aviation career and his planes were using more of these products than ever before. He was a good customer—when he paid his bills.

Imperial was the only money source with a stake in the

airline's future, McConachie told Pat Reid, the local manager
of the oil company. All he wanted, he said, was a long-term
credit for one hundred thousand dollars against owing and
future fuel bills. He cajoled the flabbergasted Reid into wiring
his head office for a McConachie interview with the board of
directors. To everyone's surprise, the request was granted.
Perhaps the directors of this mighty corporation were curious
to inspect the source of such audacity.

McConachie knew that the oil men would not readily spring
for the hundred thousand dollars, especially when they checked
the UAT credit rating. So he prepared carefully for the encounter. When he appeared two weeks later in the Toronto
board room he had copies of a brief he had put together—and
a globe and a piece of string.

"Gentlemen," he said confidently, "you all know about our
present route pattern, which forms an inverted Y starting at
Edmonton and Vancouver, joining at Fort St. John and running
up to Whitehorse, as you see on this globe. You know we have
mail contracts and that we are planning to build airports on
these routes to develop an airline type of operation. Your own
records will also tell you that we have been losing money
steadily.

"Today I am not going to talk about this route pattern and
what it will mean to the development of a great new empire
of natural resources. I won't take up your time by going into
details about the interest that both our government and the
government of the United States is showing in this sheltered
inland air route to Alaska, with all of its military as well as
commercial implications. Let us look over the horizon instead."

He rotated the globe. He had the keen interest of the board
now. He spoke confidentially,

"You will see that I have extended the route markings on
this globe over the top of the world . . . across Alaska . . .
over the Bering Sea . . . down the coast of Siberia and on to
Shanghai.

"This, gentlemen, is the route I want to talk about today, because it's the aerial northwest passage to the Orient. It's the logical extension of our route to the Yukon. It's the short route to China over the top of the world. We intend to fly it in the near future, and it will become one of the great world airways of tomorrow. You are the first to hear about it in detail because your decision today can make it possible. When it does happen it will mean a great deal to your company as well as to ours."

Some of the captains of industry leaned forward, intently studying the $3.95 schoolroom globe.

Urged on now by his own strong conviction, McConachie set forth the irresistible logic of the short route to the Orient.

"Gentlemen," he said, "since the world is a sphere, the only way you can put it on a map accurately is with a globe. The schoolroom wall map we were all brought up on would be right if we had a flat world, but for a round world it's a fraud. It distorts directions and distances.

"Let's take a look at the route from, say, Edmonton to Shanghai, on the globe." McConachie fished a piece of string from his briefcase. He knew he had the board's full attention. He placed one end of the string on Edmonton, then extended it on the globe to span the distance to Whitehorse and on over the Aleutians, down the coast of Asia to Shanghai. With a pen he blackened the spot on the string where it reached the Chinese metropolis.

"As you see, we have measured with the string the air distance from Edmonton to Shanghai over the top, the Great Circle Route, as the geographers would call it.

"Let's use the same string to compare the distance from Edmonton to Shanghai via Honolulu around the bulge of the Pacific . . . there. As you can see, the black mark on this string marking the great circle distance to Shanghai is right out in the middle of the ocean. Somewhere around Wake Island, with another four inches of string needed to reach Shanghai.

The scale of this map is five hundred miles to the inch. So, our Yukon route to Shanghai is *two thousand miles shorter* than the trans-Pacific route! What's more, over the thousands of miles of open Pacific, Pan American Airways has to use huge flying boats. The way we'd go, we can use wheel-planes, like the DC3, and carry just as big a pay load. With the stepping stones of the Aleutians, as you can see here, we'll never be more than two hundred and fifty miles from land."

"What about the weather? I hear it's pretty foul up there around the Bering Sea," broke in one of the directors.

"No problem," McConachie emphasized. "The worst weather and terrain are on the segments we're already operating, such as the mountain routes between Vancouver and Fort St. John, and Fort Nelson to Whitehorse. We've got that licked. Since the prevailing winds are from the west, we get the worst weather on the coastal fringe of this continent, from the moisture picked up over the ocean. Down the coast of Siberia and China the westerly winds are from inland, dry and clear."

That satisfied one chair-bound expert.

"How long would it take to fly this route from Edmonton to Shanghai?" he was asked.

"About forty hours with the equipment, the planes I have in mind. The distance is less than six thousand miles. The fastest ocean liner takes ten days from Vancouver to Shanghai," he replied.

"What about the Russians, flying over their territory?" was another query.

Other directors joined in. Yes, indeed. The Russians could be a problem.

McConachie grinned hugely and announced that he had already opened negotiations with the Russians, through the Amtorg Trading Company in New York, representing the USSR. They had seemed enthusiastic about the prospect of mail and passenger service over the route. Their only stipulation had been that Russian flight crews would have to be

McConachie in 1936 with fellow-pilot Art Rankin (who later became a captain and an executive with TCA), in front of the Whitepass and Yukon rail office in Atlin, B.C. The following year, when he pioneered the first air-mail service to the Yukon, McConachie was to clash with the big boss of Whitepass.

Described by the Edmonton *Journal* at the time as "the most powerful aircraft in Canada flying on pontoons," this tri-motored Ford plodded through sullen skies and bucked headwinds for twelve hours to pioneer the first air-mail service from Edmonton to Whitehorse, Yukon, on July 5, 1937.

Murray Semple, left, the executive of Canadian Car and Foundry, Ltd., Montreal, with Grant McConachie to whom he was persuaded to sell three $70,000 airliners for three dollars down plus monthly payments. The payments were never met. One of the Barkley-Grow aircraft is in the background on floats.

After midsummer 1938, pilot president Grant McConachie and the flight crews of United Air Transport wore uniforms. He is shown here, at left, with Captain Sheldon Luck. In the background is one of the three famous Barkley-Grow airliners.

With its clumsy lines, the Fleet Freighter aircraft gave the general impression of an elaborate practical joke. The first delivered to McConachie became a flaming pinwheel at the Chicago airport during a delivery flight. The second, shown here (with McConachie far left), crashed in the northern woods. It was the original "fat Albert" of Canadian aviation.

The tri-motored Ford which McConachie flew to pioneer the first air-mail service to the Yukon in 1937 met a sticky end at the Vancouver airport two years later when a runaway Hurricane fighter demolished it. McConachie sued the Crown and collected $52,000 damages and costs plus $5,200 insurance. It was another of his lucky. misadventures.

A Barkley-Grow at Grande Prairie (the domain of Mayor Percy Tooley) in 1939 or 1940 during a refuelling stop.

Loading the Barkley-Grow nose cargo compartment at Charlie Lake for the flight north of Fort St. John. Stan Emery, then mechanic, was doing the loading.

Yukon Southern's executives pose beside a Lockheed airliner which McConachie had spirited off a freighter in California and delivered to Edmonton where the war-painted plane was sand-blasted back to its original aluminum colour for civilian use. In the picture are (left to right) Grant McConachie, president; Barney Phillips, vice-president and Ted Field, operations manager of Yukon Southern.

Grant McConachie poses beside another Lockheed airliner newly delivered to Yukon Southern.

W. M. Neal (right), top boss of the CPR, poses with famous bush pilot W. R. "Wop" May in front of an Anson wartime trainer. During thirty-five years with the railway, Neal had earned a reputation as a tough driver of men, but he admired McConachie's practical enthusiasm and appointed him president of the airline.

carried between Vladivostok and Shanghai. That was no problem, he said, now confident that all was going well.

McConachie also explained that he was sure the Americans would welcome the service, too, because of the air link to the Alaska territory as well as the commercial benefits of the short route to the Orient.

"You have made out a very convincing case, Mr. McConachie," said the president of Imperial Oil. "I can assure you that our company would like to encourage such an imaginative yet practical development. Where do we fit into the scheme? What do you want from us?"

"Time," McConachie replied simply. "The time it will take to complete all the negotiations, with our own Government, with the American Government, with the Russians and the Chinese. We'll have to get traffic and landing rights, look into the operational features, and sign up mail contracts. So the big problem now is to keep our present flying operations solvent. I am asking you gentlemen to grant us a hundred-thousand-dollar credit, without interest, for gas and oil, so we can keep flying, pay off our other obligations and have a chance to get into the clear."

A spirited discussion began. McConachie's enthusiasm was contagious. The directors scanned the written presentation and the route maps showing the comparative hours of flying and distances. They were particularly intrigued by the prospect of the top-of-the-world route. This was new, but so logical.

"North to the Orient!" mused one director. "That's a new one on me!"

There was some boggling over the interest-free credit until McConachie pointed out that Imperial would be making a profit on the oil and gas. Finally, the directors voted unanimously to grant United Air Transport interest-free credit to the amount of a hundred thousand dollars.

As a result, the airline was able to operate for the next eighteen months without paying any bills for fuel and oil.

This proved to be more than a relief from the burdens of debt overloading the operation; the arrangement actually *contributed* to income.

"It could only have happened to McConachie," remarked UAT's accountant, Ab Chambers.

He explained: "The government of Alberta granted operators of aircraft a five-cents-a-gallon rebate on the six-cent gas tax, since the gas tax was intended to finance highway construction, and planes didn't use highways. McConachie wanted this tax rebate as revenue, of course, so we set up a rather strange arrangement with the local office of Imperial Oil.

"Every month I had to sign a note in favor of Imperial covering the five or six thousand dollars in fuel and oil purchases, including tax, by our company. In return I was given receipted invoices which we turned in to the government to collect our rebate. It seemed to work fine for everyone concerned, especially us. But it was a little unusual, considering that I was not a signing officer of the company."

As it was to turn out, Imperial Oil won, the Alberta government didn't lose, McConachie won—but McConachie won the most.

Chambers commented, "What a guy! Not even thirty yet and he pries a hundred-thousand-dollar credit out of Imperial Oil. No interest!"

But McConachie was just warming up. What was even more incredible was his bargain with one of the country's biggest industrial corporations, Canadian Car and Foundry Co., Ltd. A Montreal-based manufacturer of railway equipment, they were eager to break into aviation and had recently acquired five twin-engined Barkley-Grow aircraft and sales rights.

The Barkley-Grow appealed to McConachie as the ideal plane for his low-traffic-density mail and passenger runs from Edmonton and Vancouver to the Yukon. For an airliner it had the unusual virtue of being able to operate on pontoons, skis or wheels. Obviously, this feature was essential to UAT.

When he indicated to Canadian Car his company's interest in the Barkley-Grow, the manufacturing company paid McConachie's expenses to Detroit where he test flew the aircraft. Then he met Murray Semple in the St. James Street head office of the company in Montreal to talk business.

"I am very much impressed with your aircraft," McConachie told Semple, with boyish charm. "Terrific performance. It's a lot faster than anything we've ever had in the north. We can use three of them for a start. I predict you'll sell a lot of them if you give us the chance to demonstrate it over our routes. I should make clear to you, however, that we don't have any cash, although we do have mail contracts through British Columbia and up to the Yukon, and that's just like money in the bank."

The key word was "demonstrate" but Semple didn't recognize the trap. He smiled—he liked this young man's candor—so he said, "I realize seventy thousand dollars is a lot of money to pay for an aircraft to fly in the north, and you chaps aren't financed like the big airlines. We have these planes on our hands, and they don't do us any good just sitting around. We're anxious to get them working so other operators will see what they can do, so we're prepared to be generous. Suppose you just give us a nominal hundred thousand dollars for the three and you can have them."

McConachie stood up, walked over to the window, looked down on the busy street, tugged at his tie, turned around, walked back and sat down. He looked at the older man for a moment. Both men smiled.

Now, down to business—or reality.

"I'm sure that's very generous of you, Mr. Semple, but I want you to understand that I'm serious when I tell you that we don't have any ready money. We've got some terrific routes, we're opening up a great new economic empire and our airline has fabulous prospects. But we're out of real money."

Semple took a pen, deliberated some more, and then said,

"Very well, Mr. McConachie. I understand your position. Canadian Car is a big company with many interests. We have a stake in the future of this country and we want to get into aviation manufacturing, to move with the times. This seems a good way to open the door, so we'll let you have the three Barkley-Grows for ten thousand dollars each."

In a few words, Semple had cut through hours of bargaining —but the dealing was still to come. And it was McConachie's deal. He smiled ruefully.

"I guess I'm still not getting my message across, Mr. Semple. We don't have that kind of money," he said.

Murray Semple threw up his hands.

"In God's name, Mr. McConachie, you tell me what you *can* pay for them. You know they're a gift at ten thousand dollars each."

McConachie turned up his hole card.

"Let's look at it this way, Mr. Semple," he said. "Canadian Car doesn't need the cash. You can always reclaim the three planes if we don't keep our end of the bargain. We can put the Barkley-Grows to work, so they'll be earning you something as well as demonstrating their capabilities, instead of just eating up hangar rent. Here's my proposition.

"We'll pay you a token one dollar for each of the three planes, and as soon as we put them on the runs we'll pay you one thousand dollars a month for each plane on a lease-purchase arrangement. Ah, before you make your decision, I would suggest you consider what you will do with these planes if we don't take them and put them to work."

Semple chuckled.

"I don't know where you learned to bargain, Mr. McConachie, but you're right. We have these planes on our hands, and we're too busy to fiddle around with them. Take them away. Get them flying and keep them flying."

After a short discussion of details, McConachie strode to the door. Semple said, "I don't know what your particular ambitions are, young man, but somehow I think you'll get there, wherever you choose to go. Anyway, good luck, especially with those Barkleys."

McConachie grinned, waved at Semple and walked out. As he entered the elevator he exulted to himself, "Well I'll be Goddamned. It worked!"

This lease-purchase of the Barkley-Grow fleet was to prove an even greater bargain than the actual deal struck between Semple and McConachie.

Ab Chambers, the bookkeeper for UAT, said that after the acquisition of the new planes he faithfully entered three thousand dollars a month in the books as a sinking fund to pay for them. For some reason unknown to him, probably preoccupation with far more important concerns, Canadian Car never pressed for their payments and no actual money was ever put into the sinking fund. Except for the original three dollars in down payments, McConachie put out no cash for the three Barkley-Grows until they were eventually sold to make way for larger planes.

22. RUSSIAN ROULETTE

By late 1938, McConachie had miraculously managed to keep his airline aloft by contriving free gas and free planes. But he was still dedicated to cutting out frills.

Like aircraft insurance.

Ab Chambers, the bookkeeper, explained how McConachie's insurance system worked:

"We had this crazy collection of twelve aircraft, but McConachie decided we could only afford to pay insurance premiums on two of them. It was a case of choosing any two, like blindman's buff, then hoping to God that if any came to grief it would be one of the two carrying insurance. It was Russian roulette but with ten cylinders loaded and only two blank."

Aero Insurance Underwriters had agreed even to this limited coverage with reluctance. In their books McConachie's outfit was a poor risk. In three years the airline had burned up three bush planes during blow-torch warm-ups, had demolished another in a shallow-water somersault, and had put one through the ice of a northern river. They had never killed a passenger or incurred public liability, but the aircraft mortality was something else!

But the year 1938 was looking brighter. Why shucks, it was the end of October and the year's write-off record was still unblemished! Aero's Edmonton agent, Jim Slessor, was able to send reassuring reports to his principals in Chicago. McConachie was in a mood to congratulate himself on the astuteness of his two-in-twelve insurance gamble and indeed was beginning to wonder if perhaps the premiums on the two aircraft had been a needless expenditure.

And then Monday, November 3, 1938:

09.25 hours—Pilot Charlie Tweed and mechanic Limey Green were struggling with the pontoon strut bolts of a Fairchild FC2W2 on the west bank of the Peace River at Fort Vermillion, 350 air miles north of Edmonton. The plane had been trapped in the flow ice of the river after flying in with the last mail of the previous summer season. Unable to take off on floats, it had been hoisted high on to the river bank and left there.

McConachie was impatient to get the Fairchild back in the action, so he had sent Tweed and Green to Fort Vermillion with a set of skis to make the change-over from pontoons. They would then fold back the hinged wings of the Fairchild, tractor-haul it over the snowy bush trail to a near by field and take off for the Edmonton base.

They had jacked up the aircraft but were having difficulty with the grease-coated bolts and nuts securing the pontoons to the undercarriage struts. Green drained a pail of gasoline from a wing tank to rinse off the grease.

As the two men worked on the stubborn undercarriage, a farmer came along on a horse-drawn sleigh loaded with wheat. He had never seen an airplane up close, so he reined in alongside to gawk. He lit up a corncob pipe. With considerably more accuracy than judgement, he flicked the glowing match into the pail of "water" under the plane.

W-H-O-O-S-H! The gasoline exploded in a geyser of flame that was consuming the varnished fabric of the fuselage as the pilot and mechanic leaped clear. The farmer lashed his team into a flat-out run, gone, gone. The Fairchild was a ruin in about thirty seconds.

11.05 hours—Pilot Ted Field, at the controls of a north-bound Waco mail plane circled the snow platter of Watson Lake near the Yukon border and began to glide down for a ski landing. Grounded for more than a month during the freeze-up in-between season, he was flying the first mail run of the winter. A big pay trip. His departure from Edmonton the day before had been triggered by a radio signal from the operator at Watson Lake reporting the minimum four-inch ice thickness to permit a ski landing.

The air was crisp and still. Smoke rose straight from the cabin chimneys as he slid in high over the tree line. With no head-wind to slow him, he overshot the landing area in front of the trading post and the skis made contact further down the lake, sliding easily on the powder snow. As the Waco slithered to a stop on the lake surface, the pilot was startled to see water gush over his skis and cover the snow. The plane was sinking—through the ice!

Knowing there was no choice, he unbuckled his seat belt, stood on the seat and with head, arms and shoulders smashed through the fabric of the cockpit roof. He then grabbed the mail sacks from the forward end of the cabin and one by one tossed them up on to the overhead wing. As he climbed through the hole, the water was already burbling over the cockpit floor and rising to submerge the instrument panel. Seconds later, the entire fuselage of the Waco had gone under. But the wings rested on the firm ice on either side of the hole, holding the aircraft up. Field walked along a wing to safety.

He had been unlucky enough to come to a halt directly over one of the unsuspected warm springs in the lake where the ice was thin. Now the plane would have to remain under the ice until spring. If it were raised into the winter air, the water inside its hollow-steel framework would freeze and burst the structural tubing.

16.00 hours—When the flash came in about the dunking at Watson Lake, McConachie ordered Alec Dane to take off up the line in the gull-wing Stinson to pick up the mail and carry on to Whitehorse. Dane knew the boss had been under a lot of pressure about mail delays, but surely it could have waited one day.

His mood had not improved when he landed at the Grande Prairie field to discover that his arrival was unexpected. Percy Tooley, who served as United Air Transport agent and airport manager as well as local real estate dealer and mayor, was nowhere in sight. The gas pump was locked. Tooley would have the key. Dane hitched a ride three miles to town in a farm sleigh and routed Tooley out of a council meeting. As they jostled back over the ruts, the pilot had his mind on the weather. A strong westerly had sprung up and powerful gusts slapped snow against the windows of Tooley's Chevrolet.

"That's all I need to make this a perfect day," he thought bitterly. "A nice brisk head-wind so I can sit up there all day going nowhere."

As the mayor turned in at the airfield gate, Dane yelled: "I'll be go-to-hell!" The Stinson was lying on its back, skis in the air. Incredibly, the wind had flipped the plane, leaving the wings crumpled and twisted and the rudder smashed; from the look of the fuselage its back was broken.

"There's one thing for damn-sure," Alec Dane said. "The mail won't go through today. That crate will never fly again. Percy, when's the next train for Edmonton?"

The loss of three aircraft in one day was a truly astonishing record. But what really impressed his colleagues was McConachie's talent for profiting from such dire adversity. He had won his wild gamble with the insurance premiums! In the crazy game of twelve-cylinder Russian roulette he had fired the two blanks! The Fairchild burned to cinders on the bank of the Peace and the Stinson demolished in the Grande Prairie blow were the two aircraft of the fleet covered by insurance!

The only uninsured plane of the three was the Waco under the ice at Watson Lake, which could be winched out in the spring and would be in the air again after an overhaul. Meanwhile, the payments from the insurance company for the two aircraft would furnish the cash he needed for first installments on new planes.

In December McConachie placed orders for three new Fleet Freighters. These twin-engined planes, he told the press, had been specially designed by Canadians to meet the conditions of northern bush flying. They were the best; they'd do any job. He expected to take delivery of the first Fleet Freighter at the Fort Erie plant in February.

Each of the new Freighters cost fifteen thousand dollars. McConachie knew his financial backers would never sanction insurance roulette with that kind of money. He would have to get full coverage. There was a big "but." Jim Slessor, his local insurance agent, told him that head office in Chicago had decided against insuring any of his planes ever again. McConachie would have to tackle the top men in Chicago himself.

As it taxied in to the flight line after landing at the Chicago airport from Fort Erie early in February 1939, the new Fleet Freighter had already been classified by the tarmac wiseacres as "Early Wright Brothers." When McConachie parked it amongst the sleek and silver airliners of the transcontinental fleets it looked as out of place as a barefoot hillbilly at a Junior League ball.

Although a new design, the Freighter had the contours of a pregnant dragonfly. The overblown fuselage sprouted biplane wings that were already an oddity in the new era of low-wing monoplanes. A cat's-cradle of struts criss-crossed between the biplanes to support the two radial engines embedded in the roots of the upper wing. Twin vertical fin-rudders bracketing the horizontal tailplane completed the general impression of an elaborate practical joke.

As McConachie lumbered towards the flight office wearing his raw-wool siwash sweater and his deerskin mukluks, a four-stripe American Airlines captain clapped him on the back.

"That's quite an aerodyne you got there, friend," he grinned. "Make it yourself?"

"No. But it beats your fancy-pants airliners all to hell where I do my flying," McConachie replied.

The twenty-nine-year-old airline president who kept an appointment at the head office of Aero Insurance Underwriters in downtown Chicago the next morning bore slight resemblance to the bush pilot of the previous afternoon. He appeared in the chairman's outer office in a dark-grey overcoat, double-breasted, pin-stripe suit, dark blue tie, white shirt, and pearl-grey spats. He carried a snap-brim fedora and a black briefcase bulging with documents.

The courtly greeting of the chairman, Paul Harvey, was tempered with a measure of restraint—not altogether surprising in an insurance underwriter confronted with such a spectacularly poor risk. McConachie was pleased to note, however, that the man bore the obvious stamp of an outdoorsman, as Jim Slessor had indicated earlier. Harvey's cool grey eyes were almost on a level with his own. Both were big men.

The chairman of Aero Insurance introduced the youthful airline president to two of his colleagues—McIvor, the company treasurer, and Freeman, an actuary, who clutched a manila filing folder that, no doubt, contained the sorry accident record of McConachie's airline. These were the inside men, the ink-fingers, McConachie decided. They would have to be blocked out of the play if he hoped to score.

Harvey's polite inquiries about the flight down from Ontario and McConachie's impressions of Chicago in winter were followed by an expectant pause. This was it. He was on. McConachie smiled with a false confidence as he pulled a fat manila envelope from his briefcase and laid it on the polished mahogany table.

He tapped the envelope and said, "Gentlemen, before we talk about insurance, I believe you will understand the situation much better if you know something about the region in which we are flying," and he took out a large map of British Columbia and the Yukon with his airmail route from Edmonton to Whitehorse marked in red crayon.

He dipped into the envelope again and spread over the table an array of glossy photographs he had obtained—free—from the government fish and game branch. These showed big game of the Fort Nelson and Fort St. James regions—giant grizzlies, moose, deer and elk and impressive fish. Big ones. Harvey forgot about insurance statistics and was soon absorbed in a discussion of wild life in the wilderness, Grant McConachie's domain. Harvey asked questions. McConachie answered enthusiastically. The two pen-pushers fidgeted but kept quiet.

McConachie then located on the map the main air bases he had established and traced the route of the weekly mail service he had launched the previous July from Edmonton to Whitehorse and Dawson City in the Yukon.

"I note you have inked your routes in red," Harvey laughed. "Would that perchance have any significance?"

The pen-pushers smiled, ever so little.

"You're damn right it does," McConachie almost shouted. "We've never flown in the black, because we've been pioneering this new country. But we've got a fantastic future. There aren't even roads through all this huge territory. Nothing but a few bush trails. Can you imagine what part the airplane will play in the development up there? Mines, rich ones, lumber mills, new towns, even cities some day. That country is ready to bust wide open!

"Sure we've been up to our eyebrows in red ink. But that's going to change. One of the reasons is out at the airport right now, the Fleet Freighter."

The Freighter, McConachie told them, was the first aircraft ever designed for the special operating conditions of the Canadian north. Not only would it fly a good load on floats or skis, but it was the safest plane ever built for this kind of flying. The two engines gave reliability while the biplane wing provided the high-lift performance and the safety margin needed in the bush. Its greater range capability would mean few refueling landings, a good thing in a business where landings and take-offs caused many accidents.

"Examine this aircraft and you'll see that the Freighter is going to clean up our record. It will put us in the black. I'm absolutely positive of that," he said with conviction.

It worked! Before inviting his guest to lunch in the executive dining room, Harvey put through a call to Jim Slessor in Edmonton and told him to insure McConachie's first three Fleet Freighters for fifteen thousand dollars each, plus a hundred thousand dollars public liability coverage. During the convivial luncheon he accepted McConachie's suggestion that he and his two executives inspect the wonder plane and watch it take off for Canada.

23. THE GREAT CHICAGO FIRE
And Other Lucky Misadventures

As he cramped his six foot two inches into the cockpit of the Freighter, McConachie was still savoring the success of the morning's discussions. He peered out of the greenhouse of the cockpit across the tarmac to where Harvey and his two associates, in the lee of the loading ramp, were gazing in amazement at this new breed of flying machine. Having inspected it, they were waiting for it to take off for the wild northland.

McConachie moved the rudder, elevator and aileron controls to check their freedom of movement. He reached for the plunger knob to prime the cold port engine. Raw gasoline from the primer pump spewed directly into the cylinders. He flicked the number one ignition switch "on," adjusted the throttle lever to "idle," set the mixture control to "full rich" and reached for the starter button.

The starter motor groaned with the effort of rotating the crankshaft. In the cold ice-fog, the lubricating oil had congealed. He continued to depress the button, watching the slowly revolving prop, and waiting for the fiftul kick that would signal ignition. No reaction from the engine's combustion chambers. Too much prime. Cylinders flooded. Better let number one dry out, save the battery for another try. So give number two a whirl. That important audience out there wants to see some action.

After careful priming, number two engine responded with a cough. White smoke belched from the exhaust stacks. The engine shuddered on its mountings, then roared to life. McConachie nursed the throttle forward for a fast-running warm-up before returning his attention to the reluctant port engine. His peripheral vision had caught a trickle of fuel down the wing strut below the dead engine while he was busy with number two, but he had not considered it of any significance. Overflow from the flooded cylinders. It would evaporate quickly in the gusting wind.

McConachie pushed the starter button of the number one engine again and watched the propeller begin its slow thunk-thunk-thunk. Suddenly the power plant erupted with a backfire from one of the cylinders. Flame snaked through the carburetor, lapped at a puddle of raw gas in the trough of the exhaust manifold, and streaked on down a wing strut to feed on the shellacked fabric of the lower mainplane. The fire spread with astonishing speed. Even as McConachie snatched at the fire extinguisher in its wall bracket he realized the situation was already beyond control. His position was desperate. In five seconds the enclosed cockpit would be his flaming coffin. There was no exit at the front of the plane. The entire port side of the Freighter was already a roaring holocaust. The fabric of the cabin seats was smoking. He unbuckled his seat belt and dashed back through the cabin, running a gauntlet of flame and smoke to burst into the cold air of the tarmac. All the seats and the entire port wall of the Freighter were ablaze. The number-two engine, meantime, was still running at fast idling speed, the air blast from its propeller beating back the flames so that the right forward section of the plane remained intact as the rest of the craft began to disintegrate.

The smoke had alerted the airport control tower and a yellow crash truck roared up. But too late. Firemen sprayed white geysers of foamite at the blazing wreckage without effect. There was no way to shut off the starboard engine, which was feeding from a fifteen-gallon gravity tank in the top wing.

The fuselage had burned and was now sagging, twisting the undercarriage askew so that it jumped the wheel chocks. The flaming remnant, consisting of one wing, the engine, a wheel, and part of the forward fuselage, now began a pin-wheeling tour of the Chicago airport tarmac. It was a wild scene. The firemen scattered. The crash truck backed off. McConachie retreated, unwilling to believe what was happening before his eyes.

The jolt of the crumping fuselage had jogged the throttle forward so that the engine of "the thing" was now roaring at nearly full power and the remains of the fifteen-thousand-dollar machine might even have taken off except that it was careening in ever-widening circles.

By this time, the fifteen-thousand-dollar coverage on the Freighter was the least of Paul Harvey's worries. He was thinking about that hundred-thousand-dollar liability coverage—and with good reason, for there were nothing but high-priced airliners as far along the ramp as you could see. If that flaming dervish so much as brushed one of them, or swooped into a hangar, it would be good-bye hundred thousand dollars. The situation appeared to have all the ingredients of another Great Chicago Fire, airport version, with the flaming Freighter in the role of Mrs. O'Leary's cow.

A wide gyration headed the projectile directly toward the row of airliners. Then, suddenly, the engine spluttered and quit. The remains of the Fleet Freighter subsided in a heap of smouldering rubble.

McConachie walked slowly towards the three insurance men. For once he had nothing to say. Paul Harvey was shaking his head, as if trying to awaken from a bad dream.

Meantime, almost to the minute, in Edmonton, bookkeeper Ab Chambers had just returned to McConachie's headquarters from the Chapman-Slessor Insurance Agency where the coverage on the three Freighters had been documented.

Ab recalls, "Half an hour after I got back to the office, I got a phone call from McConachie in Chicago telling me that the Freighter had burned. It was rather embarrassing, particularly in view of our record, to have to go back and tell Jim Slessor that we had already written off the aircraft he had just insured an hour ago."

The scene: A fog-shrouded stretch of the Liard River at Lower Post, a few miles south of the Yukon border. The time: June 13, 1939, three and a half months after the Chicago airport fire.

It was 10:45 A.M. as Sheldon Luck taxied the Yukon Southern Air Transport's* second Freighter downstream and ruddered around into wind. On board with the mail were Danny Driscoll, the Whitehorse agent, Danny's new wife, three commercial travellers and the Driscoll dog, Woof.

After taking off, Luck found himself in fog so thick he could barely discern the wing tips. He was confident in his instrument flying and in the knowledge that he would quickly rise above the surface layer of fog. He cranked back on the elevator trim wheel to raise the nose into a normal climbing position, his eyes on the artificial horizon instrument to keep the plane flying straight and level. But the control cable linking the trim wheel in the cockpit with the movable flap on the elevator surface of the tailplane was slippery with overnight dew. It slid on the pulley, failing to activate the control surface; and so, instead of climbing, the Freighter continued in level flight, right into the invisible trees.

Three hours and forty-five minutes after watchers by the lake had seen the plane disappear into the fog and had heard its engines suddenly stop dead, Luck stumbled out of the bush to collapse in front of the radio shack. Though dazed, bruised

---

* The name had been changed from UAT in March of that year.

and bleeding from gashes on his forehead and neck, he was
not seriously injured. He reported that all aboard had survived
except Woof.

But Freighter number two was a complete write-off.

Back in Chicago, Paul Harvey must have put his head in his
hand and groaned. Perhaps his two ledger-watchers smiled
behind their slender hands.

McConachie cancelled the order for the third Freighter.
Not surprisingly, Aero Insurance Underwriters decided to get
out of the bush-plane insurance business. But Paul Harvey had
been so intrigued with McConachie's descriptions of the British
Columbia interior that he later flew up to Fort St. James on
a hunting expedition.

McConachie later reminisced: "When I got the word that
Harvey was coming north with his guns I wasn't sure whether
he was coming to hunt moose or me."

Almost as spectacular as the flaming death of the Fleet
Freighter at Chicago was the fate of the second tri-motored
Ford. Like most of the McConachie write-offs, the ruin of the
Ford had the luck of the man going for him.

In the spring of 1939, CF-BEP was on the tarmac in front
of the tiny administration building at Vancouver's Sea Island
Airport, ready for an active summer in the north. The plane's
load capacity and performance enabled McConachie to under-
bid the freight barge operators for the contracts to supply the
Hudson's Bay and the free trader at Fort Nelson.

Threat of war in Europe had stimulated Canada's modest
air-training program to the extent that an increasing number
of Air Force roundels mingled with the civilian registrations
in the traffic circuit at Sea Island. One of the Air Force training planes, a Hawker Hurricane, sat in the bay Runway Zero
Eight on the morning of June 24, its engine idling, the young
pilot nervously ticking off his cockpit check as he waited for
take-off clearance from the tower. Trained on biplane Fleet
Finches, then on Harvards at Camp Borden, the youth had just

graduated to a real warplane. It was a single-seater, so this first flight in a strange and powerful fighter was solo.

The young aviator tensed as the voice of Tower Control rasped: "Hurricane 502, you are clear to line up and take off." He ruddered the fighter into position on the centre line of the runway, advanced the throttle through its full arc and felt the surge of power as he released the toe brakes. The plane charged forward with such startling acceleration that the student momentarily froze on the controls. As the powerful torque action of the big metal propeller began pulling the fighter's nose to the left, he neglected to apply right rudder. Rigid in the cockpit, both feet jammed hard against the rudders, he had clenched his right hand around the control column. The Hurricane swerved from the centre line in a wide arc to cross the margin of the runway.

The pilot was in such a funk he was deaf to the insistent squawking of the tower in his earphones: "Hurricane pilot . . . close your throttle . . . close your throttle . . . close your throttle . . ."

The fighter was now skipping over the grass of the infield at flying speed, its wheels barely grazing the surface as the wings took up the load. And dead ahead was the Yukon Southern tri-motored Ford, dear old lovely-ugly, profit-making Ford, McConachie's money-in-the-bank freighter.

The Hurricane struck the Ford amidships. The impact exploded debris everywhere. The pilot catapulted from the cockpit and soared completely over the Ford to land on the grass, unharmed, with only scratches and bruises. The fighter bored right through the cabin of the freighter to emerge on the other side.

When McConachie arrived from Edmonton to press his claim for compensation, he encountered a total lack of sympathy. The training squadron's commanding officer said, "It's your problem. Go see your insurance company. You can't sue the Crown."

McConachie sued. The court case lasted two weeks. Judgement was in his favor. Yukon Southern Air Transport was awarded damages of $52,000 for loss of airfreight contracts, plus all court costs. He also collected $5,200 from the insurance company for the loss of the aircraft.

24. FLYING CIRCUS CLOWNS

When Grant McConachie wasn't persuading flinty-eyed ty-
coons to take leave of their senses he was having fun with his
flying circus. And on that midway-style bush airline there were
plenty of clowns and sideshows.

On one occasion McConachie flew a government mapping
crew and their supplies in to the Thutade Lake country near
the headwaters of the Finlay River. Jokingly, he asked the
surveyor, Swannell, what it would cost to have a mountain,
lake or stream named after him.

"A bottle of rum would be a fair price," Swannell replied.

Taking him at his word, McConachie added a bottle of rum
to the map camp's supply cache on the next trip. The idea
took. As a result, the charts of the Finlay territory record Gil's
Peak (for Gil McLaren), Mount Oakes, Kubicek Valley, and
McConachie Pass, all UAT pilot names.

Then there was the Shifty Schuman hoax. Shifty was probably the most experienced bush-plane passenger in British Columbia by the fall of 1939. He was a roving buyer for his
dad's Acme Fur Wholesale and one of Yukon Southern Air
Transport's best customers. He had criss-crossed the skies of
northern British Columbia so many times the bush routes were
almost as familiar to him as First Avenue in Edmonton where
he had been born in a flat above the fur warehouse. He had

flown hundreds of hours in weather so bad the eagles were walking.

So McConachie was glad to give Shifty the honour of riding up front in the gleaming cockpit of his new twin-engined Barkley-Grow. No sooner had they taken off from Edmonton airport than the silver airliner had nosed right up into the soup. Ten minutes of blind climbing and zoom, they were riding in bright sunshine.

Young Schuman knew it was a great way to fly, over the top, none of the usual bouncing over the tree-tops, no straining to pick up landmarks that would check with the map. But he was worried. Finally, he could contain his concern no longer. He asked McConachie how he could possibly know when to go down, since they hadn't seen earth since take-off.

"Very simple, Shifty," yelled McConachie, waving a half-smoked cigar and flashing his familiar grin. "This compass here keeps me headed in the right direction and my cigar does the rest."

"How d'ya mean, the cigar?"

"You remember I lit this cigar just as we reached cruising altitude up above the muck. Well, as soon as I've smoked it down to a butt I'll know we're over Grande Prairie, and we'll let down through the clouds. You'll see."

Twenty minutes later, unnoticed by Shifty, the needle of the radio compass homed on CFGP, the Grande Prairie radio station. It spun erratically, then reversed itself, indicating that they had passed directly over the station. McConachie nodded to Shifty, showed him his cigar, then, reaching forward to grind the cigar butt into the ash tray, eased back the twin throttles. Moments later the Barkley flashed out under the cloud deck directly over the roof-tops of Grande Prairie. Shifty was impressed. No matter how many times you flew with these bush pilots, he said later, they always seemed to come up with some new trick. Imagine, navigating by cigar!

But even with the introduction of bigger, better planes like the Barkley-Grow and the construction of airstrips on McConachie's routes, many of the operational problems of bush flying remained. There were no heated hangars at the northern bases. In fact, there were no aircraft shelters of any kind, except for the canvas engine covers that had to be "rassled" into position at night and removed after the blow-torch warm-up of the engines in the morning.

The gritty, greasy "black gang" mechanics were made miserable by cold in winter, tormented by black flies in summer, and numbed with the spare-time boredom of isolation—all for twenty-five dollars a month and board. It was made endurable, according to Glen Fenby, who was based at Fort St. John, only by the parties and the pranks. It was his impression that McConachie fretted in the confines of his executive office in Edmonton and looked forward eagerly to the flying and to the cameraderie of his frequent inspection trips up the line. He especially relished the parties.

"McConachie was a fun-loving guy and he seemed at his best in the midst of a party, probably because he loved people, enjoyed a laugh. In a party atmosphere he could tell his stories and put over his ideas with eloquence.

"Whenever he arrived at Charlie Lake on one of his inspection trips his first question would be, 'where's the party tonight?'

"So we'd crank up a few numbers on the party line and find out where the fireworks was going to be. It might be happening in the town or it could be at a farm-house twenty miles away. We'd always find out. Then we'd all pile into the staff truck and off we'd go.

"One reason the parties were so great was that we could get all the moonshine we could drink, and more, at just a dollar a pint. We'd mix it with Coke. As a side-line, Ted Field used to fly soft drinks, chocolate bars and cigarettes in from Edmonton and he set up a little canteen with Tony Craig, the radio apprentice, minding the store.

"There were several reasons we did business with the bootlegger. He turned out a good product, particularly his double-distilled five-star special; the price was right; but, more important, it was handy. The nearest liquor vendor was sixty-seven miles away over a dirt road that was a swamp when it rained. Our bootlegger, George Taylor, was a homesteader a few miles north of St. John.

"The Mounties had been trying for years but they could never find the bootlegging. It was a close-knit community and whenever the police moved out of town on a search everybody knew about it. Then the war came along and sugar rationing put George out of business. When his moonshine enterprise folded George worked for us as a flunky for a while. Then he joined the Army. We sure had old George to thank for a lot of good parties!"

One of the wilder bush blowouts erupted at the Yukon end of the mail run during a siege of lousy weather. The scene was the crew quarters, a back room on the main floor of the White-horse Inn. In the early rounds, the soiree was attended by Mrs. Barber, wife of Jack, the Yukon Southern agent, and Jessie Maclean who was in charge of the office. Soon after midnight the ladies bowed out to let the stag session roar on until dawn. When dawn came Barney Phillips and McConachie ruled that Jack Barber was no longer roadworthy. He was unfit to solo, so they would provide the necessary physical support and directional guidance.

It had been raining hard. The street was mud slop, precarious even for the sure-footed—which they were not. In their unsteady progression down a side street, the escort team fumbled the wobbly agent into an open storm sewer. Fished out, he was coated in mud and obviously unfit to pass domestic inspection. And Mrs. Barber would certainly be awaiting his return.

Ted Field, who had been trailing along as a reserve escort, detoured through a back yard to liberate a pair of red flannel longjohns from a clothesline. With great difficulty, the three colleagues stripped Barber and stuffed him into the freshly-laundered red underwear. Then they deposited him on the doorstep of the Barber home, knocked and ran.

"The awkward part of the whole situation," Jack said, "was that I could not for the life of me explain to my wife what had happened to my shirt and slacks, and, more important, how I came by the red underwear. It was a complete mystery to me, not to mention a source of some considerable annoyance to Mum."

The great dynamite caper at Charlie Lake was the most spectacular of the practical jokes to enliven bunk-house life on the bush routes. It was conceived and executed by three mechanics, Bill Gibbons, Stan Emery and Glen Fenby in retaliation for Ted Field's trickery. A few nights previously, the pilot had put sulphur in the stove of the mechanics' bunk-house. The fumes drove them out into the night. The next night he poured water down their chimney, dousing the fire—and it was a cold night.

In their quest for revenge, Gibbons and company were not deterred by the fact that McConachie had flown in that afternoon with two directors who were also financial backers of the airline. McConachie hoped to impress them with the business-like nature of the air-service operation.

Every great plan needs inspiration. In the back shed at the Charlie Lake base were a few sticks of dynamite left over from a recent rock-blasting project. Gibbons cut a length of garden house, wrapped it in brown paper to resemble a dynamite stick and stuck a fuse in one end. Just after lights-out, when the pilots, McConachie and the two directors, were still awake, Fenby slid up to open the bunk-house window. Gibbons lit the fuse and tossed the bogus explosive into the centre of the room. Emery yelled, "Dynamite!" while Fenby shone a flashlight on the stick.

The fuse hissed ominously. There was a second of stunned

horror. Then the bunk-house was a pandemonium of shouting, struggling men all crazy to fight free of their sleeping bags. Alec Dane, a pilot, made it first. He took the screen door with him half-way across the yard. He was followed by McConachie and the others almost in a dead heat. Scotty Moir somehow made it across the bunk-house, through the door and twenty yards out into the night while still in his sleeping bag, as if in an insane potato-sack race.

The directors were predictably impressed.

When Tony Craig arrived from Edmonton as apprentice radio operator he got the traditional mail-sack treatment. The Barkley-Grow was at the sea-plane dock. Stan Emery instructed Craig to get to the mail out of the airliner's nose compartment. This involved laying a plank across the pontoons, stacking up two dynamite kegs on the plank, clambering on to this perch to open the baggage compartment door, and pulling out the canvas mail bag. The youngster didn't realize that instead of letters and parcels, this mail sack contained eighty pounds of gold, in bars.

Unbalanced, poor Tony toppled from his perch into the muddy waters of Charlie Lake. The gold sank. Forty-five thousand dollars in gold. There was thigh-slapping laughter as Craig heaved himself on to the dock, then everyone went off to the cook-house for lunch. Someone later remembered to dive for the sunken treasure.

Such casual treatment of gold shipments was routine in the north. At Whitehorse, Jack Barber once dropped a sack of gold into the near-freezing waters of the Yukon River. He paid an Indian fifteen dollars to dive for it, and he got a line on to nearly one hundred thousand dollars in bullion.

McConachie once took off from Manson Creek leaving a fifty-thousand-dollar bag of gold bars on the shore beside a tree. When he remembered it a week later he flew back from Fort St. James to retrieve the shipment. It was, of course, still there.

High on the list of improbable characters abounding in the bush was "Tiny" Johnson, the stoker who had befriended McConachie back in 1925. He weighed three hundred pounds, stood six feet six in his bare feet, and could lift a five-hundred-pound drum of gas out of a bush-plane cabin and on to the dock without grunting. "A human crane" was how Jack Moar described him.

Moar vividly remembers meeting Tiny after Grant, always pleased to help an old friend, had hired him as a general handyman cum trainee radio operator. Tiny's first assignment was to build a dock and a cabin at Watson Lake. Moar was to fly him there, on his way up the line.

"Grant had told Tiny to carry damn little luggage up to Watson since we had a heavy pay load for the Barkley-Grow. Johnson showed up at the office carrying a pair of high leather boots and an Indian sweater over his arm. There was a tooth brush stuck into the laces of one boot and some pajamas crammed inside the flap.

" 'Where's your luggage? We want to weigh it,' said Grant. 'This here's my luggage,' said Tiny, pointing to the boots and sweater.

"When we landed on Watson Lake with the Barkley-Grow there was a strong wind blowing and the waves were bashing on the rocks, so I told Tiny I would have to let him off at the other end of the lake where there was a beach. He'd have to hike back to where our base was going to be.

" 'Don't go to that trouble,' said Tiny. 'Just shut off the motor on my side.' As soon as I had shut down the number-two engine, he looped his high boots around his neck, shoved an axe into his belt, leaped into the water and started swimming for shore.

"I had told this rare man I would be in the next day, on the southbound trip from Whitehorse. We'd bring in supplies. As it turned out, the weather socked in at Watson for the next ten days and there was no chance of getting in there. I was quite worried about Tiny because he must be close to starvation.

"I knew all the food he had taken with him was four tins of sardines he had shoved into one of his boots before going over the side.

"When I finally got into Watson it was a nice sunny day. Tiny had already built a fine sea-plane dock, and as I taxied in he was perched on top of the eight-foot wall of a log cabin he had almost completed. He was a wonder with an axe. He seemed in the best of health and spirits. When I asked him about food he said, 'This lake has the best trout you've ever tasted, and there's lots of berries around here. I've had a marvelous time.'

"I've always thought of Tiny Johnson as a sort of human crane. He's the kind of man that made McConachie's northern airline possible."

Even more colourful than Tiny was Tommy Clark, half Indian, and a rough-cast product of the northern wilds who ran his own independent trading post at Fort Nelson in rough-tough rivalry with the Hudson's Bay. Volatile and unruly, Clark was number one on the police suspect list for any wrongdoing in the area. He was once acquitted of murder. He was the major suspect in the hold-up and robbery of sixty thousand dollars in furs from the HBC post but was cleared when the two culprits who had pulled off the caper were apprehended by chance in Sweet Grass, Montana.

One thing was for sure, the Fort Nelson free trader would never be the victim of mistaken identity. He was unique. Squat, swarthy, truculent, he nourished his resentments with firewater, wore his tousled tar-black hair in a shoulder-length mop, and fancied a selection of glass eyes guaranteed to startle any stranger. He had lost his left eye in a brawl over a bottle of Scotch but had ordered a range of replacements from a catalogue and chose from them according to his whim. One was emblazoned with a Union Jack, another bore a crucifix, one was dark brown to match his good eye and still another was yellow and blue.

One day while Clark was mushing his dog team along a trail at 40° below zero, his eye-of-the-moment shattered in the extreme cold. This caused some pain and inconvenience, so he resolved never to wear a false eye on the trail again.

Before leaving his cabin Tommy always performed the ritual of removing his current eyepiece and placing it in the window of his trading post. Some claimed he did this to warn off native thieves who might be tempted to help themselves from his stock. Certainly no Indian would venture near the cabin as long as Tommy Clark's eye was watching them with its unwinking vigilance.

McConachie, who had worked out an arrangement with this free trader to fly in trade goods from Edmonton, once, almost hesitantly, asked Clark about his methods of doing business.

"You seem to be the only one making money out of our deal. How do you manage to do so well?"

"Simple," Clark replied. "I mark up only ten per cent. I get an item flown in here and I figure it costs me a buck. I just mark it up to ten dollars, which is my ten per cent to take care of expenses and profit."

Perhaps even financial wizards could learn something from this lowly Indian's formula.

But if McConachie managed to assemble a strange group of colleagues, surely the most unlikely was Clancy Craig.

Craig was a big, rough raw-boned Irishman with a college degree, who happened to be a successful professional gardener. In that role he had helped to landscape Grant McConachie's property and had got to know the pilot slightly.

Brooding over Jack Moar's advice that they had to "go wheels or go bust," McConachie had decided that Craig, used to working with the earth, was the man to carve out his airstrips for him. Or at least one airstrip—at Fort Nelson.

He called Craig to his office. It was a vintage McConachie performance—opening up the north—living close to nature—he-man exercise—spectacular sunsets—"If I weren't tied down to this damn desk I'd take the runway job myself.

"Mind you, it's no cinch. There will be problems, even hardships, but you're stubborn and resourceful. And of all the men I know, I think you could handle it best.

"Clancy, you are the man for the job. Not too much money in it, mind you, one hundred and fifty a month and expenses, but a great experience! What do you say?"

After some moments Craig looked up at McConachie with a rueful grin and said, "My wife will say I'm loony to give up my gardening business and leave home to squat up there with the Indians and scrape dirt all summer. But, hell, you make it sound like quite a challenge, sort of an adventure. I'm getting tired of city life anyway. Okay, I'm your man. When do I start?"

When Craig arrived at Fort Nelson, he looked around, remembering McConachie's recent cheerful assertion that "the word 'isolated' no longer applies to Fort Nelson." He was six hours' flight north of Edmonton and his neighbours consisted of four Indian families, several unattached braves, the factor of the Hudson's Bay trading post and his welcoming committee, the unforgettable Tommy Clark, whose glass eye of the day featured a tiny but striking Union Jack on a field of pink.

Any misgivings Craig felt on arrival were soon congealed by time and experience into the solid conviction that he had been mad to let McConachie talk him into this lunatic venture. "I've been a fool," he told himself ten times a day. In place of his comfortable bungalow in Edmonton, his new home was a patch of canvas barely adequate to shelter his sleeping bag and personal effects. A larger spread housed equipment and supplies, while beyond, in the small river-side clearing, were three dirty pup tents sometimes used for sleeping by the rotating population of Indian helpers.

Game may have been plentiful near by, as McConachie had promised. Fish could be swarming in the river eager to be caught. But his dawn-to-dusk labours left Craig too exhausted for such pursuits. His only form of hunting was the ceaseless though futile campaign to exterminate two ever-present predators, the black fly and the mosquito, both so vicious that, in their billions, they can make a northern summer one long terrible torture.

Later that summer Tony Craig flew to Fort Nelson to spend his school holidays helping his dad, and he recalled: "I got quite a shock when I laid eyes on the old man. First glance I thought it was an Indian, his face was so swollen from the insect bites and darkened by the sun and the weather. But, of course, he was a giant among those Indians, plus the mop of sandy hair, the blue eyes and the craggy nose. It was Dad, all right, but not the same guy I had seen off at the Edmonton airport a couple of months before."

Craig's ignorance of airport construction was exceeded only by that of the Indians and horses he was forced to employ. The Indians never had the time, nor the inclination, to become experienced because they disappeared as soon as they had earned a few dollars. Green and equally unenthusiastic recruits were skiffed across the river from the fort to take over the reins, the axes, picks and shovels.

The horses, accustomed only to the pack trails, had neither the strength nor the disposition for heavy work. Clancy found he had to maintain a stable of ten scrawny beasts, four in harness and six in reserve. Even so, the cayuses were unreliable.

Tony Craig recalls: "I'd say on the average of about once a day those critters would stampede and all hell would break loose. The Indians would scatter, the horses would be off at a wild gallop heading for the timber, half the time flattening the tents as they went, tangling the harness in the trees. It was beautiful! I don't know how my dad put up with it."

What gusto they lacked for working in harness, the pack ponies more than made up for once they got their noses in the feed bags. As oat-eating machines, they were extremely efficient.

McConachie recalled this ruefully, "Hardly a day went by, it seemed, but I got another signal from Craig. 'More oats for the horses.' It cost twenty cents a pound to fly those oats in. I was damn near ruined by horses!"

The details of other expenses on the Fort Nelson construction project were lost to history one hot Friday afternoon in mid-August when Clancy Craig raised his eyes from his toil to see smoke rising from his campsite. The fire, of unknown cause, wiped out the tents, most of the grub and all of the records.

But somehow, with sweat and strain, Craig and son got the job done.

On a crisp September evening in 1940 the wheels of Yukon Southern Air Transport's new Barkley-Grow rolled on the fresh gravel of the Fort Nelson airstrip.

Clancy Craig had won his war with the wilderness. He returned, gratefully, to the sweet simple life of a city gardener.

25. A PAY LOAD OF LUCK

The chain of airstrips was slowly taking shape. In the wilderness they were cleared by reluctant heroes like Clancy Craig. But near the towns McConachie had another system. Aided by enthusiasts like Mayor Percy Tooley of Grande Prairie, McConachie flew around the country convincing people that better air transport would bring prosperity to their regions.

Soon the port-of-call communities along the first six hundred miles of the Yukon route vied with each other in voting public funds to appropriate land and to level runways for McConachie's tri-motored Ford.

Slowly, more radio beams and better instruments were installed. Even the name of the company was changed. In 1939 it became Yukon Southern Air Transport.

But despite all these changes pilots had to fly by the seat of their pants for much of the time. Any aviator without "air sense" was soon in trouble in that treacherous terrain.

One young pilot sadly lacked this vital ability and so was nicknamed "The Groper." When lost he would plop on to a patch of open water and wait. Usually he was spotted by another flyer who would either land and point him in the right direction or report his location to the base. On one occasion a farmer passing Charlie Lake in a grain wagon called out that there was a yellow plane parked on a lake just ten miles away. It was "The Groper."

He was soon persuaded that northern flying just wasn't his bag.

The air sense "The Groper" so conspicuously lacked, McConachie possessed to a superlative degree. But as the record of his numerous near-misses shows, he would never have survived without a pay load of luck. On a flight from Great Falls, Montana, to Portland, Oregon, he had three passengers in a single-engined Waco on wheels. Jim Slessor, his long-suffering insurance agent; Jimmy Bell, the Edmonton airport manager; and Walter Hale, the postal chap. They were hopping down from Edmonton as delegates to an International Northwest Aviation Council convention in Portland.

They had overnighted at Great Falls in bad weather. About mid-morning the cloud base was still on the trees but a patch of blue showed, so Grant decided to give it a whirl. Using a road map marked with elevations, he flew among the mountains in milky visibility. Beyond Missoula, where they re-fuelled, the weather worsened. He escaped from several dead-end valleys only by snapping the Waco into wing-wrenching 180-degree turns. Then he found himself trapped in a mountain bowl. He decided to spiral up in the hope of breaking out over the top of the cloud cover.

As Jim Slessor described the view from the co-pilot's seat: "We seemed to climb through that cotton-wool sky forever . . . up to thirteen thousand feet . . . the Waco nudging its ceiling . . . less than an hour's gas in the tanks . . . there was just one way to go . . . down. Well, I tell you! We were spiralling down through that solid overcast encircled by rock, a corkscrew sinking into the neck of a bottle. It was the scariest experience of my life! I was breaking out in beads of sweat and flinching away from those mountain walls I knew were there in the mist, but couldn't see. Christ!

"The most amazing thing was that Grant showed no strain.

Very casual, he asked me to slide open my side window and keep a lookout for trees or rocks.

" 'Grant,' I said, 'if I spot a rock or a tree I won't be telling you about it. It'll be too late!' He just grinned.

"Well, I never would have believed it! We broke into the clear under the cloud ceiling at about four hundred feet right over a small village at the bottom of the bowl. It was Plains, Montana. We landed in a hayfield and called it a day."

Once McConachie was caught in a "white-out" while flying from Yellowknife, the northern gold camp, to Edmonton with a twitchy *Journal* reporter sharing the cockpit of the Norseman ski-plane. They were hit by a blizzard. White tundra rolled beneath the wings, merging with the snow filling the sky and wiping out the horizon. Forced to descend till the skis were brushing the tree tops, McConachie was scarcely able to maintain ground reference. He was on the point of reversing his course when his keen eyes spotted the scar of a river bank. Soon he picked up the slash of the Northern Alberta Railway right-of-way leading to the city. Flying the "iron beam," he was so low that the telegraph poles flicked by like a picket fence just beyond the Norseman's wing tips.

Then they were roaring low over the northern reaches of Edmonton. With a chuckle and a wink at his passenger, McConachie advanced the throttle to full power to rocket down Ninety-ninth Street so low his port wing tip appeared to tick the flagpole of the post office and the reporter found himself looking directly into the upper offices of the McLeod Building. White faces pressed to the windows as the Norseman whooshed by in a pane-rattling avalanche of sound.

The thunderbolt fly-by immediately started telephones jangling all over downtown as startled citizens clamored for information. A later call, to McConachie himself, was from the civil aviation inspector who was not convinced the storm had justified the shoot-up of the city. But he decided not to take disciplinary action against the resident hero.

After McConachie landed, the operator of the radio transmitter station a few miles north of the city called him. He was excited.

"Hey, Grant," he shouted, "that was sure some stunt of yours, flying right between the towers of my aerial in that snow-storm!"

McConachie whistled softly as he cradled the phone and turned to the reporter: "This guy says we flew between his radio towers. Did you see any towers?"

There was a long and thoughtful pause, and he said, grinning, "Well, I guess it helps to have luck riding with you in this business."

Luck was also his co-pilot the day he took a bush plane up for a post-overhaul flight check. The plane in question was the Fairchild FC2W2 he had acquired in trade for the first Ford. It had a unique feature for a bush plane. When two bolts were removed, the wings could be folded back against the fuselage.

Red Rose said, "Grant made a circuit but wasn't satisfied with the way it flew, so he brought it right down again. As he taxied in we could see what was wrong. We just flipped! The mechanic hadn't checked the wing bolts. They had not been secured into the bolt holes in the wing roots. McConachie had flown that plane with not even a prayer to prevent those wings from peeling back against the fuselage. It was a miracle the Fairchild didn't just fold and crash as soon as it got airborne, with the pressure of the slip stream against the leading edges of those wings.

"All that was holding the wings in place were the roots of the trailing edges butting against the tubing of the fuselage. It was a fluke. There was a six-inch gap between the front of the wing and the rest of the plane on each side. You just wouldn't believe it. Thank God he didn't put the plane through his usual aerobatics. That would have wrapped it up, but good!"

Rose said McConachie never did know how close it had been on that flight, because, as he said, "None of us was about to tell him. We weren't that crazy. We didn't want to get fired . . . again."

Maybe McConachie's flying luck infected some of his pilots.

One February afternoon, Ernie Kubicek was piloting the YSAT Norseman CF-BFR up through the wild Liard country in the vicinity of Headless Valley. Visibility was limited in heavy snow. The region was marked "unexplored" on the charts, but a pilot who had flown in there once had told Kubicek, "just follow the river." The instruction seemed clear enough. He neglected to mention, however, that the river forked into twin valleys. Kubicek took the wrong one, into a granite-walled cul-de-sac.

When the mountain suddenly loomed out of the snow-storm directly ahead of him, the pilot had neither time nor air space to reverse his course. Instinctively, he jammed the throttle to full power and pulled back on the control column to wrench the Norseman into a steep climb. By some miracle, the plane power-stalled on to the very crest of the mountain, its skis settling into the deep snow of the summit. Incredibly, the only damage was a broken undercarriage strut—plus a pilot with badly frayed nerves.

Kubicek knew he had to get word out to the nearest air base at Prince George or he would starve or freeze to death on the isolated peak. The Norseman had an air-to-ground radio transmitter that was effective only when a trailing antenna was reeled out from the plane's belly in flight.

Kubicek strung the aerial to a shovel handle planted in the snow. After some anxious moments he got through to Prince George and reported his position. Then he crawled into his sleeping bag in the shelter of a snow bank, munched emergency rations and waited. The next day Ted Field casually made a ski landing on the summit, bringing with him metal tubing for makeshift repairs to the Norseman's under-

carriage. Both planes then were flown off the mountain top.
It was adventure-fiction for the rest of the world, but rather
routine stuff for the fly-boys.

McConachie's most frightening air experience, by his own
account, occurred in a twin-engined Barkley-Grow equipped
with blind-flying instruments and a radio direction-finder. He
had taken off from Edmonton early that morning on the last
mail flight to the Yukon before the 1938 spring break-up.
There were no passengers, which was financially regrettable
but not unusual.

Flight 102 encountered strong head-winds and deteriorating
weather conditions all along the line. McConachie reached
Watson Lake late in the afternoon, but he was anxious to
get through with the mail, so he decided to press on to Whitehorse, confident because there was a Royal Canadian Corps
of Signals station there with a powerful transmitter-receiver.

But in one of the world's most forbidding areas, over the
Cassiar Mountains, he realized that with the head-winds he
could not reach Whitehorse before dark. Just when he was
planning to swing back to Watson Lake, he spotted a break
in the clouds. He could see the twisting shoreline of Teslin
Lake, the ice white against the surrounding forest. Radioing
Whitehorse signal station, he cancelled his flight plan and reported that he would be putting in at Teslin base for the
night. Whitehorse acknowledged and went off the air.

As the silver aircraft sloped over the tree line and levelled
inches above Teslin Lake, McConachie suddenly jammed both
throttles to the wall to abort the landing. At the last second
before touchdown he had detected a heaving movement of
the ice. Now, flying over the lake at low altitude he could
see dark fractures and fissures in the surface. A wind shift
must have caused a premature break-up. Landing on Teslin
was out of the question.

Grimly, he climbed the Barkley into the darkening sky and
set course once again for Whitehorse. He had no alternative

now, and even Whitehorse was a poor chance. With the radio station shut down for the night the homing compass in the aircraft was useless, and so was the air-to-ground radio. Even if he could find his way over the peaks in the darkness and get down through the clouds without smashing into a mountain, the airport would be blacked out. It was a real mess.

He was so isolated he might just as well be on another planet.

"The flight deck of the Barkley was the loneliest place in the world that night," he recalled. "There was only the pale glow from the instrument panel that was my small universe. It was a pitch-black night. I kept calling Whitehorse on the radio, but I knew it was hopeless. This was going to be the end for me. The wreckage would never even be found, most likely."

Jack Barber, the airline's agent at Whitehorse, recalls: "I was ready to settle in for an evening of light reading when I heard an aircraft roaring in the darkness overhead. It gave me quite a shock. I knew it could only be Grant and we'd have to get him down. There was just no place else.

"I ran to the signals shack and got Hurt, who had shut down for the night, back on the air again. I talked to McConachie and he said he was above solid overcast but could tell by the dark silhouettes of certain peaks that he was just about overhead Whitehorse. I told him there was only about two hundred feet of ceiling, but that forward visibility was pretty fair once you got under the stuff.

"Knowing the country pretty well, having lived in the area for a number of years by this time, I suggested to Grant he fly north. He was likely to find a break in the clouds over Lake Laberge.

"I raced up to the airport in my old Chevvy truck, threw the flare pots aboard and drove down the runway, tossing the flaming pots overboard, spacing them to mark the strip.

But in my haste I put them on the right instead of on the left side of the active runway.

"There was something uncanny the way Grant could fly an airplane. The average guy would have been scared silly up there alone in the night with mountains all around, fuel running low, no place else to go but down, and heavy cloud under the wings.

"Cool as you please, he searched out a cloud hole over Laberge, circled down through it, then came booming over the black landscape to pick up the glow of those flare pots. He even spotted that my bloody fires were on the wrong side and came in smack on the runway. Still, he was mighty glad to be down. The engines sputtered and quit half-way down the strip. The Barkley had run out of gas on the landing run! You just can't get it any closer than that, about five seconds of gas left."

In another landing crisis McConachie found his ground support less than effective. Flying a single-engined Waco on skis, he was southbound out of Whitehorse for Watson Lake in a heavy snow-storm.

The regular radio operator was off duty, and Tiny Johnson, the bull-sized handy-man, was alone in the Watson Lake radio shack. Tiny could talk into the mike when someone called, but he knew little of radio patter or flight procedures.

"BMW to Watson. BMW to Watson. Do you read me? Over."

Johnson flipped the switch, clutched the mike in a huge mitt and shouted,

"Hi, Grant. This is Tiny."

"How's the weather down there, Tiny?"

"Well, the weather isn't bad for this time of year."

"You don't understand, Tiny, I want to know what is the visibility." There was a pause, and then Tiny was back on the air. "It's pretty good as far as you can see."

Things were getting out of hand, thought McConachie.

"Tiny, I'm in trouble. It's snowing like hell up here, and I've got to know what it's like down there where you are before I let down."

"Gosh, Grant, why didn't you say what you wanted to know. It's snowing like hell down here, too."

"No. No. You haven't got the idea, Tiny. Listen. I'm up here on top of the cloud deck. I want to let down through it. What is your ceiling down there?"

The reply crackled in McConachie's earphones: "Well, I can sure give you the answer to that one. It's beaverboard. I should know. I built this shack myself."

That was the end of Tiny's hopes for a career as a radio operator. After he had made a blind letdown through the snow-storm McConachie saw to that.

The incident that finally shattered McConachie's composure came as a call to his Edmonton home on a sultry evening late in August of 1939. It conveyed the text of a telegram from P. J. Tooley, the agent/mayor at Grande Prairie, and it concerned a missing pilot, Don Patry:

URGENT. RADIO MESSAGE FROM CHARLIE LAKE AS FOLLOWS —PATRY MISSING IN BMW WITH JOHNSON HUNTING PARTY PLUS GAME COMMISSIONER VAN DYKE PLUS TWO STAFF MCKINNON AND HANNIS STOP LAST WORD FROM PATRY AFTER DARK REPORTED HE UNABLE TO PICK UP RADIO BEACON AND RUNNING LOW ON GAS ADVISED HE WAS COMMENCING BLIND LETDOWN THROUGH OVERCAST AND PLANNED USE EMERGENCY FLARES FOR WATER LANDING STOP NOT HEARD FROM SINCE STOP CONTINUING EFFORTS TO MAKE RADIO CONTACT AND PLAN SEARCH AT FIRST LIGHT TOMORROW STOP TOOLEY GP.

Don Patry's flight had been a charter assignment with the eight-passenger twin-engine Barkley-Grow CF-BMW on floats. With Bob Hannis, a mechanic, in the co-pilot's seat, he had taken off from Charlie Lake in the morning and had flown 260 miles north to a rendezvous with the hunting party of a New York sportsman, Edgar Johnson. The flight out was delayed as the huntsmen assembled their trophies and hunting gear. It was mid-afternoon when Patry and the four sportsmen and their trophy heads of a moose, two deer and two mountain sheep, took off from Deadman's Lake and headed for Fort St. John.

Twenty minutes out, Patry had picked up a radio transmission from Leo McKinnon, the agent at Fort Nelson. He was suffering from an agonizing toothache and wanted to be flown south. Also, he said, the provincial game commissioner, Arthur Van Dyke, was in Fort Nelson and wanted transportation south. The pilot veered off course, landed on the river at Fort Nelson, boarded McKinnon and Van Dyke, and resumed his flight. By now, however, it was already dusk and Patry was concerned about completing his journey before dark. He was not unduly worried, though, confident that his radio compass would lead him to Charlie Lake. As a qualified instrument pilot, he could then drop through the cloud and darkness and count on breaking into the clear over the eleven-mile-long lake. He also knew that if he arrived over the lake after dark the ground staff at the base would spread gasoline on the lake and burn it to create a landing flare for his float-plane.

Head-winds further delayed the flight, so twilight had deepened into darkness below as the Barkley-Grow cruised over an unbroken cloud base at six thousand feet. Patry's assurance dissolved into alarm as the needle of his homing compass started to swing aimlessly. Either the instrument was haywire or the operator at Charlie Lake had turned off the radio beacon. He called Charlie Lake continually but got no response. He wasn't exactly lost, he thought ruefully, but he certainly didn't know where he was. And time was running out. There was only enough gas left for another twenty minutes. He would have to go down blind in the hope of breaking into the clear and using the parachute flare to find enough water to sit down on.

As the bush airliner descended, it was enveloped in utter blackness. The pilot's world was reduced to the luminous dials of his instrument panel. He was lost and descending blind without any knowledge of the cloud ceiling height below.

After an eternity of letting down through inky cloud, Bob Hannis, look-out for Patry, shouted, "Trees! Don, trees! I can see the trees." The pilot scanned the instrument panel. The sensitive altimeter still had close to four hundred feet of altitude, enough height to release the emergency parachute-flare to light up the terrain below. Patry made his decision. He thumbed the red button. An explosive flash lit up the sky, blinding the occupants of the plane with its brilliance. That was all. The flare had misfired. The gloom seemed deeper than ever.

"This," Patry told himself grimly, "is the end."

In the radio shack at Charlie Lake, the staff were grouped around the receiver as the operator, Tony Craig, continued his attempts to make contact with the Barkley-Grow. For a time, Patry's messages, though faint, had been getting through, but he was not receiving. Then silence.

The pilot's young wife, Jean, eight months pregnant, had been listening on the 5390 frequency in her quarters and now had joined the tense group. As Patry's air time expired, Craig intensified his efforts to make contact but to no avail. Then time ran out. BMW was down somewhere.

At four the next morning, Craig, still at his radio equipment, received a message relayed through Grande Prairie. McConachie had taken off from Edmonton in a Waco on wheels and would be landing at the Fort St. John airstrip at dawn. He had with him Ted Field, chief pilot, and Hans Broten, head of Yukon Southern's communications section.

When they arrived, the base radio receiver was supplemented with a high aerial strung in the tree tops. A huge air search was to begin.

After the emergency flare fizzled, Patry knew that their

chances of survival were small, about as small as they could get. But, calmly, he reduced power on the two engines to lose altitude. Flying just above the trees he began searching for water, even a large puddle or beaver pond. Now only ten minutes' fuel remained. Then, eureka! A change in the terrain below. They were passing over a small lake. Mustn't lose it in the darkness. It was their only hope. Patry reached forward to set the gyro compass on zero. He lowered the wing flaps for maximum lift at reduced speed, and banked the Barkley into a precise rate-one turn to the left. The precision turn should take him around in a complete circle to level out on the zero heading, bringing him over the lake again.

As the gyro compass crept steadily around and steadied on "0," Patry flew with his right hand on the throttle knobs, his left holding the control wheel to maintain level flight just above the tree tops. Suddenly, again, there was that break in the darkness. The lake! Not a big one, but still a lake. He pulled the throttles back and let the plane sink. To hell with a smooth landing. The pontoons struck the surface with heavy impact. Then a second shock as the float-plane splashed down from a high bounce. Then the steady swoosh of water streaming by the pontoons. They were down! Safe!

At Charlie Lake, the high aerial was working. A faint voice signal came crackling over the base receiver.

"BMW to Charlie Lake. BMW to Charlie Lake. Do you read? Over."

McConachie leapt from his chair to seize the microphone from Craig.

"This is McConachie at Charlie Lake. How are you, Don? Is anyone injured? Over."

"Patry here, Grant. All okay. I don't know how, but I managed to put her down in one piece last night. And by the way, ask Red if he's got a job for me on his farm."

"Is the aircraft in condition to fly out of there?"

"Sure. BMW is in great shape. Only two things wrong. I'm

down to a thimble of gas. And this lake is so small it scares me. You'll have to send in a Waco with gas and ferry the customers and the crew out of here. Without any load I could just make it out again."

Patry gave his position as Cecil Lake, about twenty miles northeast of the base.

Returning from the town to Charlie Lake late that afternoon, McConachie saw the Barkley-Grow CF-BMW at the seaplane dock. As he strode down to inspect the plane he was greeted by Glen Fenby waving a piece of paper. It was a sheet torn from a pilot's logbook.

"Patry said to give this to you. He's gone to the cabin to see his wife," said the mechanic.

McConachie looked at the scribbled sheet.

TO THE PRESIDENT
YUKON SOUTHERN AIR TRANSPORT:
I QUIT.

> D. PATRY
> FORMER CAPTAIN.

McConachie chuckled as he crumpled the sheet of paper and tossed it into Charlie Lake.

26. ENTER CANADIAN PACIFIC

By 1940 Yukon Southern had the dimensions and some of the pretensions of an airline. A few of the airline's trappings, indeed, were almost impressive considering YSAT's humble origins as a fish-packer, and its constant desperate financial struggle to stay alive.

There were the landing strips (admittedly home-made, unpaved and unlighted); the sleek zippy Barkley-Grows (on which none of the payments had been met); the "homing pigeon" radio compasses in the Barkley cockpits (installments owing); the two scheduled flights a week from Edmonton and Vancouver to the Yukon (more than half-empty); the in-flight meals served on the main routes (cold sandwiches, Dad's cookies and milk in paper cups, doled out by the oil-stained flight mechanic); the fleet of fifteen planes (for the most part a gaggle of pipe-and-canvas bush planes . . . Norsemans, Wacos, Fairchilds, Fokkers and a Boeing 40-B-4 . . . too inefficient to break even); and a roster of 150 employees (all underpaid and racing each other to cash their pay-cheques at the bank, just in case).

Yukon Southern by now was up to the eyebrows in hock to the Royal Bank of Canada. The hundred-thousand-dollar Imperial Oil credit was running out, raising the horrible prospect of paying cash-on-the-barrel for oil and gas. The airline, in fact, was in financial quicksand, sinking deeper by the minute.

But if Grant McConachie endured any private agonies of despair, there was no trace of it on the bright face he presented to the public. In February 1940 he announced through service to Alaska, connecting with Pan American Airways at Whitehorse under the terms of an interline agreement. Yukon Southern also had consented to serve as licensee and operator of a Pan Am-financed chain of ground radio stations needed by the U.S. carrier on its Seattle–Fairbanks run. (Radio licenses in Canada were restricted to Canadian firms.) Juan Trippe was personally grateful to McConachie for this favor.

In April the young president of YSAT negotiated in New York with Amtorg, the Russian overseas trading agency, for rights to fly down the coast of Siberia on an Edmonton–Shanghai over-the-top service.

In May, back in Edmonton, he announced to the press that Yukon Southern would inaugurate the first stage of this route with an Edmonton–Vladivostok (Siberia) schedule "this summer."

The prediction was premature, but undaunted, McConachie accepted Juan Trippe's invitation to make a number of flights as guest co-pilot on the Pan American Clipper service between New York and Bermuda to gain personal experience in over-ocean flying, navigation equipment and techniques.

In 1940 evidence to justify Grant McConachie's apparent confidence in his dream of international air conquest was like hairs on a frog. But he continued to operate his airline on the assumption of colossal success. Meanwhile, he and his colleagues may have drawn some measure of consolation from the positive effects the war in Europe was beginning to exert on their Northwest Route.

By June 1940 defense strategists had begun to concern themselves with the frightening vulnerability of Alaska to attack from the Pacific. The Canada United States Joint Defense

Board recommended the improvement of the Northwest Route as a vital communication and logistics link to Alaska. Before the end of the year A. D. McLean, Superintendent of Airways in the Canadian Department of Transport, had ordered engineering surveys for modernization of the Edmonton–Whitehorse airway.

Because of this special defense priority, Yukon Southern alone of all the flying operations in the country, was cleared for unrestricted purchase of war-scarce airliners, aircraft parts and maintenance supplies. Permit to purchase, yes. Money or credit, no.

At the same time, the other bush operations were being slowly garrotted by the iron squeeze of these very wartime priorities. Down the Mackenzie, out of the Winnipeg base, throughout northern Ontario and Quebec, down the St. Lawrence, the bush planes were faltering. Traffic dwindled as gold and silver mines were closed to conserve manpower. Camps were abandoned. Prospecting virtually ceased. The fur trade was failing. Men of the north moved south to enlist.

Aircraft sat idle, starved for repair parts as factory output was commandeered for war. For some years most of the northern operators, including McConachie, had been bankrupt, but these pilot-presidents were so indifferent to bookkeeping they didn't know how broke they were, so they had kept their outfits staggering through the skies. But by the end of 1940 it was obvious that only heroic measures could save the bush airlines.

In this case, the required hero rode out of the east in a private car attached to the CPR's Transcontinental No. 1, his briefcase figuratively bulging with rich uncle's money to save the poor but worthy bush flyers from a fate far worse than a punctured pontoon.

The hero role was played by tall, high-domed, bespectacled L. B. Unwin, wearing a pin-stripe suit, starched collar, modest blue tie and the title of financial vice-president of the country's

Champagne is served to McConachie and guests during the CPA inaugural Vancouver-Honolulu-Fiji and Sydney, Australia, flight in July 1949. The young lady is Pamela Hookem, an Australian girl hired by McConachie.

In the summer of 1949 Canadian Pacific Airlines spread its wings over nearly 15,000 miles of ocean to serve the South Pacific and the Orient from Vancouver. President Grant McConachie, left, relaxes with the author during a stopover at Honolulu on the airline's inaugural flight to Sydney, Australia.

McConachie addresses the assembly of dignitaries at Sydney Airport during the arrival ceremony marking CPA's first flight from Canada to Australia.

Poised for a survey flight to the Orient, Captain Charles Pentland (with log book) and Grant McConachie appear with company specialists under the wing of an airliner bound for Tokyo, Shanghai and Hong Kong. McConachie did not go on this flight. The aircraft was the last to leave Shanghai as the invading Communist forces stormed the outskirts of the city. On McConachie's immediate left are Captains North Saule and Charles Pentland, both of whom died in the crash of the Comet airliner. (Photo courtesy of the Canadian Pacific Railway Company.)

Always happiest in the cockpit, McConachie tries out the controls of the new Boeing 707 aircraft during a demonstration flight non-stop from Seattle to Tokyo.

Big wheels of Canadian Pacific: (left to right) Ian D. Sinclair, general solicitor, CPR; N. R. "Buck" Crump, president, CPR; Grant McConachie, president, Canadian Pacific Airlines and L. B. Unwin, financial vice-president of CPR who is talking to a Boeing Aircraft official after the group returned from the demonstration flight in the new Boeing 707.

McConachie delighted in talking airplanes to visiting pressmen, who described him as "an irresistible force."

Grant McConachie and Mrs. McConachie during a Christmas party in Honolulu.

Grant McConachie was an early enthusiast for supersonic transports. Here he explains noteworthy features of the original U.S.-designed supersonic model to visitors.

"It's Grant McConachie . . . a little off course."

The press delighted in covering McConachie's many exploits. (The Winnipeg *Free Press,* December 2, 1964.)

For his powerful campaign for free-enterprise competition against the airline monopoly on Canada's main-line routes, Grant McConachie was awarded a plaque as "Canadian Businessman of the Year" by Sales Executive International.

As president of Canadian Pacific Air Lines, McConachie found that much of his time concerned diplomatic duties. Here he escorts VIP Field Marshal Montgomery at Vancouver Airport.

McConachie the rancher appears in Calgary Stampede "uniform" (white Stetson) to receive a plaque during the famous Stampede's Salute to Transportation in the summer of 1963. Presentation is made by H. Gordon Love, president of the Calgary Exhibition and Stampede, Ltd.

After years of searching for a hobby, Grant McConachie finally became a spare-time rancher. Here, at a cattle show, he illustrates a cliché by "taking the bull by the horns."

The last photograph of Grant McConachie was taken at his ranch on the week-end before his final business trip to Long Beach, California.

wealthiest, most powerful corporation, the Canadian Pacific Railway.

Nothing in "LB's" background had qualified him either for the dashing hero part or for the role of an aviation expert. At seventeen, fresh out from England, he had stepped off a CPR train into a five-foot snowdrift and a thirty-dollar-a-month job with the railway at the northern Ontario siding of White River. For the next three decades Unwin had applied himself to the corporation's ledgers, rising Horatio Alger-like through the inky-fingered ranks to become a vice-president.

Though Unwin himself might not have known a bush plane from a catamaran, the CPR had shown an interest in aviation as early as 1919 when the corporation obtained (but made no use of) a special government permit to own and operate aircraft commercially. In 1933 president Sir Edward Beatty had dipped in a corporate toe by venturing $250,000 in Canadian Airways, a bush-flying enterprise fostered by James A. Richardson, the Winnipeg wheat-trading tycoon.

By 1937 airline service was well established in the United States but nonexistent across Canada. Many Canadian businessmen were using the United States airlines for quick transportation across the continent. There were fears that Canada's failure to develop its own east-west air service would encourage the development of north-south services. Thus, as in the case of the railway sixty years before, a transcontinental air service was seen as essential to national cohesion.

For a time the Canadian Pacific Railway was encouraged to anticipate an equal participation with the CNR in the new airline service. But that didn't work out.

In 1937 the human dynamo from Massachusetts, the Hon. C. D. Howe, as Minister of Transport in the Canadian Government, proceeded with characteristic vigour to set up Trans-Canada Air Lines under government ownership. He imported Phillip Johnson, one of the ablest airline operators in the

United States, as vice-president of operations, with another eminent American expert, D. B. Collyer, as his assistant.

Although the government was thus firmly entrenched on the trunk air route across Canada, CPR's Sir Edward Beatty was determined that nevertheless "the world's greatest transportation system," predominant for generations in Canadian rail and sea travel, would sprout wings of its own. He commissioned Unwin to buy up all the bush routes in the country.

The purchase of Yukon Southern Air Transport by the CPR was announced on January 13, 1941. The price was four hundred thousand dollars, but the airline's debts left little more than a hundred thousand for the shareholders. Grant McConachie and his partner, Barney Phillips, held 82 per cent of the stock. In addition to a share of the cash settlement, each received a job guarantee with the new corporation, Phillips at a minimum $350 a month and McConachie at $500 or more.

For the first time in the nine years since his first commercial flight with the yellow-tailed crows, Grant McConachie was able to contemplate a future free of financial worry. But was there a destiny for him, he wondered, in the gargantuan complex known as Canadian Pacific? It seemed unlikely.

The Canadian Pacific Railway was born in 1881 out of the daring of six millionaires and the need of the Government of Canada for a twin ribbon of steel to bind the western provinces to the newly-founded nation. The CPR's charter of incorporation carried with it the challenge to build a railroad across the northern half of the continent, through the rugged wilderness of the Laurentian Shield, over the emptiness of the prairies, penetrating the rugged barrier of four mountain ranges to reach the coast of the Pacific. The steel was essential to give material substance to the dream of nationhood. Its construction within a ten-year period had been a condition of the western territories joining the Confederation.

As an inducement to take on the appalling risk of building an impossible road to nowhere, the CPR was promised $25 million in cash, 25 million acres of western land, and other considerations.

An American historian was to describe the deal as "the only case in history where a ranking nation was in a sense created by a construction project." With some accuracy he speculated that "without that railroad, all the territory west of the Great Lakes would probably now be governed by Washington."

It was thus ironic that it was a gutsy, spike-chewing American, William Van Horne from Chicago, who bossed the construction miracle that saw the railroad completed in four years and six months to beat the deadline. He was to become the second president of the CPR.

The CPR now faced another formidable challenge—to develop traffic on the line to nowhere. It proceeded to do this by spending $130 million on immigration, colonization and irrigation in the Canadian west, and by diversifying in many directions.

At about the time Grant McConachie became one of its 81,000 jobholders (out of a total Canadian population of only 11½ million), the Canadian Pacific Railway was assessed in the following terms by the noted American journalist Temple Fielding, writing in the *Saturday Evening Post:*

More than a railroad system, a skein of corporations, an industrial colossus, CPR is the empire upon which Canada expanded. In physical size, diversity of operations and importance to the basic economy of the country, there are few parallels. In the hands of eight CPR directors lies the destiny of hundreds of thousands of Canadians.

There is a quip that the CPR owns everything in Canada that isn't nailed down, but it's the country's largest taxpayer. It's no monopoly of the privileged rich, because ownership is spread among close to 100,000 separate stockholders in Canada, Great

Britain, the United States and other countries.

Biggest asset of the $1.7 billion corporation is the 21,000-mile railway (83,000 cars, 1,800 locomotives). Other interests: a fleet of forty-two ocean, coastal and inland steamships, a chain of fourteen hotels, a 200,000-mile national and international telegraph network, more than a million acres of real estate, a mining and smelting company producing a large share of the world's fertilizer and non-ferrous metals.

To pioneer a new country and make its own traffic, necessity has forced CPR into a score of strange businesses. Turkish baths, a dance palace, fire stations, bus companies, the largest salt-water swimming pool under glass. It owns a trolley company, a police force of 377 professional cops, and more trucks than anybody in Canada. It manufactures heavy water, sleeping cars, fine art, hockey rinks, golf courses and macaroni.

The universality of the CPR in Canada is illustrated by the anecdote of a Bond Street haberdashery traveller who crossed the Atlantic on a Canadian Pacific steamer. At Montreal a Canadian Pacific agent cashed his Canadian Pacific travellers cheques, transferred his samples to the Canadian Pacific express company, then transmitted his safe-arrival cables by Canadian Pacific Communications.

A crack Canadian Pacific train whisked him to Quebec where he booked into the Chateau Frontenac, a Canadian Pacific hotel. In the elevator he dropped his watch on the floor. The Canadian Pacific bellboy returning it to him said, "Your watch reads one hour slow. It's exactly eleven-o-five, Canadian Pacific time."

The Englishman neither knew nor cared that CP also transmitted authentic time signals from Greenwich.

"Good heavens!" he exploded. "Does your ruddy railroad own the time here, too?"

Such awesome presence and power did not win widespread popularity in Canada, of course. Prairie farmers, impoverished and embittered by the depression of the early thirties, nurtured resentments against the CPR. These were usually illogical, since the company had spent millions in fostering settlement of the wheatlands, had assisted homesteaders with generous loans, and had written off $37 million in mortgages in the depth of the depression.

But the dust farmer's view of the giant corporation was fairly reflected in the anecdote of one who had endured three crop failures in a row. The next year, just before harvest, he came home to discover lightning had struck his farmhouse, burning it to the ground, a hailstorm had flattened his wheat crop, and his wife had run off with the hired man.

This was too much! The farmer raised his eyes to heaven, shook his fist in rage, and bellowed, "Goddamn the CPR!"

27. STRIFE IN THE CORPORATION

For Grant McConachie and his wilderness cronies the CPR purchase of the bush routes of Canada marked the end of an era—and the start of new careers. No longer would they guide their tattered tramp freighters on marginal missions, sniffing out pay loads where they could, never sure when duff weather would ground their seat-of-the-pants flights, forcing pilot and passengers to take to their sleeping bags. In 1941 northern aviation began its transition from bedroll to bankroll.

But life at the head office of Yukon Southern Air Transport continued much as before during most of McConachie's first year on the payroll of the great corporation. With the ten flying companies, the CPR had on its corporate hands a baffling complex of aircraft and route patterns, not to mention the personal rivalries and vendettas of dozens of potential executives. It took Windsor Station (the Kremlin of the CPR in Montreal) more than a year to sort things out.

Meantime, Yukon Southern, until so recently the airline of despair, was flying high on the abundant resources of the parent corporation and the war priorities granted to no other Canadian air service—including the national airline, Trans-Canada.

Barney Phillips remembers how McConachie used his persuasive powers to spirit a fleet of high-speed military transports away from under the noses of the U.S. command.

"Somehow, in 1941, Grant got C. D. Howe, who controlled Canada's wartime priorities, to agree to the purchase, and then he used his personal friendship with Carl Squier, the Lockheed sales manager, to snaffle nine Lodestars over the period of a year. Most of them came off the end of the military assembly line, but two were actually lifted by crane right off the deck of a freighter for us just before it sailed.

"There was the damnedest thing, too, about those Lockheeds. We had the serial numbers and could watch our planes going down the assembly line in the Burbank plant. But at the end of the line were guys with big spray guns plastering on coat after coat of green and brown paint . . . just the thing we least needed as a commercial airline, especially flying over the bush where if a camouflaged plane went down you'd never find it in a million years. But do you think we could stop them? No sir! It was in the specifications, so they kept squirting on the paint.

"After we got the planes up to Edmonton it took hundreds of man-hours to sandblast them back to silver again. There was one small benefit though. When our ferry pilots landed those war-painted transports at the Great Falls military airport, the U. S. Air Force pumped them full of gas. No way we could convince them these were civilian, and no way we could pay for the gas."

While the Lodestars (advertised by McConachie as "the fastest commercial aircraft in the world") were joining Yukon Southern's fleet, the Canadian Government had pushed through in less than a year a $9 million airway system from Edmonton to the Yukon. Known as the Northwest Staging Route, it featured paved and lighted runways, radio range equipment and improved air-to-ground communication facilities. Obviously, better times were ahead for the underpaid, overworked and long-suffering northern breed of plane jockey.

When CPR bought the ten bush lines they didn't realize the enmities they were inheriting. McConachie said, "There were ten presidents, most of them senior to me in age if not experience, ten operations managers, ten sales managers; each had his own ideas, ambitions and staff, all in conflict."

Barney Phillips put it more bluntly: "There was more venom than a snake farm! These guys had been clawing each other so long they didn't know any other way to act. It was worst between the Mackenzie Air Service (MAS), Leigh Brintnell's gang, and the Canadian Airways (CAL) crowd with Punch Dickins and Wop May in the Mackenzie Valley region north of Edmonton.

"Their hostility continued long after they were all working for the same CPR outfit. Say the Norseman CF-BUA landed at Edmonton with pilot North Sawle up front. All the mechanics had 'Canadian Pacific Airlines' on the back of their overalls by this time, but do you think a former MAS grease-jockey would go out to meet that ex-CAL plane and pilot? Not bloody likely! Hell, if the plane was on fire he wouldn't leak on it!"

The same rancorous rivalry extended right up the executive ladder. Barney Phillips recalls: "There'd been hot argument ever since the CPR took over about who would run the show in the west. Most of the bets were on Brintnell, but some said Wop May. They never dreamed it would go to the fish pilot, McConachie. The arctic pilots didn't even rate him as one of their class."

So the bush-flying fraternity was shocked and, in some quarters, deeply chagrined when on November 28, 1941, CPR vice-president W. M. Neal announced the appointment of Grant McConachie as assistant to the vice-president, Western Lines (Air Services) in Winnipeg.

Barney Phillips was not so surprised. "It was pretty obvious that he got the nod mainly because he wasn't in the dogfight. I think Neal was canny enough to realize he needed a neutral. I'm not saying Grant didn't make a good impression on Neal. That proved itself later. But normally he wouldn't have got the job, with his lack of seniority."

In any event, the youthful veteran of the northern air trails breezed through the musty corridors of the Royal Alexandra Station in Winnipeg in a refreshing style that shook the tradition-bound railroaders to the heels of their button shoes. Hugh Main was McConachie's secretary in the new Winnipeg posting. He still remembers his new boss's non-conformist behaviour.

"Grant would come loping into the VP's outer office and bellow across the ranks of desks to me, a lowly secretary, 'Hey Hugh. Let's get up to the "Y" for a swim and a workout.'

"The clerks were conditioned to think of the railway's top brass in terms of The Almighty, though somewhat less approachable. Suddenly here was Grant in their midst. Everybody's pal. He rode a bicycle to work because he needed the exercise. When he chose to see Neal he'd whoosh past the dumbfounded secretary, right into the inner sanctum. Likely as not he'd sit on the corner of the VP's desk with that big boyish grin of his and he'd say, 'And how are-yuh today, Mr. Neal?'

"Mind you, Neal wasn't the kind of boss you trifled with. He didn't get the nickname "Old Slaughterhouse" for sweetness and light. Some of the staff claimed his normal breakfast was barbed wire and acid. But McConachie's brashness must have struck him as a pleasant contrast to the servility everywhere else. In any case, McConachie didn't get thrown out on his ass. From Neal that was quite a tribute under the circumstances."

Another of McConachie's new associates in Winnipeg was Harry Porteous, assigned to him as chief clerk, who later became treasurer of the airline until his retirement.

He said, "When Mr. Neal told me I was to work for this new man, McConachie, I went into the small office he had

next to Mr. Neal. There he was, sitting on the floor, which
was covered with maps. Right away he started to show me
how he was going to fly to the Orient and to Australia. It
was a tremendous revelation to me. I had never even thought
of anything beyond the two ends of the railroad."

Soon after getting established in Winnipeg, McConachie was
dispatched to Edmonton for a top-level secret conference with
high officers of the United States Army.

Less than a month before, the Japanese had attacked
Pearl Harbor. The United States was at war in the Pacific,
and so was Canada. Their common problem was obvious.

"Alaska is wide-open to attack and we're in no position
to defend it," said Brigadier-General William Hoge, of the U. S.
Army.

"We know the Japs have a naval and air base in the
Kuriles. Just seven hundred and fifty miles away is Attu, the
western tip of the Aleutians. Right now we have no way of
stopping them if they decide to come swarming up the Aleu-
tian island chain or if they launch a bomber attack on
Fairbanks direct from the Kurile base. It's that serious.

"Surrounded by sea and wilderness, Alaska might as well
be an island, like Hawaii, were it not for the airway from
Edmonton north to Fairbanks.

"That's where you and your flyers can be of enormous
help to us," Hoge directed the remark to Grant McConachie,
who sat with Barney Phillips and two pilots, Ted Field and
Ralph Oakes, in their new dark-blue Canadian Pacific Airlines uniforms.

"It hasn't been announced yet, gentlemen," the General
continued, "but our government, with the co-operation of
yours, will build a military road from the end of steel at
Dawson Creek right through to Fairbanks.

"We selected your inland route because it's mostly flat terrain, it's out of strike range of carrier-based planes from the
Pacific, and, of course, there's the airway. The road will

serve two purposes—a supply route and also a track to be followed by our pilots who will soon be ferrying military planes to Alaska."

Hoge declared the U. S. Army would need the advice of McConachie and his colleagues in selecting the best route for the highway. They would need civilian planes for aerial photography of the terrain. They would use the civilian air service for personnel transport and supply. The Americans, in effect, would need a great deal of help from Canada's bush pilots.

Two months later, on March 9, 1942, a troop of U. S. Army Engineers stepped down from the red wooden coaches of the Northern Alberta Railway at Dawson Creek to begin a project that would occupy much of the attention of Grant McConachie and his colleagues in CPA for nearly two years.

The engineers pushed through a narrow tote road. They were followed by a work force of seven thousand civilians employed by the U. S. Public Roads Administration to widen and improve the road. By the first of October 1943, the builders celebrated completion of the biggest job since the Panama Canal: a two-way graded, gravel military highway running 1,600 miles from Dawson Creek to Fairbanks through a land with only one settlement, Whitehorse, big enough to be called a town. It cost $75,000 a mile, a total of $125 million—really big money in those days. It was the first all-year land connection of Alaska to Canada and the United States. The project had ensured the security of the vast territory. It had also provided the traffic to establish, finally, the stability of the airline that Grant McConachie had toiled so long and so hard to build.

Early in 1942 the CPR got around to melding the ten bush air services into one organization, Canadian Pacific Airlines; it was to be a subsidiary of the railway, with a capital stock of eight hundred thousand shares at a value of $4 million. L. B. Unwin was elected as the first president, much to the disgust of W. M. Neal, who considered the western air routes part of the rail empire he ruled from Winnipeg. Unwin appointed C. H. "Punch" Dickins, the dean of the bush pilots, as vice-president and general manager of the airline in Montreal. Neal named Grant McConachie as CPA general manager, western lines, to be located in Edmonton but reporting directly to him on matters of policy.

With that arrangement, friction was inevitable. Personal differences of philosophy as well as the internal politics of the corporation soon built up a strong rivalry between Dickins and McConachie, although Grant was never to lose his high regard for Punch and his notable air achievements.

A former war ace, Dickins was pioneering the prairie airmail early in 1928, before Grant had taken his first flying lesson. Between 1927 and 1939 he had covered 80,000 miles in bush planes, mostly over mapless northern regions, often in temperatures of fifty below. First to wing across the subarctic Barrens, first to fly the mail to the Arctic Ocean, Dickins had been chosen by the CPR in 1940 to direct the operations of the Atlantic bomber ferry service.

Dickins was personally congenial, but he possessed his own peculiarities. In the north he was known as the Beau Brummel of the bush. Lean and handsome, he flew in a deerskin jacket with matching breeches fitted into gleaming high-top boots, his jet-black crew cut encased in a leather helmet. In winter he wore an Eskimo parka and enormous fur gauntlets made to his own specifications. To the mechanics he was a martinet, extremely fussy about the planes he flew, a quirk that perhaps had aided his survival—for the north does not tolerate mistakes.

Dickins brought to his administration of Canadian Pacific Airlines his meticulous regard for detail, plus an abiding devotion to economy. Grant McConachie did not share Dickins' dedication to the purse strings of the CPR.

As Harry Porteous, McConachie's chief clerk and later airline treasurer, said, "Once the CPR moved in, Grant defined success as expanding the airline rather than making money. If there was any money left over at the end of a year, I think he had the feeling he should have used it up in extending the routes."

Thus, in the early years of CPA, Dickins' strangle-hold on the CPR moneybag was to frustrate and infuriate McConachie. Vaughan Perry, who was in charge of the CPA base at Whitehorse, Yukon, remembers the situation well:

"Dickins was a prince in most ways but where company bucks were involved, he had a reputation for deep pockets and short arms. So when Windsor Station got alarmed by the mounting losses of the airline and ordered tight economies, Dickins was right on their wave-length.

"First the word came down that any expenditure over a hundred dollars had to get prior approval by mailing a Form 175 (purchase order) to Dickins' office in Windsor Station. As things got tougher, Dickins kept tightening the strings. The hundred dollars was trimmed to fifty, then twenty-five. Finally we got the order that *every* purchase had to get the Dickins okay, regardless. This was an impossible situation, as anyone could see.

"When McConachie came up the line on inspection I told him flatly I couldn't run the base that way. Our bus breaks down, for instance. What do we do? I said, do we route-march the passengers and their baggage to the airport until we get that precious Form 175 to Montreal and back?

"Grant just grinned. Then he looked thoughtfully at the huge pile of coal we had on the base. 'I'd be surprised if even Punch has had time to count all those lumps of coal.' That's all he said, but I got the idea. From then on whenever I needed a rush item, like a new tire for a vehicle, I'd sell off enough coal to make the deal. We also developed a lively trade in gas and oil from the base 'drum farm.'"

On policy, however, McConachie was able to exert influence through Neal's powerful voice on the airline's board of directors.

"Because of the high operating costs and tremendous losses that were being incurred in the northern operations, I persuaded Mr. Neal that we should operate year-round with big efficient wheel-planes down the Mackenzie," McConachie said. "So the CPR appropriated the money to build airports at Fort McMurray, Fort Smith and Yellowknife. This was so successful that we carried it on into the Pickle Lake and Red Lake areas of northern Ontario."

The airports on the Mackenzie were soon to be justified by another important military project for the defense of Alaska. The United States needed aviation gasoline in Alaska to fuel the growing squadrons of warplanes based there. They decided to tap the oil fields at Norman Wells on the Mackenzie, 1,400 miles north of Edmonton, by building a pipe-line across six hundred miles of mountainous terrain to serve a refinery at Whitehorse. CPA provided the air supply for this formidable task.

Many years later, McConachie was to pay a sincere tribute to the CPR for its financial support in sustaining air service to the northern communities during the difficult war years and for its legacy of privately-financed airports.

"The CPR did a tremendous job in northern Canada and never received any credit for it," he said.

The CPR was also open-handed in its support of the air war program. The corporation organized the Atlantic ferry operation in the summer of 1940 and ran it successfully for fourteen months until the Royal Air Force took it over. From the spring of 1940 until the end of March in 1945 CPA personnel operated seven flying schools and five overhaul plants for the British Commonwealth Air Training Plan, with all the profits returned to the government.

28. THE PATH TO THE PRESIDENCY

"Get that Goddamn McConachie down here! By air!" The voice of W. M. Neal rasped through his secretary's intercom box in Windsor Station, headquarters of the CPR. Recently elevated to the post of senior vice-president of the great corporation, Neal now occupied a spacious office in the ancient stone edifice in downtown Montreal. The spark that had ignited his explosive ire was a feature article in the Toronto *Telegram,* now spread across his desk. Here the writer had quoted a disclosure by McConachie of the heavy operating losses of Canadian Pacific Airlines.

This was outrageous. Not even the president of the CPR had ever presumed to reveal to the press such details of the corporation's finances. It was none of their blasted business.

Later the CPR was to develop an enlightened public information policy, but in the era of the forties the zipped lip was mandatory in all ranks, inspiring one frustrated newsman to speculate, "I don't think they even tell each other what's going on."

When Grant McConachie reported to Windsor Station, he was greeted by Dickins and his airline associates with the embarrassed solicitude usually reserved for a resident of death row. They knew his career was dead. All that remained was for Neal to pronounce the coroner's verdict.

Grant himself, being familiar with the top vice-president and his whiplash methods, had braced himself to go along with this gloomy prophecy. During his thirty-five years with the railway Neal had become known and feared as a tough irascible driver of men, as hard on himself as anyone on the payroll. His venomous tongue, no-excuse stance and ruthless firings were the gossip of the smallest whistle stops. Barney Phillips described him in appearance and methods as "very much like Mussolini . . . but, hell, beside him Il Duce was a powder puff . . ."

Such was the top VP in Canada's greatest corporation whom McConachie had had the ill fortune to antagonize.

His progress along the marble corridors of Windsor Station's executive row, the processing past two secretaries, the long wait in the ante-room, then the eventual entry through the heavy oak door into the hushed opulence of the senior VP's sanctum might well have unnerved most offenders summoned for rebuke. As McConachie stood silently before the massive throne-desk the great man went on attending to the papers on his side-table. The offender's survey took in the bronze telephone, the eighteen-switch intercom console, the gold pen set on the ivory base, and Neal himself. He did resemble Mussolini, McConachie decided—compact, exuding controlled energy, egg-bald except for the fringes of grey at the temples, firm jaw line, bristling dark eyebrows, square-set shoulders sheathed in executive blue.

When Neal suddenly swivelled angrily to confront his visitor, he was surprised to see that McConachie wore an unrepentant grin, with no sign of the trembles.

"Young man! What do you think our directors are going to say when they read this newspaper story about all the money the airline has been losing?" Neal flung a copy of the offending *Telegram* piece across the desk, stepping up the candlepower of his glare.

McConachie glanced casually at the already-familiar article, then smiled at his inquisitor.

"I suppose they won't be very happy about it," he replied. "But they should be."

"What the hell should they be happy about?" Neal bellowed, half rising from his swivel chair.

McConachie later admitted that he was telling himself he could always go back to flying on his own. But he refused to abandon his convictions.

"How would they have liked to see a head-line and story berating the CPR as a robber baron stealing from the people of the north by charging them excessive rates for air service?"

"Just what do you mean by that?" Neal was incredulous.

"I mean that that is the story the reporter had obtained in his tour of the northern communities. That's the story you and the directors would be reading in the *Telegram* if I hadn't shown him our ledgers."

Neal was thoughtful for a few moments.

"Now that we're on the subject, Grant," he went on. "What the blazes is wrong with our airline? Why should we be losing so *much* money? Sure, I know about the closing down of the mines, the problems getting equipment, but I can't see us losing our shirts like this."

"I think we may have to live with our losses until the war is over. But the long-range answer is obvious to me," McConachie spoke with assurance, warming to his subject.

"I should know; I went through the same wringer with United Air Transport and Yukon Southern. There's no way the bush plane on floats and skis can break even. Too small and unreliable to make it. The economics don't work out. You've seen what can be done since we've put landing strips and wheel-planes down the Mackenzie. What's more, in our hundred-plane fleet we've got twenty types and fifteen makes of engines. That runs our maintenance and pilot-training costs sky high."

"So what's the answer? We can't go on losing money like this forever."

"There's only one solution." McConachie was emphatic. "Get rid of the short-haul bush routes. Hand them back to the original operators. Concentrate on the main runs, to the Yukon and down the Mackenzie. Fly only on wheels, year-round with big fast planes, and get into the international picture."

The discussion in the office of the senior vice-president continued. The ante-room on the other side of the oak door buzzed with whispered speculation. This was no ordinary execution. It should have been short, explosive enough to be heard through the door, and terminated by the abrupt expulsion of the culprit.

At length Mr. Neal's door opened.

The stocky vice-president himself emerged, a friendly hand clapping McConachie on the shoulder.

"It's been most interesting, Grant," he was saying. "I like your ideas. As you were saying, there's not much trimming we can do till the war's over, but I think we should start some studies right away . . . I'll see that you get down here more often . . ."

He didn't realize it then, but that interview put Grant McConachie on the path to the presidency.

CPR had high hopes for their future in air transportation. This had been revealed in March 1942, just two months after CPA was formed, when Neal had said in a speech to CP staffers:

"The Company now controls a commercial aviation system which serves the central and northern sections of Canada, with terminals on the Pacific and Atlantic oceans as well as the Arctic Ocean . . . these services are highly elastic and permit a tremendous expansion, both as to interior operations and trans-ocean routes.

"Just what forms this expansion may take is at present a

matter of speculation, but you may be assured that Canadian Pacific will not fail to take advantage of any opportunity to maintain a position of preeminence in world transportation. . . ."

It soon became clear that the CPR's ambitions for an air empire were on a collision course with government policy. In April 1943, Mackenzie King, the Prime Minister of Canada, made an air policy statement—"TCA will continue to be the instrument of the government in maintaining all transcontinental air transport services and in operating service across the international boundary lines outside of Canada . . . TCA is the sole agency which may operate Canadian international services . . ."

CPA president L. B. Unwin and his general manager, Punch Dickins, proceeded to mount a powerful propaganda campaign against this declaration, appealing directly to the public. They prepared a brief that traced the CPR's historic interest in aviation back to 1919, recounting its pioneering participation in the first prairie air services and in the development of northern aviation. It noted that to date the CPR had invested $8 million in the northern air services and suggested that this was probably more than the government had put into TCA.

The brief then launched a frontal attack on the government's domestic and international aviation policies. Within Canada, the argument went, CPA must have access to large population centres to support its extensive thin-traffic-density lines in the north. Here the brief stated: "Today CPA is virtually as large as TCA in most respects and is rendering far more vital air transportation service than that provided by the publicly-owned airline which essentially parallels existing surface transport."

Opposing also the government's designation of TCA as the "chosen instrument" in international aviation, the CPA brief claimed that "by not using the experience, facilities and world-wide organization of Canadian Pacific, which has carried a great part of Canada's trans-ocean traffic for the past 60 years, it would seem that the country as a whole will suffer materially . . .

"If equity and justice have any place in the Canadian Government's plan, Canadian Pacific should be allowed to carry traffic in the air to supplement its long-established sea routes."

This bold attempt to subvert the government's air policy assailed the nostrils of C. D. Howe like the stench of a polecat. The reaction of the tough-minded minister of transport was typically abrupt and forceful. In March 1944 he rammed through a government order which amounted to a death certificate for Canadian Pacific Airlines. It decreed:

"Steps will be taken to require our railways to divest themselves of ownership of airlines within a period of one year from the ending of the European war. Transport by air will be entirely separate from surface transportation."

Gloom prevailed in Windsor Station and deepened as the war ended on August 15, 1945 and CPA's twelve-month countdown began. There seemed little hope of a reprieve. Yet early in 1946 Neal had himself elected president of Canadian Pacific Airlines; then, three months later he summoned Grant McConachie to Montreal with the title, assistant to the president, and with virtual jurisdiction over the airlines. (Punch Dickins was given the innocuous title of Director of Northern Development, a large office, and no authority. He soon resigned to take up a successful new career with de Havilland of Canada helping to direct the design, manufacture and marketing of bush planes.)

The new team of Neal and McConachie was successful in deflecting the axe of the Ottawa executioner, which lopped off a number of the smaller regional air services but left the main CPA route structure intact.

With the retirement of D. C. Coleman, W. M. Neal was elected president and chairman of the CPR. Six days later, on February 7, 1947, Grant McConachie became president of

Canadian Pacific Airlines. The bush pilot's rise through the corporate ranks had been meteoric. He was thirty-seven.

Now McConachie was able to start working on international expansion.

He began his campaign at home with the Canadian Government. It required the full voltage of his persuasive power to convince C. D. Howe that he should consider breaching the government's declared "chosen instrument" air policy so that the private airline rather than the national carrier might be allowed to fly the Pacific. He treated the gruff hard-nosed cabinet minister to a touched-up rerun of the great-circle-to-the-Orient spiel—complete with the globe and the string—that he had previously employed to such good effect on the directors of the Imperial Oil Company.

Howe seemed impressed but was non-committal until he checked with TCA president Symington. The government airline wasn't in business to squander the taxpayer's money, Symington decided. Let CPA have the Pacific. So Howe decreed that McConachie could fly his dream route to Shanghai on two conditions: 1. That he buy North Star aircraft from the Canadian manufacturer, Canadair, thus supporting home industry; 2. That he also serve Australia for reasons of British Commonwealth prestige and solidarity, since the Aussies were already flying to Canada. Obviously, it was time for McConachie to visit Australia.

29. WINGS ACROSS THE PACIFIC

"Ladies and gentlemen . . . Welcome aboard Pan American Clipper Flight to Honolulu, Fiji and Sydney, Australia. Our flight time to Hawaii will be ten hours and twenty-five minutes. . . ." The voice of the purser crackled from the PA speaker in the first-class cabin as Grant McConachie reclined his seat and watched San Francisco's Golden Gate bridge recede behind the wing of the DC-4.

It was mid-November 1948, and the thirty-nine-year-old president of Canadian Pacific Airlines was in a jubilant mood. He was off on a diplomatic mission to Australia to obtain an operating license for the airline's first overseas route. Beside him sat Hugh Main, his sales and traffic manager. In the two seats ahead were Wally Townley, general manager of operations for CPA, and Ian Warren, traffic manager of the CPR. Warren had been instructed to make the trip to introduce McConachie to CP's long-established steamship staff in the South Pacific.

"We're on our way, Hugh," McConachie exulted to his seatmate as the airliner climbed for altitude. "It won't take long to get through the formalities with the Minister of Civil Aviation in Australia, Drakeford, then early next year I'll hop over to Tokyo and Shanghai to set up arrangements for our Orient run."

"That's great, but what about revenue?" Main put in. "Perhaps Symington was smart in passing up the Pacific. We'll have to fill a lot of seats. The fare will be over twelve hundred dollars Canada-Australia return, about the same to Tokyo and back. That's a pile of money. Is there enough business across this big puddle to make it pay?"

"Well, that's going to be your job, Hugh. I figure the C-4 will run us about five hundred dollars an hour, direct and indirect operating costs, so figuring thirty-seven air hours Vancouver to Sydney on the average, we'll need $18,500 revenue to break even. At $685 fare one-way, that means twenty-seven passengers to cover our cost, and we're putting in thirty-six seats. But with cargo revenue I calculate we can make it with twenty-one passengers, a sixty per cent load factor."

"That's a hefty load factor, especially on a new service. So what happens if we get less than break-even loads?" Main asked.

"The CPR has to haul a few more boxcars of freight to make up our losses," McConachie smiled. "I told the directors to expect us to lose our shirts on the Pacific for maybe ten years until we'd built up these routes. They're still better off than replacing the White Empresses. Ships have no future on these long hauls. Too slow. Too expensive.

"I'll tell you my philosophy of this airline business," McConachie said, gazing at a balloon of pipe smoke as it swirled into a cabin vent overhead. "Make the big decisions, and the details will fall into line. If I had fussed around with market studies and cost ratios I'd still be hauling fish out of Peter Pond Lake, or perhaps I'd even still be selling socks in the Hudson's Bay store. We've got to expand while the options are open. If we wait till the new routes prove out, we'll be too late. Others will be ahead of us." He puffed thoughtfully on his briar.

"Do you realize that by this time next year we'll be serving

both Sydney and Hong Kong!" McConachie waved his pipe
in a great circle arc. "Combined with our domestic runs that'll
be a route pattern of over twenty-four thousand miles! Just
the thought of it puts me in a poetic mood, Hugh. Here's an
idea you can use in your advertising: Canadian Pacific Airlines, wings of the world's greatest travel system . . . flying
from the Northern Lights to the Southern Cross, from the
estuary of the St. Lawrence to the shores of the South China
Sea."

"Sounds poetic, all right, but I'm damned if it'll sell twelve-
hundred-dollar tickets," Main grumbled.

During a two-day lay-over in Honolulu, the CP foursome
luxuriated in the pink opulence of the Royal Hawaiian Hotel
and the November sunshine on the sands of Waikiki Beach. As
they floated in the Pacific surf McConachie reminded Main of
their conversation in the Clipper cabin.

"You may be right, Hugh," he said. "My poetic bit about the
Northern Lights and the Southern Cross won't sell tickets, but
this will. Sun, sand and surf. That's our product. We'll get
Hawaii traffic rights, then watch our frozen fellow-Canadians
flock over here in the winter. I've got another idea, too. We'll
throw in a twenty-four hour expense-paid stop-over in Hawaii
en route between Canada and Australia. That should flummox
the competition. They fly right through."

During the long overnight flight from Honolulu to Fiji with
a fuel stop at Canton Island McConachie meditated on the human achievement represented by this routine air crossing of the
Pacific. It was over this same route twenty years before, he
mused, that the Australian pioneers, Kingsford-Smith and Ulm,
had piloted their tri-motored Fokker, *The Southern Cross*.
This had been their longest hop, Hawaii to Fiji. He tried to
imagine their ordeal as they shared the controls of the creaky
monoplane for thirty-four hours of unbroken flight across the
featureless ocean, fighting through tropical storms, drenched

and half-frozen in the leaking cabin, and finally groping for the tiny target of Suva.

He thought also of Pan Am's Captain Musick who had surveyed the commercial air route to the South Pacific in the famous Samoan Clipper in 1937 only to be killed a year later when his flying boat crashed near Pago Pago. It was not until 1940, a full twelve years after the *Southern Cross* epic, that commercial air service had been established across the South Pacific.

Now, eight years later, Grant McConachie was sure that, like the pioneers, he, too, was making a significant contribution to air progress by spreading the wings of Canadian Pacific half-way around the world.

Meanwhile, no such pleasant thoughts were being enjoyed by Ian Warren, the rail member of the CP foursome on the flight to Australia. A twenty-eight-year veteran of CPR service, he shared with most railroaders of his vintage a vigorous antipathy to even the notion of flight. He had embarked on this (his first) air trip only as a result of a direct order from the president of the CPR, and he seemed determined not to enjoy it. As Hugh remembers, "On the ground Ian was a warm, witty chap with a puckish grin. In the air he was more like an unwrapped mummy. When we took off from Honolulu for the overnight hop to Fiji via Canton Island, Ian was sitting across the aisle from me. He had let the stewardess take his topcoat, but that was all. The rest of us took off our jackets, put on sweaters or dressing gowns, removed our shoes, doused the lights, reclined our seats and got comfortable.

"Not our rail friend. I kept waking up during the night and there was Ian, sitting shock upright, his black Homburg jammed squarely on his head, suit jacket and yellow waistcoat buttoned, tie firmly knotted in his stiff collar, still wearing his yellow kid gloves that were as much a part of his Windsor Station uniform as the grey spats he adopted from October on in Montreal and was still wearing over the South Pacific.

"Every time I woke up I'd say to Ian, 'If you just push that little button there your seat will go back . . .' But he'd only take a tighter grip on the arm-rests and say, 'No, I'm trying something here.' Finally I said, 'Ian, what the hell are you trying?' He said, 'I just want to see how uncomfortable these airplanes can be.'"

The bright expectations with which McConachie and his party landed in Australia were soon dimmed. For days they met with evasions and procrastinations from government bureaucrats on the question of the operating permit for the CPA service. Even a cable from the Canadian Minister of Transport re-affirming the airline's credentials as the "chosen instrument" failed to get action. After two weeks, the Canadian delegation seemed no closer to their objective than on the date of their arrival.

Finally, McConachie was able to confront Drakeford, the Minister of Transport, in his Canberra office.

"I am sorry, Mr. McConachie," Drakeford said, "but we are a government of labor. We are socialists. We believe in government operation of vital public services such as air transportation. That's why we recently put Australian National Airlines off the Pacific and have joined with the British and New Zealand governments in British Commonwealth Pacific Airlines.

"When we made the air agreement with Canada it was our understanding that your government service, Trans-Canada Air Lines, would be designated for the Australia route. This is a matter of principle with us. We don't propose to issue an operating permit to a capitalistic corporation such as Canadian Pacific."

Later, "Crofty," Croft, the senior Canadian trade commissioner for Australia, summed up the debacle of their mission for McConachie and his colleagues in a suite of the Canberra Hotel.

"It's a damn shame you gentlemen have been put to the trouble of flying all the way down here to Australia for nothing," he said. "I can assure you we have laid on all the diplomatic pressure possible, right up to the PM, but aside from straining international relations somewhat, it's had no effect."

"I can't understand why they're so mule-stubborn about this," Townley put in. "After all, there is an air agreement."

"It's a lethal combination of prejudice and politics," Crofty explained. "These chaps are very decent and quite friendly on a personal level. After all, the PM himself has invited us all to a farewell luncheon tomorrow. Some of his cabinet will be there. But that's just a pleasantry; won't make any difference to what you're after.

"You have to understand their background, small town, been nowhere, almost fanatically pro-labour. Ben Chiffley, the Prime Minister, was a driver before he got elected in the socialist sweep. So was Drakeford."

"What's a driver?" Ian Warren interjected. "Does he herd sheep?"

"Nothing like it. They were both in your business, Ian. Worked for the railroad. In Canada you'd call them engineers —driving trains."

"Railway engineers, you say." McConachie set his Scotch on the side-table, fished for his wallet, began searching through an assortment of cards and papers. Suddenly he grinned cheerfully. "All is not lost, fellows," he said. "This luncheon tomorrow may not be a total waste of our time after all."

The atmosphere of the Australian Prime Minister's luncheon for the CP delegation was correct if not cordial, the flow of conversation polite but restrained around the U-shaped table in the maroon executive dining room of the parliament building. McConachie sat on the PM's right, flanked by the Canadian High Commissioner. The assembly included Drakeford, the New Zeland High Commissioner, a few top civil servants and four cabinet ministers, plus a selection of airline and business executives.

Ben Chiffley, the Prime Minister, a large shaggy grey-haired man with John L. Lewis eyebrows, a florid complexion and a rumpled blue pin-stripe suit, impressed McConachie as being a remarkably shy and diffident man for his exalted post.

Later he told his colleagues, "During lunch I got the distinct impression that Chiffley assumed that I was head of the whole CPR, and that I must be a nephew of Sir Edward Beatty or have some such family connection to be at the top so young."

When the burly PM rose to his feet it was to express his regrets in a booming voice. "Our government has not been in a position to meet your wishes," he explained, "but I hope you will understand our views even if you do not agree with them. In any case, we did not want you Canadian visitors to think of us as savages, even if we are socialists, so we have arranged this luncheon to get better acquainted. I am sure, Mr. McConachie, that we are all curious to know how you got to be the president of Canadian Pacific at such an early age, and perhaps you would tell us your story."

"Mr. Prime Minister, honourable ministers, gentlemen," McConachie began. "It may surprise you to know that like Mr. Chiffley and Mr. Drakeford, I am a 'brother of the plates,' a railway engineer, or, as you would say here, a driver. Here is my union card." He held it aloft.

"My father was a railman all his life. I grew up on the tracks and at the age of seventeen was an ash wheeler during school holidays. I worked for the railroad for seven summers, then full-time for a while after finishing high school, working my way up from the ash pits to be a wiper, a watchman, a hostler, a fireman, and finally an engineer. . . ." He went on to regale his astonished listeners with anecdotes of his railroad career, then told of his struggles for survival in bush flying, culminating in his emergence as a CP executive.

As he spoke he could sense new warmth in his labourite listeners. He found the Australian politicians amazed and de-

lighted to learn that in Canada, and particularly in the great
Canadian Pacific organization, a man could rise from the ash
pits of the rail yards to become a top executive, even as they
themselves had come from humble origins to the highest political offices in the land.

As McConachie concluded his speech, the Prime Minister
leapt to his feet to shake his hand. "I welcome you, Mr.
McConachie as a brother of the plates," he grinned. "We had
no idea you were one of us—and I must say this puts a new
complexion on the situation. We have enjoyed your remarks
this afternoon, and I believe I can assure you that Mr. Drakeford may have some good news for you."

After the luncheon and a brief conference between the PM
and the Minister of Transport, McConachie was invited to
Drakeford's office where Canadian Pacific Airlines was issued a
temporary operating permit, "while this whole question is
being reviewed." (Many years later, CPA was still flying to
Australia on the same "temporary" permit.)

One of his close associates observed that Grant McConachie
was never happier than in the midst of a party but had a
shrewd talent for using such convivial occasions to advantage.
Such an event followed the unexpected success in Canberra, as
reported later by Hugh Main.

"Back in Sydney, Grant suggested a celebration, so we piled
into a hack and sniffed out a hideaway called Double Bay.
Drinking happened to be illegal in Australia at the time, but
the place was so jammed we had to stand at the bar where
we couldn't help noticing there were some very attractive
dollies on the premises, all escorted.

"Grant surprised me by remarking in a loud voice that it
would be great to hire some Australian girls as stewardesses,
but he didn't suppose they would be interested in flying the
Pacific with a Canadian airline.

"In a few minutes, as we sipped our drinks, sure enough

a young girl came over and, boy, if you ever saw a dream walking, she was it—glistening black hair, big dark eyes, lovely complexion and a figure to stop traffic.

" 'Pardon me,' she said, 'but I couldn't help overhearing your remark about Australian girls as stewardesses. My name is Pamela Hookham and I would just love to fly with your airline.'

"Well, before you knew it, Grant and I had joined the table, met her friends, and Grant was launched into some exciting yarns about flying in the Canadian north. They were fascinated. It was great fun, but it helped the airline, too. Pamela and a lovely blond friend, Shirley, came around to the hotel the next morning for formal interviews, and Grant instructed me to note their biographical details and addresses 'for Company purposes only.'

"Later, back in Vancouver, he told Reg Sargeant, in charge of in-flight service, it might be a good idea to hire some Australian stewardesses for the Pacific run. 'Fine,' said Reg, 'I'd better go down there and look into it.' 'I've saved you the trouble,' McConachie chuckled. 'Get their names from Hugh Main.'

"It worked out perfectly. Both girls were CPA stewardesses for a number of years. Pamela had been the Jantzen bathing-suit model for Australia. Whenever the Waikiki girl-watchers saw her on the beach in her yellow-silk strapless swim suit they knew the CPA flight was going through."

Before returning to Canada, McConachie and his companions flew across the 1,300 miles of the Tasman Sea to Auckland, where a permit for CPA to fly the Canada-New Zealand route was readily granted on the precedent of the Australian approval. The air crossing of the Tasman in 1948 was a ten-hour journey in a Solent flying boat operated by Tasman Empire Airlines. This tedious, squirmy ocean-watching ordeal did nothing to convert Ian Warren to air travel, particularly when he learned that on the previous flight head-winds had caused a fuel crisis. The Solent had reached its destination only after all of the cargo and the passengers' baggage had been tossed overboard into the Tasman to lighten the load.

30. NORTH TO THE ORIENT

Shortly after 2 P.M. on the hot sultry afternoon of August 30, 1945, a silver C-54 aircraft with "Bataan" emblazoned on its prow dipped a wing over Mount Fuji, spiralled into a long descent and landed at Yokohama's Atsugi Airfield. Wearing dark glasses and an open-necked shirt, his corncob pipe clenched at a jaunty angle, General Douglas MacArthur, master of the Pacific, strode from the airplane to begin his occupation of Japan.

The triumphal procession of the Commander in Chief and his entourage in ancient automobiles, including a wheezy fire engine, drove to Tokyo through a former industrial area bombed to dust. The capital itself was a wasteland of shanties built of rubble on the ruins, except for the area of hotels and office buildings in the vicinity of the Imperial Palace, which was virtually intact.

Here MacArthur installed GHQ SCAP, General Headquarters of the Supreme Commander for the Allied Powers, in the twelve-storey Dai-Ichi Insurance Building alongside the outer moat of the palace. Here was the fountainhead of all political and military power in Japan, a vast complex entirely dominated by the aloof and lordly Supreme Commander MacArthur.

Three years and four months later, early in January 1949,

Grant McConachie arrived at Tokyo airport on a Northwest Airlines flight on the second major diplomatic mission of his career. His assignment was to obtain for Canadian Pacific Airlines the operating permits to begin a scheduled air service from Vancouver to serve Tokyo, Shanghai and Hong Kong. To succeed, he had to win the approvals of General MacArthur, Chiang Kai-shek and the Governor of Hong Kong. He was accompanied on this mission by the World War One flying ace and famed bush pilot, Wop May, whose CPA title was Director of Northern Development, but who was along because of a personal contact that might be useful in Shanghai.

The two were fortunate to obtain scarce accommodation in a hotel, also named Dai-Ichi, which had been built in 1940 to house visitors to the Olympic Games for which the Japanese had been preparing when they launched a war instead. The designers must have anticipated lilliputian guests, for the Dai-Ichi's rooms and facilities were small even by Japanese standards. As McConachie recalled,

"Both Wop and I were over six feet, but the beds were about five foot five. The wash basins were so low we had to kneel to use them. In the bath tub my knees were beside my ears. I had to duck through doorways. The menu relied heavily on raw fish. It was all a joke for the first few days because we didn't expect any problem in getting our permit and pushing on to Shanghai in a hurry."

Wrong again.

Three weeks later the two bush pilots were desperate. The melange of midget quarters, raw fish and frustration were too much. In McConachie's words,

"I had no idea there were so many generals in the entire United States Army, but I saw them all during those weird weeks in Tokyo. We would need a food permit for staff and passengers. A general looked after that; fuel for the aircraft, another general to see; permit to export money, the general in charge of financial administration; another general for radio permit; yet another for housing and office space, and so on. Every one of those generals gave me the same answer. See MacArthur first.

"Our Canadian ambassador to Japan, Mr. Norman, had a regular meeting with the Supreme Commander every Thursday, and every Thursday he would try to get me an appointment without success. It was getting on to the end of January and I was beginning to think I was in Japan for the year. So were my directors. Every night I was sending a cable to Windsor Station, 'Nothing today,' and of course there's no better way to upset CPR headquarters than reporting you have accomplished nothing today.

"Finally, the break came. Mr. Norman phoned to report that I had a fifteen-minute audience with the Supreme Commander at six P.M. on the following Wednesday. Fifteen minutes. For the next six days I went over and over my presentation, trying to get it all compressed into fifteen minutes. I wrote down all the points, CPA's designation by the Canadian Government, the importance of the additional transport capacity to the economy of Japan, the list of permits we would need and so on.

"I was told to report at four in the afternoon of that fateful Wednesday and soon found out why. They screened me on the first floor of the Dai-Ichi Building, then cleared me to the second floor where they probed into my ancestral history until five o'clock. They seemed mildly perturbed because I didn't know who my grandmother's parents were. I figured if I had to work my way up twelve floors at this rate I'd never make it, but finally I was promoted to the sixth where they checked me for firearms, then boosted me direct to the twelfth.

"A portly self-important colonel presided at the appointment desk in the ante-room of General MacArthur's office. He checked my name in his book, then looked at his watch, reminding me of those precision military operations in the movies. 'The time is now seventeen hours, forty-five minutes, fifty-three seconds,' he said. 'You will be ready to go in in exactly fourteen minutes, seven seconds.' For some reason this countdown, after days of preparation, made me nervous. As I sat on the edge of a big leather chair I suddenly realized that my carefully-rehearsed fifteen-minute speech had gone right out of my head. I couldn't remember a thing. My mind was blank.

"I made a grab for my notes, spilling a pipeful of tobacco into my briefcase and making a mess of the papers. By the time I got my spiel sorted out again the Colonel was saying, 'You will be ready to go in in exactly one minute, Mr. McConachie.'

"By this time I was visualizing what to expect . . . probably a huge desk stacked with important documents, the General frantically signing papers between calls on direct lines from world capitals, the whole office bustling with activity. This was the power base for all of Japan and much of the Pacific.

"I was ushered into a spacious but plain living room with a highly polished desk, one telephone, no papers in sight, a small window looking out on a wall, brown broadloom rug, and a big crumpled leather divan beside a glowing fireplace. (I was to learn later that the General had selected this back room which the Japanese insurance executives had used for storage, while assigning his aide a much larger office with a view of the palace.)

"As I entered, a big handsome and jovial man lunged from the leather desk chair to shake my hand warmly. 'Good afternoon, Mr. McConachie,' General MacArthur said. 'I'm very glad to see you. Come and sit down.'

"He showed me to the leather sofa and we sat in front of the fireplace. He seemed in no hurry. 'Well now,' he said, 'you're from Canada.'

" 'Yes,' I said, 'I am representing Canadian Pacific Airlines.'

" 'Canadian Pacific,' he said, tamping some tobacco into a large long-stemmed corn-cob pipe. 'If you'll just put your ships

back on the Pacific here, I'll give you a charter to keep them
busy for the next three or four years. We are very short of
shipping. Why not move them over from the Atlantic? We'll
pay the charges through the Panama Canal . . .'

"I kept trying to interrupt to get on to my airline pitch, but
he went on about ships. 'When you get back to Canada,' he
said, 'you tell your people I need shipping here. We need
supplies, we've got families and their furniture to move.' As
he talked on about this I was getting slightly frantic because
now I had only ten minutes left and hadn't got in a word of
my presentation.

"After he had talked at some length about shipping and
Canadian Pacific, he offered me some of his Hudson's Bay
Mixture tobacco, and this started him off on the Hudson's Bay
Company, how they had pioneered the northern fur trade, then
built retail stores, and what a wonderful blend of tobacco this
was . . . By now I had only five minutes left and I was in a
mild panic trying to listen to him and at the same time figure
what parts of my fifteen-minute speech I could cut out.

"Without a pause he began to tell me about the engine
trouble he was having with his DC-4. At least we're finally
on aviation at last, I thought. But there was still no chance to
talk about permits. He was telling me about the engines back-
firing and what did I think was the solution to this problem.
Well, it seemed obvious to me that the engine manufacturer
was the one with the solution and I wasn't the one to fix it
for him, especially with just three minutes left to present
Canada's case for an air service to Japan, but I wanted to get
it over with, so I quickly told him we had had similar trouble
with our engines and found the spark plugs were running too
cool in long-range cruise power. We had corrected the back-
firing by installing hotter-running plugs.

"Both of us were sitting there drawing on our pipes like a
couple of pensioners on a park bench, except that I had a bad
case of the fidgets. The General was gazing into the fire.

'Canadian Pacific Railway,' he said, 'a great corporation.'
(This I knew.) 'I've taken the CPR train to Banff and Lake
Louise . . . have never seen a more beautiful place anywhere
in the world . . .' My fifteen minutes was up, but he rambled
on about the wonders of the Rockies while I was deep in gloom
because I had missed the big opportunity and there was no
telling when, if ever, I would get another interview.

"Suddenly the great man looked at his watch. 'I've got to go
to an embassy dinner tonight,' he said, 'I'm awfully sorry I
can't spend more time with you, Mr. McConachie, but when
you get back to Canada say hello to General McNaughton,
and if you can get those ships for us I'll give you the char-
ters . . .'

"I realized I had nothing to lose by now, so I said, 'I'll
do that, General, but I came here on another problem. My
airline is planning to fly the Pacific as the Canadian flag carrier, and we'll need a lot of permits to operate to Japan.'

"'I don't think you have a problem,' he said. 'You see
General Wedemeyer downstairs at nine tomorrow morning and
it will be all fixed up. Don't worry about the permits.' He
shook hands and I left, with the impression that General
MacArthur was a fine congenial gentleman, but I had serious
doubts about the permits. I couldn't believe they would be
cleared in the morning.

"When I returned to the Dai-Ichi Building at nine A.M.,
however, General Wedemeyer was expecting me. 'You're all
cleared,' he said. 'I have phoned all the generals and all you
have to do is take this document to be stamped by each of
them.' By four that same afternoon I had all my permits and
was ready to leave for Shanghai."

In Shanghai, McConachie and Wop May approached Generalissimo Chiang Kai-shek, head of the Nationalist Government of China. He had come down from his Canton headquarters to confer with his military chiefs on the defense of

the great seaport, which was in the path of the Communist armies sweeping south.

To help their bargaining position, Wop May made a point of renewing his old Edmonton acquaintance with General Morris "Two-Gun" Cohen, now in Shanghai as personal bodyguard to the Generalissimo. Squat, balding, heavy-jowled, Cohen's appearance belied his heroic story. Born in England but exiled to Canada by his family as a sixteen-year-old incorrigible, he had worked on a ranch on the Canadian prairies. From the cowhands he learned how to handle cards and six-guns before touring the west as a pedlar and gambler.

In Edmonton he became a hero to the small Chinese community when he knocked out a burglar who was robbing a Chinese restaurant. It was thus he later came to meet the Chinese Nationalist leader Sun Yat-sen who visited Edmonton in 1911 while on a fund-raising tour of Chinese communities abroad. Sun hired "Two-Gun" as his bodyguard, made him a colonel of the Nationalist Army, and when Sun died in 1926 his will decreed that Cohen be made a general.

Although captured in Hong Kong by the Japanese, General Cohen survived to join Chiang Kai-shek after the war.

It was never established to what extent, if any, the Jewish general of the Chinese army influenced Chiang in favor of the CPA air-rights pitch, for while May was dealing with Cohen, Grant McConachie was working through the more normal channels of the Canadian embassy. One evening the Canadian Ambassador, Tom Davis, invited McConachie to a reception where he met Mme. Chiang. At the end of that evening Davis reported that Chiang had approved the Canadian airline's application to serve Shanghai on a trans-Pacific route.

"It was the easiest permit I ever got, but the least fruitful," McConachie later reflected.

He went on to Hong Kong, where he used the influence of the Canadian embassy to obtain operating and traffic rights, then returned to Shanghai. What he saw and heard alarmed him, as he reported when he returned to Vancouver.

"The situation in Shanghai appeared desperate. Currency was inflating so fast it made you dizzy. The U.S. dollar would be worth a hundred dollars Shanghai today, one thousand tomorrow, two thousand the next day. The printing presses couldn't keep up with the demand for banknotes. Northwest Airlines was flying them in from the United States by the planeload.

"Meantime there were reports that the Communists were winning and would soon be attacking Shanghai. However, our embassy said it was just a rural uprising, a farmer protest, and would soon settle down. Don King, the Northwest Airlines resident manager, thought I was an alarmist. 'Business as usual,' he said.

"I think what bothered me most in Shanghai was the arrogance of the white residents towards the Chinese population. In Calder where I grew up there were people of many races, including Chinese, and everyone was judged as an individual. That white superiority attitude upset me."

Two weeks after his return to Canada, McConachie was at the Vancouver airport to witness the departure of the first CPA plane to fly the Orient route. It was one of two North Star airliners he had leased from the Royal Canadian Air Force to get the new Pacific services going.

Captain Charles Pentland with eighteen company personnel and a spare engine on board flew the plane to Tokyo and on to Shanghai. As they landed they could see fires on the city's outskirts. They soon learned that the Communists were battering the suburbs of Shanghai and would conquer the city in a matter of hours.

Pentland took on fuel, loaded his passengers and departed for Manila just before dark. His was the last plane to leave Shanghai before its surrender to the Communist forces. Northwest Airlines' "business as usual" Don King was captured and held hostage by the Communists for six months before he was allowed to leave on a refugee ship.

Grant McConachie had realized at last his bush-pilot dream of an air route over the top of the world to the Orient. But he knew that without Shanghai and the Chinese mainland, its prospects were dismal indeed.

31. HARD TIMES
AND FORTUNE COOKIES

In the summer of 1949 Canadian Pacific Airlines spread its wings over nearly fifteen thousand miles of ocean on nothing more substantial than Grant McConachie's hunch. No market surveys. No economic projections. There was not even a smudge of tablecloth arithmetic to justify the venture of some $10 million in capital and first-year operating expenditure.

Thus the scheduled air services that gangled from Vancouver 8,400 miles southwest to Australia and 6,500 miles northwest to the Orient were the creatures of a bush pilot's dream—the "great-circle" airway to China—supported only by his conviction that the fabled seaport of Shanghai, commercial gateway to all China, just had to be a great destination.

But even as the first commercial flights took off to ply the freshly-plotted Pacific routes, they seemed financially hopeless. Shanghai and the entire China mainland had vanished behind the Communist curtain early in 1949. More potential revenue had trickled away when Australia's sterling currency slid into devaluation, shrinking by 25 per cent the dollar yield of airline tickets sold down under. And there was more bad news on the horizon. During the second winter of the Pacific services, the anticipated build-up of sun-seeker traffic on the Canada-Hawaii run was effectively squelched by a Canadian Government currency restriction.

But for McConachie the Pacific venture was merely a replay on a more heroic scale of the pioneering air service to the Yukon. He applied to the new overseas routes the same confidence in his own intuition that had inspired him to inaugurate weekly schedules over 1,200 miles of wilderness in the summer of 1937, in defiance of experts who had labelled it economic suicide.

This optimism, which was to remain a source of board-room bemusement during the great expansion years of Canadian Pacific Airlines, appeared to spring from a booster's philosophy and, closer to hand, from McConachie's belief in his own personal Santa Claus.

He once expressed the philosophy in a press interview. "I have always believed in making the bold move first, then the profits will find their way home eventually . . ." he said. "If a route is flyable, it should be flown."

In mid-1949 McConachie needed all of the moral support he could find, of whatever origin. For CPA, the Pacific horizons could not have been murkier. The total complement of passengers booked on the Australia service might have been housed in a cloak-room. Not one customer had been found for the Orient run which was to start in a few weeks.

There was as yet no business or tourist community of interest between North America and the Orient. Japan, under MacArthur, was still in economic rags and tatters. Its nationals were not allowed to travel out of the country, even if they had the resources, and no tourists were allowed in. Hong Kong, the other traffic terminal, was a warren of bewildered refugees, most of them dirt-poor.

In the executive corridors of the airline McConachie alone was unfailingly cheerful. In the words of a colleague:

"In the summer of 1949 the outlook was completely hopeless and the rest of us were secretly convinced the airline was doomed. Grant would take a long pull on his cigar, flash his confident grin and tell us not to worry, something would turn up. As it turned out, of course, something always did turn up, either from dumb luck or because he made it happen. It was incredible!"

However, neither his dedication to the bold move, nor his lucky-charm assurance, nor even the substantial financial backing of the CPR were to liberate McConachie from the penny-pinching legacy of his bush-flying years. Thus, though his far-horizon policy was prodigal and he was personally a free-spender, his daily administration of the airline was a haggle and scrimp affair.

When he convinced his directors, at the end of 1948, that the executive and operational headquarters of CPA should be uprooted from Montreal to the route pattern hub in Vancouver, he was not thinking in terms of a corporate Taj Mahal. He haggled a deal with Crown Assets Disposal, the government's war-surplus corporation, to acquire for $20,000 a million-dollar war plant at Vancouver airport. (In August 1949 CPA moved its fleet, facilities and HQ staff into the vast Sea Island hangar where Boeing had built wartime coastal-patrol amphibians.)

When CPA joined the elite fraternity of international airlines the gain in prestige was not reflected in the salaries of the staff, most of whom continued to rely on the deferred expectations nurtured by the McConachie mystique. A senior officer at headquarters considered himself lucky to subsist on a seven-hundred-dollar-a-month salary and the promise of a brilliant future. Junior officers drew three to four hundred dollars. A salesman was paid two hundred dollars until he found more lucrative employment elsewhere.

Harry Porteous, the treasurer, recalls the occasion he summoned up the courage to broach the subject of a long-overdue pay raise, citing to McConachie the escalating cost of living.

"A year ago," Porteous said by way of illustration, "it cost fifty cents to have new heels put on a pair of shoes. Today the same heels cost seventy-five cents."

"I don't think you have much to worry about, Harry,"
McConachie grinned. "After all, how often do you need new
heels on your shoes?" Then he deftly changed the subject.

The president's parsimony showed in his distrust of commercial advertising and his limited faith in the efficacy of sales
staff. Both of these quirks were traceable to the limitations of
his executive experience—running a monopoly air service to
isolated communities. Once, in the bush days, when a colleague
suggested advertising in the press of a northern community,
McConachie had replied, "Why should we advertise in Fort
St. John when our planes practically fly down the main street?
Besides, how else can they get in and out? The walking sure
isn't good." For similar reasons, and despite his own formidable
talents as a persuader, he seemed incapable of seeing a salesman other than as what he termed "a stomach and glove
man" whose only function was to mollify disgruntled customers via the drink and handshake route.

During the first few years as an international carrier, CPA's
advertising budget was so minimal the ad agencies just couldn't
believe it. In 1950, for example, with a route pattern serving
seventy communities and a gross revenue of nearly $9 mil-
lions, the airline's advertising appropriation for all purposes
was a piddling fifteen thousand. At that, the president insisted on personally scrutinizing and approving each requisition
of a hundred dollars or more. He would approve the budget,
then cancel it a few weeks later after contemplating the revenue sheets, only to reinstate it again later in a whim of
affluence. For some years he employed an advertising manager
who was not only nude of authority but was afflicted with a
mortal fear of flying so intense that he refused to leave the
ground under any conditions.

Both advertising and sales, for McConachie's money, were
poor seconds to word-of-mouth repute. He once said, "We
don't need an expensive staff of commercial missionaries to

preach our gospel. Flying CPA should be like getting religion, with every happy customer a convert spreading the good word."

McConachie employed his favored person-to-person device freely during the first winter of CPA's service to Hawaii on the South Pacific run. Of the 125 passengers from Vancouver to Hawaii that season, forty were the surprised recipients of presidential passes. One morning after a board-of-trade ball, McConachie grinned rather sheepishly over coffee and mused, "I wonder how many passes to Hawaii I gave away last night?"

This give-away program may have been impulsive, but it was in line with his conviction that influential free-loaders, who were only taking up otherwise empty seats anyway, represented the most effective form of propaganda. (It took time, but he was to see the winter when his airline would convey more than seven thousand passengers from Vancouver to the sunshine of Hawaii in a four-month period.)

This sell-by-reputation presidential philosophy showed most clearly in CPA's in-flight service. Reg Sargeant was a $750-a-month catering chef in charge of BOAC's Montreal base flight kitchen when McConachie enticed him on to the CPA payroll for $350 a month and the promise of a fabulous career as Director of In-Flight Service. He selected Sargeant, he told a colleague, because of his apprenticeship in the gracious old-world passenger service traditions of Imperial Airways plus his fearsome reputation as a perfectionist tyrant in flight kitchen and cabin.

He explained to Sargeant that Canadian Pacific was fighting for the market against airlines subsidized by their governments.

"We don't get a sniff of subsidy. What's more, we've got buck-conscious directors breathing on our backs. So there's no hope we can come within miles of our competitors in advertising, ticket offices, sales staffs or flight frequencies.

"But there's one way we can whip them, Reg, and that's your assignment. In-flight service! Write your own budget, but

I want the best service in the sky. I want every one of our passengers to be a *talking* advertisement for CPA."

First to sample the delicious fruits of this were the thirty-five inaugural guests McConachie hosted on the initial Australia flight that took off from Vancouver airport on the morning of July 10, 1949. During their thirty-seven hours aloft on the leisurely return flight over the South Pacific they savoured high living such as few of them had ever known . . . fine imported wines . . . succulent viands . . . the featherbed luxury of fully-reclining "loungeair" seats . . . attentive stewardesses to wipe the beads of champagne from the brows of the dreamily sated air pioneers.

Reporting after arrival in Australia on the inaugural flight a journalist wrote:

"My most pronounced impression of the flight was of unreality. We boarded after breakfast in Vancouver, spent an indolent and pampered day in the sky then surprisingly found ourselves swimming in the moonlit surf of Waikiki the same evening.

"Two nights and a day in Hawaii, then another luxurious day at 18,000 feet, lazing along at 240 mph, then a night-landing at Fiji where a lavish party occupied our attention for some hours.

"The swish of Fijian grass skirts, the memory of breakfast served by fuzzy-topped waiters, were still vivid as we harkened to the distinctive Australian accents in the streets of Sydney the next afternoon.

"It seems to the writer that the opportunity of resting on the beach at Waikiki and in the tropical-lagoon setting of Fiji with expenses included in the fare, when combined with out-of-this-world in-flight service should prove an overwhelming argument for flying CPA."

The dearth of advance advertising and sales effort, nonetheless, was reflected in the meagre passenger boardings as the new Pacific services went commercial. The first revenue flight to Australia carried a pay load of *one* in the person of Pat Reid, a one-time famous bush pilot, now head of Imperial Oil's aviation division for Canada. Reid shared the thirty-six-passenger cabin all the way to Australia with CPA treasurer Harry Porteous.

"You better go along," McConachie had instructed Porteous. "We wouldn't want our entire passenger load to get lonesome."

Harry happily made the return flight northbound with another solitary passenger, a gorgeous Australian girl going back to her husband in Germany.

The South Pacific was to remain for CPA a financial disaster area for years. But CPA's Orient route very soon justified McConachie's belief in his Santa Claus. For, much as the impoverished Yukon run a decade before had suddenly thrived on the wartime contingency of the Alaska Highway construction, the apparently doomed North Pacific route was to prosper from the unexpected bounties of Chinese immigration and U.S. military logistics.

For the cheerful McConachie and his gloomy colleagues, the immigration traffic came as a delightful surprise package.

During the thirties and forties, even the smallest hamlet and almost every urban community across Western Canada had its Chinese cafe and its Chinese hand laundry. The proprietors were naturalized Canadians from China. Their staffs were relatives imported under the provisions of the immigrations laws. There was a constant demand for more relatives from China as rice-bowl labour for these humble but thriving establishments.

To facilitate this movement, there existed in Hong Kong a prospering commercial community of middlemen known as "compradores." They had clandestine connections inside Communist China to locate the relatives and to smuggle them out to Hong Kong for the right price. The compradore service also included documentation and transportation of the immigrants to North America.

A few weeks before the North Pacific service was to start, CPA's traffic manager, Bert Riley, found himself in Hong Kong as McConachie's commercial emissary with the difficult task of selecting a Chinese sales representative. Riley recalls:

"Our office was crowded with candidates for the appointment, all eager for the 'face' of representing an overseas airline. One of them was Bill Wong, a sharp bouncy young man whose father had worked with CP Steamships when the White Empress fleet plied the Pacific. Wong's English was self-taught and I understood perhaps two words in ten, but somehow he got his message across and I appointed him our commission agent. It was the most fortunate decision I ever made in my life."

The wily Mr. Wong contrived to corner the immigration market of the compradores. So every CPA flight out of Hong Kong from the beginning carried a full load of immigrants. There was no economy fare, only first class, and the sponsoring relative, through a compradore, paid the full Hong Kong–Vancouver fare of $798.60 in Canadian funds for each immigrant carried. Each load represented a revenue to CPA of nearly $29,000, less commissions.

Young Mr. Wong was to serve CPA for many years. His English never quite attained the plateau of intelligibility, but he prospered on the CPA commissions.

Nothing in Grant McConachie's experience had prepared him for his first encounter with CPA's Oriental benefactors, the compradores of Hong Kong. Hugh Main, who was with him on the first inspection visit, describes the occasion.

"Bill Wong first took us down a narrow alley between tenements in one of the unsavoury sections of the colony and up a rickety flight of stairs. He gave some kind of a secret knock. A door creaked open to admit us to a small filthy room with a tiny cooking stove in the centre but not a stick of furniture. The walls were ribbed with wooden bunks from floor to ceiling and on every one of those bunks huddled a smuggled immigrant. They were all prisoners of the compradore until he could obtain their papers and herd them on to the plane for Canada."

That same evening Wong escorted McConachie and Main to a compradore dinner he had organized to introduce the president of the immigrant airline. In Main's words:

"When we arrived there must have been a hundred Chinese guests but none were at the dinner tables. They were all in cubicles playing mahjong. Then on signal they trooped to the tables and got busy with the chop sticks. But Bill didn't give us a chance to sit down. We had to pay a formal visit to each table. Close beside us on that diplomatic tour was a waitress with a full bottle of Scotch and a tray of glasses.

"At every one of those ten tables we each had to down a half tumbler of Scotch as a toast to the assembled compradores. We learned all too soon that 'Yum Sing' meant 'Bottoms Up.'

"Well, sir, finally we were allowed to stagger back to our own table, but just as we were picking up our chop sticks everyone in the room got up and left. The banquet was over. Back at our hotel we called room service for dinner."

The Chinese immigration market from Hong Kong proved to be a fantastic fortune cookie for the Canadian airline. It provided a seemingly boundless reservoir of revenue traffic to fill the seats and the coffers of Canadian Pacific Airlines. It salvaged the Pacific operation from the depths of economic disaster.

This was sheer luck. But the other horn-of-plenty that was to pour close to $17 million into the airline's till during the next five years was a direct result of McConachie's initiative and persuasive talent.

By the end of 1949 the Korean War had broken out. Canada was not directly involved in the conflict but had a United Nations commitment in a supporting role, had assigned two destroyers for duty in the Korean theatre and was pondering other means of assistance. McConachie made an inspired pitch to Ottawa: "Assign CPA to provide airlift for American troops and supplies." The result was a contract between CPA and the Canadian defense department.

Between August 1950 and March 1955 more than 39,000 U.S. military personnel filed into the cabins of CPA airliners at Vancouver airport and were shuttled across the Pacific to Tokyo for activity in the Korean war theatre. The airline made 703 airlift flights, most of which returned with loads of Chinese immigrants. Airlift payments from the Canadian Government amounted to $16,839,790.

Although the contract specified only the meagre essentials of military transport, McConachie, with his predilection for "word of mouth" advertising, insisted that the troops get the full first-class champagne treatment. A colleague recalls:

"Grant saw this as a great opportunity to boost CPA's reputation. He reasoned that today's military officer would be tomorrow's executive. 'We want those people talking us up,' he said."

Word of the super-service on CPA airlift flights spread like chain lightning. "Before long," one airline officer noted, "you never saw anyone less than a colonel on our flights."

While junior officers and GI's rode canvas benches and chomped cold sandwiches on the U.S. troop planes, the top brass winged to war feasting on the tender steaks and imported wines of CPA's élite cabin service.

The fortune cookie of Hong Kong immigration and the fortunes of war had once again justified the legend of the McConachie luck. At the same time the abundant revenues from the Orient route provided a launching pad for even more spectacular McConachie initiatives.

32. THE COMET

On the afternoon of September 6, 1949, Grant McConachie occupied a deck chair in the de Havilland guest enclosure witnessing the fourth postwar air show staged by the Society of British Aircraft Constructors at Farnborough Aerodrome, England. A sleek silver airliner flashed overhead in a dazzling display of speed. Yet it flew so quietly that the whoosh of its fly-past was submerged in the spontaneous roar of the crowd's approval.

This was the world premiere performance of the first jet-powered airliner, the D.H. 106 Comet I. The date marked the false dawn of the jet age. (The first U.S. jet airliner was still no more than a sketch on paper and would not fly commercially for another nine years.)

In its Farnborough debut, the Comet rocketed over the spectators at nearly five hundred miles an hour, almost twice the speed of any other airliner flying, yet the sound of its passage was so muted that some observers swore it must have been coasting with power off.

The major airlines were intensely interested, but cautious. The Comet was spectacular but unproven. Not even the vast and venturesome Pan American had made a move. Only the British Government's airline, BOAC, had ordered the jet. The prevailing attitude was wait and see.

But not McConachie. Directly after Farnborough he went
to Hatfield with Frank Lloyd, the D.H. sales director. Lloyd
recalls the occasion:

"When Grant came down from his first flight in the Comet
he took over my job, as it were. He was so high on the jet
that he did the talking while I listened. He became a joy to
all of us around the plant, a total enthusiast. Mind you, when
it came to talking contract he was as sharp and tough as they
come. But by jove he was enthusiastic!"

The joy was more confined back at CPA's Vancouver headquarters when the president returned from England with his
jet enthusiasm still on high burner. Captain Charles Pentland,
director of overseas flight operations, was heard to mutter,
"Don't tell me the boss is sucking on the opium pipe again!"
McConachie's handicap in the vital business of choosing new
aircraft was well known. It wasn't ignorance—he knew planes
intimately. It was just that when he was sold on a new plane
he became even more enthusiastic about it than its designer.

Even Frank Lloyd was harbouring some secret misgivings as
he later confessed. "Honolulu–Vancouver was one helluva
stretch for the Comet I. Its practical range was about two
thousand miles, and beyond that you started shedding pay
load rather drastically. I could never really see the plane as
being very economical on CPA's Pacific routes."

The views of CPA's chief engineer, Ian Gray, were no
secret. He recalled, "I told the boss the Comet would break
the airline. There was no way it could pay its way across
the Pacific. I could have saved my breath. He just wasn't
tuned to my frequency. He had already made up his mind to
go jet."

Indeed, the Comet-doubters did not deter Grant McConachie
in the least. He had spurned scoffers before, when he
launched his visionary airmail service to the Yukon back
in the summer of '37, and again when he spanned the
Pacific to the Orient and Australia. He was now being swept

forward on another tidal wave of conviction that overwhelmed
the quibblings of sceptics and narrow specialists.

But McConachie realized he would need more than mere
enthusiasm to win the approval of his directors for the pioneering jet purchase. The CPA board in 1949 was ruled by a
quartet of steel-eyed executives all reared on the tracks. W. A.
Mather, N. R. Crump, L. B. Unwin and G. A. Walker
between them had spent more than 150 years as railroad
men. They were tough and realistic and abhorred flights of
fancy. Flights of any nature, in fact, were still viewed with
strong, sometimes profane, suspicion. Already the CPR was
carrying an $11-million investment in the air—"and mostly
McConachie's hot air," Walker had grumbled when the board
had approved another $3 million to launch the Pacific routes.

Now McConachie had to persuade these veteran railmen
to plunge another $3 million on a novel untried airliner that
had no propellers and was squirted through the air by the
ejection of hot gas. With the exception of BOAC (which, as
a government airline had no real choice), no other airline
had bought it. Those who knew the CPA directors did not
fancy McConachie's chances.

Montreal, November 28, 1949—A scale model of the
Comet 1-A bearing the CPA "Canada Goose" insignia was
centred on the board-room table in the Windsor Station headquarters of the CPR where a meeting of the airline's directors
was in session. A large wall map of the Pacific displayed
flight-time comparisons of jet against conventional airliner performance over the vast expanses of ocean. In front of each
director lay a brochure with illustrations, performance charts,
and specifications of the only jet-powered airliner in the
world.

McConachie's presentation was low-keyed, forceful, factual.
"In the airline business," he told the directors, "our product
is speed. A big competitive feature is passenger comfort.
On both counts the Comet will put us light-years ahead of

the competition. We're now the underdog on the Pacific routes. We can be on top with the Comet matched against the old-fashioned 6-B's and Constellations." Then came the shaker. McConachie pointed to the Comet model.

"This jet airliner is the most efficient transportation machine in the history of man. Just one of these planes can turn out more transportation at less cost than your greatest ocean liner, the thirty-thousand-ton *Empress of Scotland*." Mather shook his head. Crump squinted his ice-blue eyes. Walker grunted. Unwin looked up from his doodling. McConachie continued as if unaware of the shock-wave agitating the members of the board. "The yardstick of transportation, as you well know, is passenger-miles-per-hour, or pmh. A train with two hundred seats moving at 50 mph is producing 10,000 pmh. The DC-3 aircraft with thirty passengers at 160 mph turns out 4,800 pmh.

"But look what happens at jet speed. The Comet can carry fifty passengers at 500 mph and thus will provide 25,000 passenger-miles-per-hour! This is better than the *Empress of Scotland* with one thousand passengers cruising at 20 mph, producing only 20,000 pmh. The comparison is even more meaningful when you consider that the ocean liner cost nearly three times as much as the Comet and requires an operating crew of 450 compared with a crew of seven on the jet." The directors appeared to be impressed. McConachie paused for effect, then pressed on.

"This year, 1949, will be recorded in history as the start of a new era in transportation. Canadian Pacific has a proud tradition of leadership in transportation. We now have the opportunity to be pioneers of the jet age.

"But there is more than prestige involved. The Comet makes economic sense. I do not believe we can afford to operate anything less than the most efficient air transportation vehicle available. Also, we must bear in mind that air transportation

is a hotly competitive business. We cannot afford to be
second fastest or second best in the air . . ."

A colleague of McConachie, Bob Elsey, who was with
him in Montreal for the Comet presentation recalls, "Before
the directors' meeting Grant got a haircut, put on a freshly-
pressed blue suit, a sincere new tie and off he went to
Windsor Station with his briefcase. When he returned to the
hotel suite later his jacket was open, his hair ruffled, his tie
slightly askew and his shirt was soaked with perspiration.
As he came into the room he flashed a big grin and said,
'Well, I sold the bastards, anyway.'"

No mere transcript of his remarks could convey to the
reader the persuasive power of a McConachie pitch. N. R.
Crump, reflecting in later years on the CPA president's influence on the board of directors, said:

"Grant was able to mesmerize George Walker, a member of
our board, who told me that after a meeting with McConachie
he had to go back to his office to sort out his impressions,
to snap back to reality. Walker once advised the other members of the board that they should make no decisions based
on a McConachie appeal until they had taken time to re-
consider the matter while out from under his spell."

The decision of the airline directors was recorded in the
staid prose of the 1949 Annual Report of the Canadian
Pacific Railway Company:

> To provide more efficient and economical operation, an order
> has been placed for the delivery of two De Havilland Comet jet-
> propelled aircraft which are expected to be in service by 1952.
> These aircraft are particularly suitable for operation over the long
> distances encountered in the Pacific services, due, in part, to their
> considerably higher cruising speed.

Karachi, March 3, 1953—"Comet C-U-N. You are cleared
for take-off." The rasp of tower control in his earphones

snapped Captain Charles Pentland out of his pre-dawn drowsi-
ness and the fatigue of yesterday's flight from London. He
knew he would need all his powers of skill and concentration
for the critical task of taking off in darkness from a strange
runway with this unfamiliar type of aircraft with a maximum
load, including nearly two tons of kerosene in the wing tanks.
On board with Pentland were four other crew members and
six technicians from the D.H. factory. They were on a rather
unusual delivery run.

In planning the first jet air service across the Pacific,
McConachie had been forced into a compromise because of
the Comet's limited range. He had conceded he would have
to base the jet airliner in Australia and operate it up the line
as far as Honolulu to connect there with the piston-powered
DC-6B for the long shuttle to Vancouver. The *Empress of
Hawaii,* the first of the two CPA Comets, would have to
be ferried from England to Australia to start the service.
But it was not intended to be a simple delivery flight.
McConachie ballyhooed it as a record-setter—the Comet was
to establish a new elapsed-time air record from England to
Australia. Great publicity—but, as Pentland put it, "bloody
rough on us cockpit help."

The captains he chose for this assignment were tops in
their trade, both veterans of twelve years at the controls:
Pentland with Imperial Airways and British Overseas Airways, Sawle as a bush pilot in the rugged Canadian north.
Pentland was CPA's manager of overseas operations. Sawle
was chief pilot, overseas.

At the de Havilland aerodrome, Hatfield, England, the CPA
captains took a crash course in flying the Comet. They were
annoyed to find themselves regarded as old-fashioned "wind-
mill jockeys," and novices in the mysteries of jet flight. Some
of the new procedures, they discovered, clashed with flying
instincts formed by many thousands of hours at the controls
of conventional planes. However, after a short course of

ground study and flight instruction, Pentland and Sawle were pronounced qualified for Comet command. Neither had experienced a night take-off in the jet, nor had they flown it heavily loaded. They made preparations to depart from London airport for the flight to Australia.

Thus, Captain Charles Pentland found himself reaching for the throttles in the gloom of the Comet flight deck on a runway of Karachi Airport a few minutes after three in the morning of March 3. As he pushed the throttles forward to take-off position he set the brakes against the surging thrust of the four Ghosts submerged in the Comet's wing roots. Conserve runway by starting the roll at full bore. Without the air-bite of the big props, these gassers were sluggish on initial acceleration, especially when fuelled to the gills like this. In seconds the luminous gauges were clocking take-off rpm. The Comet shuddered with restrained power. Pentland released the brakes. The *Empress of Hawaii* lurched forward to roll down the runway into the pitch blackness that enveloped Karachi Airport.

What happened then inside the cockpit of the CPA Comet? The evidence included a smear of aluminum on the runway surface 1,250 yards from the starting point, and tire tracks in the hard sand of the overrun strip between the far end of the runway and the perimeter fence. This was enough to piece together the story.

As the heavily-loaded jet picked up speed Pentland concentrated his attention on steering a course between the runway lights. Sawle called off the airspeed readings. At 85 knots Pentland exerted firm back pressure on the control column to reduce ground friction by raising the nose wheel off the runway. At this point he made his first error. He should have levelled the plane until the forward wheel was almost skimming the surface. Instead he continued to roll nose-high. The design of the Comet 1-A wing and the shape of the jet's air intakes were such that in this nose-high position the wing drag in-

creased and the jet thrust diminished. Instead of accelerating
to the 122-knot take-off speed, the Comet rumbled on at less
than 100 knots, using up precious runway but gaining no
more speed. Pentland had ignored the procedure he had been
taught during his Comet check-out at de Havilland. At 1,250
yards along the runway the situation was desperate. Pentland
tried to hoist the Comet into the air by pulling the nose up
sharply. The tail scraped on the runway, leaving a smear of
metal, but the Comet continued to hug the ground. Then the
captain must have recognized his error. He pushed forward
on the controls. The plane levelled. The nose wheel came
down. The Comet picked up flying speed. But there was no
more runway. Tire tracks on the sand beyond showed the
imprint of the nose wheel as well as the main undercarriage.
Then the tracks skipped. The Comet was ready to fly. Three
seconds more and it would have been up and away. But
time had run out for the *Empress of Hawaii* and for the eleven
people on board.

A wheel on the starboard undercarriage struck the culvert
of a perimeter drainage ditch. The airliner swerved, staggered,
then plunged into a dry canal used for the run-off of monsoon
rainwater. At a speed of more than 138 mph, the Comet
shattered against the forty-foot embankment on the far side
of the canal. The explosion lit up the entire airport and several
miles of surrounding countryside.

The waking nightmare that follows a fatal crash is the
most dreaded ordeal of an airline president. The numbing
news may strike with the shrilling of his bedside phone in
the deep of night or with the routine buzz of his office
intercom. But it comes in like an exploding grenade. Its
repercussions wreck office routine and make a mish-mash of
normal working schedules in many departments of the airline.

The world press moves in fast on the publicity department
with insistent, relentless demands for information . . . names
and origins of passengers, identities of relatives, biographies

and pictures of crew, details on the aircraft, the flight, the
accident . . . They want it all NOW. Airline traffic personnel
are engaged in the delicate and agonizing task of tracing, noti-
fying and making arrangements for the next-of-kin. Flight
operations are mounting an investigation and dispatching an
aircraft to the scene. Reservations, ticket offices, and switch-
boards are jammed with calls from the concerned and the
merely curious.

But the president squirms in the hottest seat in the airline.
Jangling phones, briefings, urgent conferences, public state-
ments, interviews, decisions . . . the pressure builds on him
around the clock during the crisis. He is further strained by
personal bereavement, the loss of close colleagues. He makes
personal visits to comfort their families. Over it all is the
ultimate responsibility that weighs heavily on the president
of an airline at such a time.

The Comet crash was the fourth air fatality Grant McConachie had had to endure in his presidency. But the crash of
the Comet at Karachi was the cruelest blow of his career up
to that time. To his personal distress—he had lost good friends
—was added the shattering of his dream of pioneering jet
flight over the Pacific.

But the shock of this set-back did not diminish his enthusiasm for the jet airliner. By November of the same year,
1953, he was able to mesmerize his directors into approving
a new order, for three longer-range Comets equipped with
the more powerful Avon engines in place of the original
Ghosts.

Four months later, front-page headlines around the world
announced the unexplained disappearance of a British Overseas Airways Comet while flying with six crew and twenty-nine
passengers over the Mediterranean near the island of Elba.
Two months after that another BOAC Comet went missing
near Naples with seven crew and fourteen passengers. All
Comets were grounded; unless the mystery of the vanishing

airliners could be solved, the pioneering jet would remain suspect.

McConachie arranged for Frank Lloyd of de Havilland to appear with him before the CPR board of directors in Montreal to describe the lines of investigation being pursued by his company and the government agencies concerned. The directors were persuaded to leave CPA's jet order on the books.

The case of the vanishing Comets became one of the most fascinating true science-detective stories on record. The water near Naples was too deep for search, but near Elba the remains of the first Comet were discovered in six hundred feet of water. Using deep dredges and grappling devices, the Royal Navy was able to recover all four engines as well as most of the metal fragments composing the wing and fuselage of the stricken airliner. These thousands of bits and pieces were taken to a hangar at Farnborough, England, where they were sorted, identified and fastened into their proper locations on a full-sized mock-up or tailor's dummy of the original plane.

From a study of the metal fragments, the scientific sleuths were able to deduce that the flexing of the metal skin of the aircraft with pressure changes between sea level and great altitudes had caused a fatigue crack on top of the fuselage just behind the cockpit. The cabin's internal air pressure (necessary in the rarified outer atmosphere of cruising height) had sent the fatigue crack right down the spine of the airliner. Near Elba, explosive decompression had blown the airliner apart.

The price of this lesson was high, as in other pioneering ventures; but the knowledge was applied to modifications of the Comet IIs and was to benefit the design of future jet airliners.

For McConachie there was the sobering implication that if CPA's original Comet had not crashed at Karachi, if it had completed its delivery flight to Australia and gone into service on the South Pacific, it might well have blown apart from explosive decompression with a load of passengers.

33. FIGHTING THE MONOPOLY

There is a hoary vaudeville routine in which a man is going wild with frustration trying to complete a local phone call while in an adjoining booth a succession of callers are connected promptly with Rome, Athens, Cairo, Hong Kong and Singapore. Grant McConachie must have felt like that while developing the route pattern of Canadian Pacific Airlines during the fifties.

Above all, CPA aspired to compete with government-owned Trans-Canada Airlines on the main-line domestic air route linking Vancouver and Montreal. But the Canadian Government was determined to protect the TCA monopoly. The message from Ottawa was loud and clear: Private enterprise need not apply.

What's more, by government decree, TCA had first claim on any *international* routes. But the government's airline didn't fancy money-losers. When Gordon McGregor had taken the controls of TCA, his boss, tough, bluff C. D. Howe, Minister of Transport, had given him only one directive—"You keep out of the taxpayer's pocket and I'll stay out of your hair." This harmonized with McGregor's own Scottish-Presbyterian philosophy. "The function of a government airline," he said frequently, "is to provide safe, reliable air service and to avoid a deficit." He had no yen for marginal air routes, so by default they went to CPA.

This suited McConachie, since his credo was expansionist. "If a route is flyable and available, we should fly it," he said. Later, in retrospect, he was to reflect, "If we had relied on market studies and economic advisers, we'd still be a bush airline."

Thus, in the just over four years to the end of 1957, CPA inaugurated seven international air routes, adding nearly sixteen thousand miles to its route pattern. The CPA service was extended to Mexico Ciy, Lima, Buenos Aires, Amsterdam, Lisbon and Madrid. These brave new ventures were launched from the pad of CPR financial support but propelled by the president's rocket-powered enthusiasm.

The thrust came from McConachie's route-expansion pitches staged in the directors' board room, in government offices, in hotel suites, on the public platform, indeed wherever he could find an audience. The visual aids he used with telling effect were, of course, his faithful inflatable plastic globe and piece of string. When McConachie's name came up in a press interview during this period, his rival Gordon McGregor remarked, somewhat ruefully, "Grant always carries that damned globe in his briefcase. On the slightest provocation he fills it with a mixture of hot air and cigar smoke. Then he sits on it." It was true; no matter how distinguished the gathering, when McConachie's globe-and-string pitch had been made he would open the valve and sit on the globe to deflate it.

The CPA directors showed remarkable faith and foresight in committing millions of dollars to McConachie's hope-deferred air route ventures, but sometimes they were bewildered by it all. On one occasion as they were filing in to the board room, G. A. Walker, the chairman, was heard to mutter, "I wonder which way McConachie is going to stretch the globe today." Another said, "McConachie is the greatest next-year man I've ever met. Things are always going to be terrific next year."

Soon McConachie was up to more tricks with his ever-ready plastic globe. He came up with the then-novel idea of a polar route from Vancouver over the Arctic Circle to Europe. There were delays. He had to find an available destination in Europe, to wait for the government to confer with TCA, and to sort out diplomatic and technical clearances. To McConachie's chagrin, Scandinavian Airlines, inspired with the same idea at about the same time, was first over the polar route with a Copenhagen–Winnipeg–Los Angeles service in November 1954. CPA was second with its route from Vancouver over the polar ice cap to Amsterdam in June 1955.

McConachie's "folly" in flying polar provoked guffaws in government and TCA offices and even the astute Howe grumped that "CPA's planes will be as empty as the regions over which they'll be flying." But the derision was short-lived. The polar route had unsuspected advantages, of which McConachie was shrewdly aware. From the west coast to Europe the top-of-the-world span was a thousand miles shorter than conventional air routes via Montreal or New York. The passenger cheerfully paid the same fare for less flying, thus boosting the airline's revenue yield per mile flown. The publicity-wise president had the slogans ready. Safety? "Flying our polar route you are never more than 100 miles from an airport." (He was counting abandoned wartime ferry-route airstrips and pinching his plastic globe considerably at that.) Flying conditions? "As any northern bush pilot knows, the arctic air holds no moisture, no turbulence, few storms. The visibility is excellent. Weatherwise it's the best route in the world."

Those who ridiculed the economics of the polar route could not see beyond the small puddles of traffic at either end of the actual run. Vancouver? Amsterdam? But McConachie was already sharply aware of what was to become a vital consideration in the future development of global air transportation:

connecting traffic. Via connecting air links, traffic from half a hemisphere could be channelled through the terminal intakes at either end of a cannon-ball air route such as the polar line. Thus goods and people from all over northern Europe could board at Amsterdam for fast direct polar passage to the Pacific coast of North America and onward to the Orient or the South Pacific. In the other direction, Vancouver could take in people not only from that city itself but also from the entire Pacific perimeter, and whisk them by polar pipe-line to Europe.

So, in March 1956 McConachie was able to tell a board-of-trade dinner audience:

"To the surprise of certain experts, the polar route has proved to be very popular from the start. In the first nine months with only one flight a week we have already carried more than two thousand passengers on this service."

It would not be long, in fact, before TCA would introduce its own semi-polar run, the "Hudson's Bay Route" Vancouver–Winnipeg–London. Some years later the government would deprive CPA of the richest rewards of its polar pioneering by granting TCA a Vancouver–London polar route.

Another winner was the Mexico run. In March 1956, just four months after the start of CPA's non-stop Toronto–Mexico service, McConachie told another after-dinner audience:

"Our biggest problem since we started this Mexico service from Toronto last November has been to supply enough flights and enough seats to meet the demand. Our planes have been booked to capacity since the day we started, and when we doubled the service to twice weekly we still had long waiting lines."

In the same speech he announced plans to extend the Latin America line to Buenos Aires, Argentina, and this was accomplished two months later, in May 1956. Soon after, Santiago, Chile, also became a port-of-call on the South America run. The following year he was able to ink in on his plastic globe two more major extensions—from Montreal across the mid-

Atlantic to Lisbon, Portugal; then on to Madrid in the same year.

Thus by the end of 1957 CPA's *White Empress* fleet was plying a 32,750-mile international route pattern and flying the Canada Goose insignia in the skies of twelve foreign countries. The bush route of 1949 in eight years had acquired the prestige —if not the revenues—of a major international airline.

Early flying was once described as hours and hours of boredom interrupted by occasional moments of stark terror. For McConachie this was never true of flying, but in the early fifties it did apply to his increasing involvement with luncheon and dinner meetings. The terror struck when he was called upon to make a speech. As head of the country's most spectacular airline and an air pioneer of some renown, he was much in demand to address service clubs and boards of trade. Though superbly self-assured and eloquent in small gatherings, he confessed that, "I would rather take a sound beating than give a speech."

He recognized, however, that public speaking gave him the chance to influence public opinion, less in terms of the immediate audience than the publicity coverage. So he fought down the panic, perspired over manuscripts, and rose to his feet to blush and stammer through a seemingly never-ending succession of painfully-rehearsed speeches.

With experience gradually came confidence. The panic subsided. He was soon able to imbue his speeches with the freshness and excitement of his own ever-renewed astonishment at the wonders of aviation. He could inject drama into the most mundane occasions, such as the opening of a new runway at the Regina airport when he told the audience:

"I landed here this morning in a forty-passenger three-hundred-mile-an-hour Convair. Twenty years ago I arrived overhead struggling through a snow-storm at eighty-five miles an hour in a four-passenger fabric-covered bush plane. There was only a small tin hangar here and I landed not far from it, only to discover I was sitting in a farmer's field. The startled farmer explained the airport was on the other side of the hangar. So I took off again and set course over the roof of the hangar to the airport.

"To those of us who have lived aviation for more than twenty years, flying on floats and skis and finally wheels, this strip of concrete is the most important piece of real estate in the entire countryside. It is the portal to the skyways from Regina to everywhere."

He enjoyed recounting to city audiences the miraculous transformation of the northern wilderness with the advent of the first bush planes. "In terms of transport, the north moved from the Stone Age to the Age of Flight overnight!"

His own astonishment at the broader impact of aviation on the world came through forcefully during his platform appearances.

"Some three hundred and fifty years ago," he said on one such occasion, "it took Magellan one thousand days to sail around the world. Three centuries later after the invention of steam power, history was made with a voyage around the world in eighty days. Today, after just half a century of aviation, the globe can be circled in eighty hours!

"If Magellan's world could be equated to a watermelon, it took three hundred years and steam power to shrink it to the size of an apple. But in half a century the airplane has shrivelled it to the size of a pea, and in another fifty years will reduce it further to the size of a pinhead," McConachie proclaimed.

Such progress flourished only in an atmosphere of freedom. McConachie expressed this conviction with a fervor that inspired some of his audiences to standing ovations. He saw "free-enterprise democracy" as providing "the ideal climate for original thinking." His public commitment to free enterprise approached that of a zealot. Thus, he told a convention of the Canadian Chamber of Commerce:

"We must not be satisfied merely to recognize the superiority of our free-enterprise system. If it is to survive . . . and to prosper . . . we must also combat the forces working to threaten its very existence . . . We must renew our dedication to free enterprise as a positive and dynamic faith." The enemies were not only "the militant creeds of socialism and communism" but also "the encroachment of government in business and the trend to state control." McConachie called for "vigorous and enlightened efforts to fight these enemies of our freedom."

The president of the private-enterprise CPA left his audiences in no doubt that the most striking example of "encroachment of government in business" was the TCA air monopoly on the main-line route across Canada. He referred to this as "the largest pool of air traffic anywhere in the world monopolized by a single carrier, with one exception . . . RUSSIA."

The ultimate objective of McConachie's campaign was to break this monopoly, but in the early fifties, even he recognized that the cause was forlorn indeed. The only hope for such a drastic about-face in government air policy lay with the Minister of Transport. But he was also the minister responsible to parliament and the people for the success of Trans-Canada Airlines. It was like having the captain of the opposing team as referee.

But when the crusading Conservative John Diefenbaker unexpectedly toppled the federal Liberals from their twenty-two-year pinnacle of power on June 10, 1957, Grant McConachie was jubilant. He believed that with the Conservatives on record in favour of air competition, the chance to crack the TCA monopoly had arrived at long last. And when George Hees, a flamboyant supporter of private enterprise, was appointed Minister of Transport in the new government, the odds for CPA appeared to have shifted to sure-fire certainty. Hees had declared from the campaign platform that like any other business TCA should stand up to competition or go under.

CPA was further encouraged when, soon after taking office, Hees commissioned the noted British air-economist, Stephen Wheatcroft, to make a survey and report on the economic viability of airline competition in Canada. This report was awaited with suspense by monopolist and foe alike, for the findings of a highly-respected neutral could go far to justify or damn duplication of air service on the country's main-line air route.

The British economist found that by the next year, 1958, TCA should be in a position to withstand restricted competition up to four transcontinental flights a day without suffering a deficit.

Thus, the CPA president was optimistic in November 1957 when he submitted to the government a formal CPA application for a license to operate air service across Canada in direct competition with TCA. He was convinced that the Conservatives were committed to competition on principle, and that the public hearings of his application would be no more than a formality.

Thus, in preparing the CPA submission for the Air Transport Board hearing, McConachie saw no reason to depart from the arm-waving, cigar-puffing, plastic-globe style of route expansion that had served him to such good effect in the overseas theatre of operations. He dispensed with economic studies and market research. The proposed CPA route pattern and schedule emerged full-blown as he deliberated with his colleagues in the airline's executive board room at the Vancouver headquarters. It was McConachie's intuition that five return flights a day would be about right. The city-pair pattern should be different from TCA's, so how about Edmonton–Regina–Toronto . . . Vancouver–Calgary–Saskatoon–Ottawa–Montreal . . . Vancouver–Edmonton–Montreal . . . Vancouver–Winnipeg–Toronto–Montreal . . . and, oh yes, better give the capital another . . . Winnipeg–Ottawa–Montreal.

It was only then that McConachie decided it was time to retain an airline economist whose assignment would be to put together traffic estimates to substantiate the revenue inputs required.

The flight-operation's planning was equally casual. Seven DC-6B's from the airline's pool of fifteen would be assigned to the new transcon routes. No spare aircraft would be allocated on the theory that a plane could be borrowed from the overseas pool as required. No overhead charges would go into the transcon budget, which would function on the "added-cost principle." This meant that only out-of-pocket costs would count.

McConachie also theorized that . . . say . . . only one passenger in three flocking to the new CPA service would be drawn away from TCA. The other two would represent new business stimulated by the extra sales efforts, advertising, publicity and facilities of the competition.

The written presentation, while skimpy on research and fact, was impressive in the force and eloquence of its assertions, some derived from the McConachie speech files. Typical was the president's affirmation, "I am firmly convinced that only under competition does the public secure the best service at the lowest price. . . . Competition will benefit not only the public but TCA as well. . . . TCA's monopoly within Canada is the largest non-competitive pool of aviation business in the free world. . . . If this market cannot support competition, there are few in the world that can."

But when the Air Transport Board hearing began on October 20, 1958, it soon became apparent that the hearing was to be conducted in deadly earnest. The three-man board, flanked by its own economic advisers and legal counsel, betrayed not the slightest predisposition in favor of the CPA contention. It was soon also evident that TCA had come to the fray with a thoroughly-researched brief and the services of one of the most formidable courtroom inquisitors in the land, John D. Edison, Q.C.

He roasted McConachie to a frazzle. Edison's ruthless, incisive cross-examination demolished the rhetorical super-structure of the CPA case to lay bare its fragile foundations of assumption, conjecture and hope. Edison ridiculed the added-cost budgeting, sneered at the conspicuous absence of market research, attacked the "unrealistic" scheduling of aircraft, and exposed the inadequacy of hastily-conceived maintenance allowances. On the fourth day of the hearing the conduct of the CPA case was in the hands of Ian Sinclair, the brilliant, towering black-thatched chief legal counsel of the CPR.

Being pulled off the CPA case at the outset of the ATB hearing was for Grant McConachie a public humiliation. He was certainly no stranger to adversity, but now, for the first time in his career, his power of persuasion had let him down. There was no doubt—he had flubbed this one.

But although saddened and considerably subdued, he was still able to manage a rueful grin as a badly-shaken and disarrayed CPA contingent assembled for the first of many sessions in the command headquarters suite Sinclair established in the Chateau Laurier Hotel.

"At least we have one consolation," McConachie quipped, "the only way we can go is up, because we can't go any lower."

Sinclair put up a powerful case. He demonstrated by factual comparison with U.S. airlines that the price tag of TCA's inefficiency was $17 million a year. He attacked McGregor's refusal to adjust to competition. And thus he sought to demolish the claim that a rival air service would cost the Canadian taxpayer dearly in TCA deficits.

His summing-up argument was that "TCA can adjust to competition by abandoning the sheer economic folly of inflexibility and by increasing its efficiency."

It was a heroic try (backed by hard cold facts and figures), but it didn't work.

In its comprehensive report the Air Transport Board refused

to accept statistical comparisons with other airlines as valid yardsticks of TCA's efficiency, concluding that "the Board is not satisfied that TCA's costs are at an unwarranted level."

Its conclusion: "It would not be in the public interest to recommend competitive transcontinental air services in Canada at this time."

However, "to strengthen CPA in the international field by allowing it to penetrate the Canadian market" the Board recommended that the private airline be granted one return flight a day serving Vancouver, Winnipeg, Toronto and Montreal.

The small measure of competition approved was the first crack in the monolith of the TCA monopoly. In the ensuing years, much of Grant McConachie's formidable energy was to be engaged in striving to widen the crack. He would be satisfied with nothing short of full and equal competition.

34. THE IRRESISTIBLE FORCE

Grant McConachie jetted into the sixties at the age of fifty-one in buoyant spirits, fifteen pounds overweight at 205 and smoking twenty cigars a day. His thinning hair had greyed at the temples and under stress his normally tawny complexion sometimes blanched with fatigue. But he retained the almost boyish enthusiasm, the sparkling eyes and the high-voltage personality of his early days.

With two sons, Bill, 20, and Don, 21, an attractive wife and a spacious Shaughnessy district home with swimming pool, the CPA president enjoyed the relaxation of a happy home life in the intervals between business trips. But his frequent and sometimes prolonged absences from Vancouver made him a frustrated family man. He told a reporter he was riding airliners up to 125,000 miles a year, had averaged four hundred miles of travel for every working day over the past eleven years, and was away from home about half the time.

He regretted the gaps in his home life. "I never could attend the PTA or take the boys on camping trips, but when I was home I took an interest in their schooling and their problems. I hated being away so much, but it was a choice I had to make, and I think the family understood."

A milder frustration was his quest for a hobby. Nothing but the airline could hold more than his casual interest. His idea of a great Saturday outing was to mooch through the CPA hangar yarning with foremen and mechanics, poking through planes, examining the sludge from engines in overhaul. He tried golf. For a time he had an under-powered amphibian Seabee aircraft for commuting to a summer cottage on a near by island but found himself taking unwarranted risks in bad weather. His staff dubbed the Seabee "Grant's tomb." Then he experimented with a cabin cruiser until "I calculated it was costing me more per mile than one of our aircraft."

Finally, in 1958 he had found his perfect hobby. He explained,

"The boys were lying around watching TV too much, not getting enough exercise, so I bought a ranch." It was the "Flying 20," a 2,200-acre spread of undulant sun-browned grazing land near Merritt in the famous Cariboo country of the British Columbia interior. He started ambitiously with 350 head of Herefords but found he could not raise enough feed to tide over the winter. As in his fish-flying days, he discovered costs exceeded revenues.

"After a couple of years I realized I was getting twenty-one cents a pound for beef that was costing me thirty cents to raise. On a ranch you have to watch the pennies more than in big business."

Sometimes he commuted to the ranch by light plane. More often he took long week-ends to justify the four-and-a-half-hour drive from Vancouver. He rode a hefty beast he described as "half quarter horse, half plow horse" and exulted in the tranquility of the open range. His hobby was also his retirement plan, he said. He would eventually spend his summers on the Flying 20 and his winters in Hawaii. Such was his distant dream. Meantime, there were more immediate dreams to be realized.

He sighted far horizons, and McConachie was too involved with them to spend much time fretting about the administrative chores on his money-losing airline during the early sixties. He delegated most of the daily worries to Executive VP, R. W. Ryan, and Comptroller, John C. Gilmer. He himself would be in Ottawa for weeks at a time prowling the corridors of power, pitching for a new air policy, striving for the glittering prizes . . . more competition with TCA . . . the coveted London destination on the polar route . . . a crack at the trans-border routes to major U.S. cities . . . triumph of free enterprise over monopoly . . . a CPA round-the-world hook-up and to heck with the economics.

He was ideally equipped for this sort of campaigning. Contemporary journalists saw him as "a genial bear of a man . . . big physically, in vision, in habits, in determination . . . a rugged individualist, sometimes the despair of the board room . . ."

One writer observed that "during his years as president of CPA, he has projected a personality so powerful that his character and that of the airline are virtually synonymous. . . . If CPA has a good corporate image it is because Grant McConachie can't help making friends . . .

"There is a strong temptation to describe his personality as dynamic, disarming, vibrant, manly or compelling. But more revealing is a picture of this high-salaried corporation chief carrying a tray of food in CPA's head-office cafeteria looking for any group of employees with a spare seat at the table . . ."

Another concluded, "few executives have been so closely identified with their company's image. In McConachie's case, he is the image . . .

"He is still the tough, resourceful and imaginative individual who cut his flying teeth flying fish along Canada's wild frontier."

A business columnist who confessed to boredom with most corporate heads described him in print as "an electric ebullient executive" and continued, "Grant McConachie's supersonic salesmanship becomes quickly apparent when he talks about his company's progress. He moves so fast you don't actually see him, you merely get an impression of height, broad shoulders and an alarming amount of energy.

"It is impossible to keep up with him as he roams his office, spinning a lighted globe to show the CPA route system, swiping the air with model jets. All you do is hold a central position and try to make contact with him as he orbits within range . . ."

He was described in a national magazine as, "a king-sized bundle of shrewdness and energy who sometimes takes big-money chances but usually has the odds figured. His round open face once boasted freckles set off by a shock of sandy hair, now greying. If he were in the ice-cream business, he'd be the picture of a cheerful street vendor . . . aging slightly now . . . but still peddling ten-cent cones for a nickel. Moreover, he'd be working out a way to sell fifteen-cent cones, still for a nickel . . . He's a quick thinker with a ready smile and no little suave aplomb."

One of McConachie's main objectives early in the '60s was CPA access to London, on the polar route from Vancouver. TCA was running to London from eastern Canada, but the air agreement permitted more than one Canadian airline to serve the U.K. capital. So why not let CPA in, McConachie argued. "Our polar planes are flying right through the smoke of London as they descend into Amsterdam. The London-bound passengers suffer the inconvenience of back-tracking on another airline."

His plea in the press and in Ottawa was so effective that a special committee of the Canadian Cabinet was assigned to witness a confrontation between McConachie and TCA's McGregor on the London issue. McConachie's presentation, supported by the effective documentation of Ian Sinclair, won the crucial debate.

On September 30, 1961, the Toronto *Globe and Mail* carried the following report:

"Next week, the goose on the CPA emblem will have reason

to flap its wings. The airline will begin its first flights into London. Permission was announced in mid-August by Transport Minister Leon Balcer. To many observers, including executives of TCA, the announcement came as a surprise.

"The present federal cabinet had once before turned down a CPA application for London. The rejection was so firm few thought the cabinet would ever change its mind.

"What budged this apparently immovable object? The answer could be a freckled, cheerful, well-nigh irresistible force named Grant McConachie . . ."

Then came a nasty shock. Even as the CPA goose was spreading its wings for the London flight, the British Minister of Transport advised that a second Canadian carrier serving the United Kingdom would be "politically unacceptable at this time."

This was more than a blatant refusal to honour the terms of a treaty. It was a public insult to the Canadian Government which had announced its decision. Some observers are convinced that if Canada had talked tough and even threatened to bar BOAC from Toronto, the U.K. would have capitulated. Instead, the Diefenbaker Government meekly submitted.

It was another jolting disappointment for McConachie.

But he was too supercharged to brood over the loss of London. He promptly opened fire from the public platform on the war-vintage air service pact between Canada and the United States which he termed "a DC-3 agreement in the jet age."

"We are the only two countries in the free world with an air barrier at our border," he proclaimed. "Canadian and U.S. airlines are prevented from linking our largest cities across the border, though foreign carriers are allowed to do so."

The largest city in Canada, Montreal, and the second largest city in the United States, Chicago, were not linked by a direct air service of either country. Yet a French and a German airline were flying Montreal–Chicago non-stop. The same applied between Vancouver and San Francisco with only an Australian airline operating non-stop. A comparable situation in Europe, McConachie said, would require the London-to-Paris air passenger to land at Calais and transfer to a French airline.

"The real victim is the air passenger who is dumped at the first stop over the border to change planes for no other reason than to preserve tight little air monopolies." He called for a get-tough policy to force an overhaul of the creaky agreement.

"Somehow we Canadians are like bumpkins at a country fair watching a slick but legitimate shell game . . . Our American neighbours have opened their sky to many other countries but have slammed it shut in the face of Canada, their good neighbour and best customer. . . ."

Every trans-border city pair that could justify direct air service should be double-tracked, with an airline of each country competing for the traffic, he urged.

It was implicit, of course, that CPA would be dealt some of the new trans-border routes to become available in the process.

As a direct result of this one-man crusade Prime Minister Lester Pearson eventually raised the bilateral question with the late President John F. Kennedy, who then dispatched his special emissary, John Kenneth Galbraith, to Ottawa on a fact-finding mission in the summer of 1963. Bilateral talks between Canada and the United States opened in April 1964. A new agreement on the direct-service principle was signed on January 15, 1966. CPA was awarded Vancouver–San Francisco with hopes for more in the next review.

35. McCONACHIE VS McGREGOR

January 9, 1962—While stoking his living-room fireplace, Grant McConachie experienced sharp pains in his chest and shortage of breath. After lying down for a while, he decided not to consult a doctor.

The cure, he told himself, was fitness. He heated his back-yard pool the next day and entered on a regimen of daily swims. He found that with continuation of this regular exercise he was able to increase the number of lengths he could swim before getting chest pains. This, he convinced himself, was progress.

In February 1962 McConachie reported to the directors that the 1961 CPA loss had hit $7.6 million. There was shocked dismay in the high echelons of the parent company. The sacrosanct CPR dividend would be diminished! This could not go on! The fate of the airline appeared to hang in the balance as the directors assembled for a crisis conference in Vancouver. A harried frown had replaced McConachie's usual smile as he entered the board room.

Ian Sinclair summed up succinctly. "This airline has been running on a mixture of glamour and gasoline for twenty years. Now we've got to inject a strong dose of economics, or else."

McConachie put it down to the "jet indigestion" that was affecting every airline.

The international airlines had plunged $6 billion on jet fleets, super-saturating the market, turning a 1960 profit of $70 million into a $140 million loss for 1961. After the jet transition, the industry would be in the chips again, McConachie predicted.

He was right. CPA turned the corner in 1962, whittling the loss to $1.2 million, then moved into profit . . . $500,000 in 1963, $4.8 million in 1964, and $7.2 million in 1965.

The CPA loss was matched by TCA's 1961 deficit of more than $6 million, a fact that provided Gordon McGregor with a fresh slogan for air monopoly.

"The country can't afford it," he warned. "The two airlines ran more than $13 million in the red last year, $25 million over the past three years. Merger is the only solution." When an interviewer asked him who would head the resulting super-airline, the TCA chief suggested that "Mr. McConachie would make a very good general sales manager."

Once again, the two giants of Canadian air transportation, McConachie and McGregor, were locked in combat. They presented a fascinating contrast of personalities and philosophies, as noted at the time by Charles King, editor of the Ottawa *Journal:*

"The story of these two is the story of the enterprises they run . . . one dedicated to serving the essential requirements of the greatest number of Canadians, the other imbued with the vision of providing a mixture of panache and profit.

"Grant is the ex-bush pilot and swinger with the imaginative glow of a man dedicated to flying Canada's—and his airline's —flag to the distant corners of the world. He happily quaffs champagne where McGregor soberly sips his native Scotch. One worries about balancing the books while the other concentrates on expansion and pizazz."

Gordon McGregor made the most of the "financial ruin" ploy to push for merger, but it quickly became obvious that, deficit or no, CPR president N. R. "Buck" Crump would have no truck with any merger on McGregor terms. When a reporter quoted the TCA president on the subject, Crump's reply was abrupt,

"How much do they want for TCA?"

A shrewd CP-watcher was to assess the Canadian airline crisis as follows. "The McConachie story might have been quite different had it not merged with the Buck Crump saga. Few would know the staunchness that held the traditionally ultra-conservative CPR firm in backing McConachie's dreams through the heavy losses following jet introduction."

McConachie's reaction to the merger proposal was predictably forceful. He told a service club audience:

"Take a look at the skies around us and see who believes in this one-airline concept. Britain has eleven international airlines, the United States eighteen, Australia three, France three. Even Iceland, Ireland and Finland each have two. Who are the one-airline countries? Morocco, the Ivory Coast, Mozambique, Kenya, Baihran and Bermuda. Is this our league in world aviation? I hope not!"

In April 1962 a strange event gave CPA a temporary advantage over its rival. TCA introduced an 8 per cent economy fare increase on its domestic routes. McGregor had advised McConachie of this well in advance and either assumed or understood that CPA would do likewise. CPA refrained, because McConachie didn't believe that this was the way to fill empty seats.

June 5, 1962—Grant McConachie arrived home from an Ottawa sojourn in a state of exhaustion. He had difficulty breathing and Mrs. McConachie, a trained nurse, was alarmed to note that his complexion was chalk-white, his lips purple. He went to bed insisting that all he needed was rest. His wife called the doctor. That night the patient was taken to St. Vincent's Hospital where his ailment was diagnosed as arterial schlerosis. The coronary arteries supplying vital blood to the heart muscles were constricted. Under stress, they could not expand to carry the increased blood supply required. Oxygen-starvation of the heart muscles had caused the chest pains and semi-suffocation.

The doctors were horrified when they learned of the patient's self-cure swimming project. It had been the worst of all possible prescriptions. They told him, "You must avoid all excitement, physical stress, emotional strain. Drop all major responsibilities. Take it easy." The patient silently refused to resign himself to a rocking-chair existence. He elected to press on.

Undaunted, he continued to lob verbal grenades into the TCA stronghold. After a year of lopsided domestic competition with TCA unfettered and CPA shackled to one flight a day it was time to give the private airline a better shake, he argued. He accused the government carrier of "a policy of fantastic and deliberate overexpansion of its domestic fleet to frustrate the competition policy by saturating the market and by deliberately courting substantial losses." He told an audience he had discovered a TCA plan to step up capacity as much as 76 per cent on one segment of the competitive route.

In this context, McConachie made a sly reference to his supposed arch-enemy, Gordon McGregor.

"Actually, Gordon and I are good personal friends. The only flaw in our friendship is the fact that I envy him. I would envy anyone who can eliminate his competition by the simple device of losing money, and the more money he loses, the more secure his monopoly."

On May 20, 1963, in recognition of his great crusade for private enterprise, Grant McConachie was selected by the New York-based forty-thousand-member Sales Executive International as "Canadian Businessman of the Year." He was also featured in a cover story in the United States publication *Business Week.*

A reporter asked him, "Why were you named Canadian Businessman of the Year?" McConachie stood stock still for a

minute. "I don't know," he said in wonder, "I've been a cowboy most of the year."

Such self-mocking humour was characteristic of the man.
"There is one big advantage in having a ranch," he told a
friend. "In the ranch owners' association they know I'm a
pretty dumb rancher, but they figure I must be a very successful
airline president. The airline people know I make stupid mistakes in the flying business but figure I must be a damn smart
rancher."

A business associate said to him, "Grant, with all the setbacks
and discouragements you've had, how come you're not hardboiled?" He grinned, "I've certainly been in enough hot water
to be hardboiled."

His geniality was a hallmark of his personality, but he could
be firm and quietly angry. When one of his executives told
the president that a long-time staffer was threatening to quit
unless he got a raise, McConachie said, "You tell Frank this
is not jail. The door swings both ways. The answer is no."

Most of his anger and frustration were reserved for what
he considered the failings of air policy, the lost opportunities
for CPA and for Canadian aviation. Ian Sinclair commented,

"Grant never really adjusted himself to not being front
runner and was much distressed by the government's chosen
instrument and monopoly policies. He was fascinated by the
big U.S. airlines that had been developed by strong imaginative individuals, mostly former pilots like himself, men like
C. R. Smith of American, Eddie Rickenbacker of Eastern,
and particularly Juan Trippe of Pan American. He could see
how their initiative and drive brought results."

Sinclair did not have a high regard for McConachie's abilities
as an administrator. He said then, "Grant is not an organization man, doesn't like lines of communication, cuts across them
all the time. He has never lost the techniques of the proprietor."

Symbolic of the CPA president's personalized approach to

his job was his little blue notebook in which he was continuously jotting ideas for improving the airline. A muddy aisle carpet on a rainy day. Notation: Use removable mats until the passengers are seated. A stewardess on a U.S. airline noted McConachie carried cigars but was not smoking. She told him the airline permitted cigar and pipe smoking because the air conditioning system kept the air fresh. Notation: "Why don't we do this?"

On a CPA aircraft he noted an attendant removing the white linen headrests from the backs of the seats while another followed, replacing them with fresh linen. Notation: "Why not flip the doilies over, double utilization, cut laundry bills, reduce man-hours?"

On one occasion he arrived in Montreal from Europe. With the six-hour time difference, he awoke at four A.M. "By this time," he said later, "all of last night's parties were over and it was too early to start a new one." Instead of reading, he caught a cab to the airport to see what went on. When he returned to Vancouver he opened his blue notebook during a meeting of his executives. He had watched the cleaners at work in a CPA plane early that morning.

"There was this chap trying to sweep the aisle carpet with a whisk. He was pushing this little pile of dirt down the aisle but the pile never got any bigger because the dirt sifted back into the carpet as he whisked it along. What the hell's the matter with you guys in maintenance? I'm damn sure they had a better method of cleaning Cleopatra's barge on the Nile!" he fumed.

Most of the time, however, McConachie was thinking big. When he got DC-8 jets, which TCA already had, his were "Super DC-8s." A reporter asked Gordon McGregor to explain the difference. He replied with a wry grin, "A Super DC-8 is an ordinary DC-8 with CPA markings."

Although deeply engrossed in world aviation, McConachie never forgot the north. Out of loyalty he carried on his staff

a number of old-time bush pilots filling such make-work posi-
tions as Director of Research and Director of Northern Development. At one time he had the airline finance the refitting of
a paddle-wheel steamer on the Yukon, and instructed his sales
staff to develop package tours by air to Whitehorse connecting
with a steamer cruise to Dawson City. The venture cost CPA
$300,000.

John Baldwin once told a colleague, "Grant knows a helluva
lot more about gold dredging in the Yukon than he does about
the art galleries in Rome." However, he conceded, McConachie
was a potent force in Ottawa. "As deputy minister of transport,
I had a serious problem in not allowing his personality and
my regard for him to interfere with my neutrality and judgement on government matters."

Another close associate, Vancouver businessman Howard
Mitchell, recalled visiting Stratford-on-Avon with the CPA
chief.

"The sacred and anointed bard just wasn't in McConachie's
book. As we strolled, savouring the carefully-restored atmosphere of Shakespeare's home town, Grant was telling me how
Canada had been gypped on air routes. To heck with Shakespeare, why did CPA have to overfly the United States en
route to Mexico?"

His preoccupation was with Canada's destiny in the air. As
he frequently proclaimed, "With freedom to plan and expand
our air services, I do not believe we can be driven from the
skies as we have been driven from the seas. We are potentially
one of the great airfaring nations of the world."

*August 7, 1963—Grant McConachie was admitted to St.
Vincent's Hospital with the symptoms of partial heart failure.
He was put under sedation. He remained in the hospital until
October 27. In the meantime, N. R. Crump issued instructions
to relieve the president of most administrative duties when he
returned to the office.*

McConachie emerged from his recuperation into an office

stint restricted to two hours a day. But he was rebellious. When one of his doctors advised against the 3,500-foot altitude of the ranch he protested. "The cabin atmosphere in an airliner flying at thirty thousand feet is pressurized to eight thousand feet. If the ranch is bad for my heart that means I can't fly either. I intend to ranch and I intend to fly." He did both. And he hated the pills. He told a friend at the time,

"My doctors have me swallowing the damnedest collection of pills . . . green pills, purple pills, yellow pills, polka dot pills. One day I emptied the whole selection, one day's dose, into a glass of water and do you know what happened? It exploded!"

Early in 1964, Bill Herbert, a veteran radio commentator and producer proposed the idea of a one-hour radio biography of Grant McConachie. The president's initial response was negative, but he finally consented to the extensive interviews required. Preparations for the national broadcast included eleven hours of tape-recording McConachie's reminiscences and sixteen hours of interviews with his friends and associates. The Canadian Broadcasting Corporation then had the voluminous tapes transcribed by a corps of typists, and edited to the one-hour dimension by journalist Himie Koshevoy. Then the tapes were cut and spliced to correspond with the script.

The hour-long broadcast of the McConachie life story was aired right across Canada on May 4, 1964. One listener made the entire effort a huge success for CPA and the president. By sheer chance, the Minister of Transport, J. W. Pickersgill, driving from Ottawa to Montreal with another cabinet minister, Paul Martin, tuned in the program. As he told McConachie later,

"Paul and I became so fascinated with the story that we pulled off to the side of the road and listened for the full hour. And Martin kept digging me in the ribs and chiding me for not giving a better break to this great pioneer of Canadian aviation."

(There was another unsuspected benefit. The full transcript of the interviews provided invaluable reference material in the preparation of this biography.)

Even under wraps, McConachie was a formidable schemer. He was intrigued by "the supersonic seventies" and what lay beyond. On February 25, 1965, he announced that Canadian Pacific Airlines had put down a $300,000 deposit on three U.S.-designed supersonic transports, the first Canadian airline to opt for SST.

The idea of supersonic travel excited him:

"Imagine taking off from Montreal at dawn to fly west outspeeding the sun. You would look back over your shoulder to see the newly-risen sun setting in the east as you cruise westward into the night before."

In the spring of 1964, the Minister of Transport, Mr. Pickersgill made a long-awaited air policy pronouncement. It was an affirmative response to McConachie's plea for recognition of CPA as an official flag carrier with a confirmed future in the international skies. CPA was named as the official flag carrier over the South Pacific, South America and South-east Europe, as well as the North Europe gateway of Amsterdam. For McConachie it was a rare and treasured success in a succession of disappointments.

(McConachie's other great campaign, for a share of the market growth on his country's main-line air route was to meet success in March 1967 when CPA was allowed to increase its capacity on the route up to 25 per cent of the total capacity provided and to continue in that ratio.)

June 25, 1965—From 4 till 7 p.m. Grant McConachie entertained members of his board of directors and airline officers for cocktails in his garden. At 8 p.m. with his family he drove the 160 miles to his ranch. On the week-end he painted fences and entertained friends who had flown in to show him a new airplane. He drove back to Vancouver Monday morning and worked at his office for part of the afternoon. At noon on

Tuesday, June 29, Mrs. McConachie reluctantly took a flight to Winnipeg to visit their son, Don. Grant looked pale and haggard. She had wanted to go with him later in the afternoon on a business trip to California, but he had insisted she not disappoint Don, who was expecting her. At 2 p.m. McConachie took a flight to Long Beach where he checked into the Edgewater Motel. He planned a meeting the next morning in the nearby executive offices of Western Airlines to discuss the leasing of a DC-6B aircraft.

36. EMPRESS FLIGHT 90

CPA Captain Aubry Weatherbe had been off duty, test-piloting a new power mower on the back lawn, when the call came from Crew Routing. One hour and forty-five minutes later, flight plan completed, he was lifting *White Empress* CZZ off Runway Zero Eight at Vancouver International and wheeling into a climbing turn that would intercept the airway beam to California.

Four hours and ten minutes after the take-off from Vancouver, *Empress* 90 reported at 15,000 feet over Green Meadows range beacon, requested clearance for let-down into the congested air-traffic pattern of Los Angeles Area Control that embraced Long Beach Airport.

A zero-visibility smog was obscuring the entire airspace of the L. A. Control Block. Blind-flying airliners were circling in a traffic stack two miles high. Captain Weatherbe had flight-planned for a two-hour hold in this traffic queue. *Empress* 90 would have to shuffle down from the top of the deck by tedious thousand-foot holding stages, eventually skimming off the bottom of the stack to join the landing circuit. Brisk, impersonal, the voice of L. A. Control rasped in Weatherbe's earphones. *"Empress* 90 we have you at 15,000 over Green Meadows. Contact Long Beach Approach Control . . . Frequency 605.3 . . . for *direct radar-vectored descent,* repeat, direct radar-vectored descent, to Long Beach Airport." Direct descent! By-passing the entire traffic stack! Obviously, the special nature of the mission had been recognized at a very high level. No detail neglected.

McConachie, pilot-president of the airline, would have loved that radar-guided let-down, Weatherbe mused. On all his travels the chief had never missed an opportunity to visit the flight deck, to relive the tension and excitement of his own flying career, to chat about flight planning, engine performance, fuel reserves, long-range cruise configuration, the aerodynamics of the new jet breed. Some of the flight-deck veterans had flown with him on the pioneering bush routes. All the captains recognized McConachie as a fellow-pilot who also happened to be president of the airline.

Eighteen minutes after retarding the throttles for his radar descent, Captain Weatherbe banked CZZ into final approach, checked the beady green eye of the "gear down" signal, chopped the throttle levers full back, and settled the 6-B smoothly onto the paved surface of Runway Two Seven, Long Beach.

Empress 90 was cleared for a quick reverse on the live runway, then across Highway 65 to the sprawling complex of the Douglas commercial aircraft plant. Red traffic lights flashed. Bells shrilled. Striped barriers swung down. Road traffic halted. The Canadian airliner rumbled across the highway and taxied directly into the open cavern of a Douglas hangar. The ground arrangements were unobtrusive and quietly efficient. Seventy-five minutes later, the big doors yawned again to emit CZZ, props already spinning, ready for priority take-off to Vancouver.

As CZZ climbed away from the airport, the voice of the Long Beach Tower operator came through.

"*Empress* 90 you are cleared to Area Control." Then a pause. It should have been the end of the transmission, but there was an audible click. Probably the operator had shut off the tape-record monitor, for the next words were a breach of the strict rule against personal utterances on the airway radio frequencies.

"Sorry, Canadian Pacific!" That was all. Another click and the impersonal staccato of airway patter resumed.

The sorrow would be widely shared, Weatherbe mused.

Empress 90, taking off from Long Beach Airport at 16:19 hours, Pacific Daylight Time on June 30, 1965, was the final flight of Grant McConachie.

On Tuesday evening, June 29, at 9 p.m. while walking in the corridor of his Long Beach motel after a solitary dinner, McConachie had collapsed with a heart attack. He did not survive the ambulance trip to the hospital. His age was 56.

Empress Flight 90 had the distinction of flying him home.

There were only three passengers in the 62-seat DC-6B cabin behind the closed door of Captain Weatherbe's flight deck as *Empress* 90 droned northward along the airway to Vancouver. Each sat alone, silent, immersed in his own private world.

Don McConachie, the husky twenty-six-year-old son of the president, occupied 15B, an aisle seat over the wing. He had little interest in the flight's progress, even less in the scenery. His broad-shouldered six-foot-four frame, a heritage from his father, was slumped heedlessly in the seat.

He was lost in a vision of the sun-baked acres of the Flying-20 spread, his father, high in the saddle, grinning exuberantly, waving the big white stetson, galloping over the cattle trails on his big-boned mare, Doll, "the only beast in the country that can carry me over these hills without collapsing from exhaustion."

In a window seat up forward, just behind the flight-deck bulkhead, the operations vice-president of the airline, Barney Phillips, hunched over a half-emptied tumbler of Scotch. The scowl darkening his rugged features would not have diminished the reputation for toughness he had so carefully nurtured over the years. McConachie's closest friend and business associate from the bush-flying era, he had always seen himself as the counterbalance to the chief's easygoing nature. He had secretly enjoyed being known at the hatchetman, the fixer, the hard-nosed bargainer. He relished the story that had got back to him about the pilots' union negotiator who had described Phillips as a man of steel with a heart of gold. "Gold, hell," said a colleague, "that's brass, only twice as hard."

Phillips frowned into his drink, the third since the take-off at Long Beach. He was not a daytime drinker but assured himself the circumstances justified the exception. He noted with absent-minded satisfaction the even pattern of vibrations rippling the surface of the amber liquid in his glass. All four engines were perfectly synchronized, purring smoothly. You couldn't beat those big brutes, the Pratt & Whitney CB-17s, for dependability. Christ, he muttered to himself, who cares about the fumbling ruddy engines at a time like this! Years of responsibility, he supposed, had triggered the reaction.

Thirty years in the flying business, Phillips reflected moodily, and he still hated to ride in airplanes. Of course, he had only fallen into it by chance in the first place, when he had found himself involved in a faltering bush-flying air service.

The other partner in United Air Transport, with its fleet of five small single-engine planes, was also the president and chief pilot, a stalwart twenty-three-year-old cockpit-happy youth wearing a leather helmet, a siwash Indian sweater and wrinkled pants. That was Grant McConachie in the thirties, Phillips reminisced, a big, good-natured bruin of a man with a contagious grin, a remarkable talent for persuasion, and a confidence in his own flying future that was not shaken by an unbroken record of financial failure. McConachie was the only man in the world, Phillips knew, who could have talked him into devoting his entire working life to a business he didn't really like.

He recalled the young pilot's incurable enthusiasm. When they had cracked up four of their five planes in a single season and the insurance companies cancelled out, McConachie had lost none of his bounce. He came up with the big confident grin, the talk of the new planes coming from the factory. Phillips thought of the crack-up and the fish-hauler's determination to fly again and to hell with the doctors . . . the all-or-nothing rescue flights . . . the crazy barnstorming days . . . the opening of the Yukon run . . . then the transition from flying helmet to Homburg hat and neat blue suit, McConachie the diplomat exploring the Pacific perimeter for airline opportunities, tracing his "great circle" routes on the air map of the world. . . .

"Hi, Mr. Phillips. The stew said you wanted to see me about the landing arrangements." Captain Weatherbe had entered the cabin unnoticed. His manner conveyed a discreet apology for having disturbed the vice-president's reveries.

"Yes, Aubry, this is very important." Phillips was still scowling, but spoke with the respect due the captain of the flight. "When we land I don't want any bother with the press or the public. I want you to get our Dispatch on the blower. Have them set it up so we don't have to go to the terminal at all. I want us to taxi right into our own hangar and close the doors, so we can have privacy. They'll have to have the Customs and Immigration chaps come over to our hangar for this one. You got that?"

As the door closed behind the captain, Barney Phillips had already returned his attention to his Scotch and his memories.

Across the aisle, the third passenger on *Empress* Flight 90 was tilted back in a fully-reclined seat, seemingly in a deep slumber. But John C. Gilmer, the tall, silver-templed, executive vice-president of Canadian Pacific Airlines, was not sleeping. He was utterly exhausted.

For more than three years now, ever since the chief's first warning of heart trouble, as number two in the multi-million-dollar complex of a modern international airline, Gilmer had been bearing a crushing administrative load. Now, a grey pallor overlay his features, a testimony to the sleepless hours, the emotional havoc, and the new pressures of responsibility that all stemmed from that midnight phone call from Long Beach.

Gilmer found himself envying, once again, Grant McConachie's free-wheeling high spirits and bubbling optimism, his ability to sparkle, to effervesce, to thrive on adversity. McConachie had delighted in telling the CPA story in terms of the gross revenues. From $3 million in 1942 to $14 million in 1952 to over $61 million in 1964! How he had loved to talk in those big, fat numbers, in multiple millions!

But J. C. Gilmer was a chartered accountant by training and by disposition. Since his concern was the balance sheet of the airline, he knew well, and the CPR top brass never let him forget, that the gross figures didn't mean a damn. It was the net financial results that told the real story. His thoughts went back to the early sixties, to the financial agonies of the airline's transition from piston-engined to jet fleets.

He marvelled anew as he recalled McConachie in action on that fateful day, April 22, 1962. N. R. "Buck" Crump, the calm, competent top executive of a $3 billion complex, "the world's greatest transportation system," had presided at that special directors' meeting called to decide the fate of the airline. Fire was in his steel-blue eyes. The airline deficit had shrunk that CPR shareholder dividend, and that would not be tolerated.

The unflappable McConachie was at his best in the crisis atmosphere of that meeting. Self-assured, confident, he had related the losses to the larger picture, to the fabulous efficiency and earning power of the new jets. The tension had eased, and the outlook brightened visibly as McConachie's enthusiasm began to infuse the meeting. By force of sheer persuasion, and some logic, he had wrested from the directors a vote of confidence in the future of the airline.

"*Empress* 90 you are number one to land. Cleared on final approach Runway Zero Eight. Gear Green. Over." The voice of Vancouver Tower was loud in Captain Weatherbe's earphones as he banked 446 steeply over the tidal flat approaches to Vancouver International and levelled into a steep glide to the runway. He took particular care with the landing. The touchdown was a pilot's dream, only a slight tremor of vibration signalling the plane's transition from air to ground. The smooth landing of *Empress* Flight 90 gave Weatherbe unusual satisfaction. Perhaps he was being sentimental, he thought, but somehow it seemed important to make this last one a landing the chief would have appreciated.

Ronald A. Keith was editor for many years of *Canadian Aviation* magazine. Also a pilot with over 2,000 hours logged at the controls, he served as Grant McConachie's personal assistant for twelve years. Ronald Keith died in 1985.

Sean Rossiter is the author of eight books, including three on aviation. His most recent title is *The Immortal Beaver: The World's Greatest Bush Plane.*